LYNNE TRUSS is a writer and broadcaster who started out as a literary editor with a blue pen and then got side-tracked. She is the author of three novels and two books of non-fiction: *Talk to the Hand* and *Eats, Shoots & Leaves*, which has sold over three million copies worldwide and was Book of the Year 2004. She lives in Brighton.

From the reviews of *Get Her Off the Pitch!*:

'A fabulous memoir. She writes about sport in a way that men never could. Hilarious, unpredictable and controversial. It's a terrific read whether you love sport or are still wondering what all the fuss is about'   *Mail on Sunday*

'Very funny . . . like a travel writer, she negotiated a foreign country and brought to bear the outsider's clear view'
                                         CHRIS MAUME, *Independent*

'Truss would rather saw off her own leg than construct a boring sentence. Indeed, this book is loaded with snort-inducing jokes. Get her back on the pitch'   *Sunday Times*

'Sheer, unexpected joy . . . You don't have to like sport to start with: it's probably better not to. But gradually she discovers things to admire about almost everything (she's that kind of woman) and she takes you, Valkyrie-like, with her'
       SUE GAISFORD, *Independent on Sunday*, Books of the Year

'Who will want to read this book? Just people like me who are largely indifferent to sport but enjoy literate, amusing, properly punctuated writing about anything'
                                         PETER LEWIS, *Daily Mail*

By the same author:

With One Lousy Free Packet of Seed
Making the Cat Laugh:
One Woman's Journal of Single Life on the Margins
Tennyson's Gift
Going Loco
Tennyson and His Circle
Eats, Shoots & Leaves:
The Zero Tolerance Approach to Punctuation
Talk to the Hand: The Utter Bloody Rudeness of Everyday Life
(or Six Good Reasons to Stay Home and Bolt the Door)
A Certain Age: Twelve Monologues from the Classic Radio Series

FOR CHILDREN
Eats, Shoots & Leaves: Why, Commas Really Do Make a Difference
The Girl's Like Spaghetti:
Why, You Can't Manage Without Apostrophes!
Twenty-Odd Ducks: Why, Every Punctuation Mark Counts!

GET HER OFF THE PITCH!

How Sport Took Over My Life

LYNNE TRUSS

FOURTH ESTATE • *London*

Fourth Estate
An imprint of HarperCollins*Publishers*
77–85 Fulham Palace Road
Hammersmith
London W6 8JB

Visit our authors' blog at www.fifthestate.co.uk
Love this book? www.bookarmy.com

This Fourth Estate paperback edition published 2010
1

First published in Great Britain by Fourth Estate in 2009

A catalogue record for this book is available from the British Library

ISBN 978-0-00-730575-9

Set in Adobe Caslon by Palimpsest Book Production Limited,
Falkirk, Stirlingshire

Printed and bound in Great Britain by Clays Ltd, St Ives plc

Mixed Sources
Product group from well-managed
forests and other controlled sources
www.fsc.org   Cert no. SW-COC-001806
© 1996 Forest Stewardship Council

FSC is a non-profit international organisation established to promote the
responsible management of the world's forests. Products carrying the FSC
label are independently certified to assure consumers that they come
from forests that are managed to meet the social, economic and
ecological needs of present and future generations.

Find out more about HarperCollins and the environment at
www.harpercollins.co.uk/green

To David Chappell and Keith Blackmore,
who sent me to football.

You bastards.

CONTENTS

Boxing and the Thrill of the Unknown

Looking back on events some years later, I remember the moment quite clearly. The place was Madison Square Garden in New York City, and the occasion was a press conference, just a couple of days before the fight between Evander Holyfield and Lennox Lewis on Saturday March 13, 1999. Boxing promoter Don King had been bellowing at us for about an hour already, and the air was hanging heavy. Two very big bored boxers sat awkwardly, in clothes, with their heads in their hands; those of us who had tape recorders had long since switched them off; I was doodling a large and complicated doodle with a lot of dense cross-hatching. And then King announced, 'And this fight is dedicated to women!' And for a second, I reacted. I flipped a page in my notebook. 'Dedicated to women? That's quite interesting!' I thought – and then, just as quickly, I kicked myself for being suckered like a patsy. How shaming. I prayed that no one had noticed. At this point, I had been in the world of international heavyweight boxing for three whole days, which was quite long enough to know the first rule of the business, which is never to allow anything said by Don King actually to penetrate your brain.

Two or three weeks before this, I would have asked without embarrassment, 'Who is this Don King, then; and what does he do?' but the assimilation of sudden and improbable expertise was the story of my life in those days. 'You will be covering the Holyfield–Lewis fight at Madison Square Garden on March 13,' they would tell me, those amusing sports-editor bosses at *The Times* in London; and, luckily for me, they didn't expect much by way of an intelligent reply. Sporting knowledge was not what I'd been hired for by the *Times* sports desk; just a cheerful nature, an open mind, a clean driving licence, and an idiot willingness to deliver 900 words on deadline from any live sporting event, including those I didn't remotely understand. 'And this Holyfield–Lewis thing will be quite a big deal, I suppose?' I might ask; and they would say, 'Yes, Lynne, it's a *very* big deal.' I would momentarily consider mentioning that I did know one rather interesting fact about the American fighter Evander Holyfield – that the top of his ear had been bitten off, during a fight, by Mike Tyson – but then I'd think better of it. They could never disguise their pity when I said pathetic teacher's-pet things like, 'Ooh, Wembley's the one with big white towers, isn't it?' or 'Thierry Henry? I believe I'm right in thinking he's *French*.' So they would tell me I was going to this mysterious fight, and it was best policy just to say, 'Well, you're the boss,' and start to arrange (in order of importance): a cat-feeding rota for my absence; a couple of opportunistic Broadway theatre outings; and a bit of basic remedial homework in the general subject area of boxing, to help me appreciate, simultaneously, both the significance of the event I had let myself in for, and the great bottomless chasm of my own ignorance.

I always really enjoyed the homework. In the week before travelling to Madison Square Garden in March 1999 for this heavyweight 'unification' title fight, I bought some serious books on boxing to read on the flight (Joyce Carol Oates, Donald McRae, Norman Mailer), plus the video of *When We Were Kings*. This famous documentary movie deals with the 1974 Muhammad Ali–George Foreman fight in Zaire known as 'The Rumble in the Jungle', and I have to say I watched it one dark February evening at home in Brighton with considerable interest. What a great film. For one thing, it was terribly well put together, with all those twinkle-eyed ringside-seat recollections from Norman Mailer and George Plimpton. And for another – well, Ali actually won the fight, and I really didn't see that coming. Yes, alone among all the millions of people who have watched that terrific account of a (then) 25-year-old iconic sporting occasion of legendary proportions, I hadn't the faintest idea of the outcome. Ali leaned back on the ropes for ages, you see, allowing the more powerful Foreman to exhaust himself with huge, heavy, battering-ram punches, and then – all of a sudden, in the eighth round – sprang into elastic action and knocked Foreman out with a combination of deft, lightning blows. Well, good heavens, I thought, as I rewound the tape and munched a biscuit. More people really ought to take an interest in boxing.

And now, after just three days in the orbit of Don King, I was already sick of him. What an appalling man to be with in a confined space. 'Do you know WHAT?' he yelled at me, as I bravely held up my tape recorder in front of him, one afternoon when the Garden was otherwise oddly quiet, and a *Times* colleague had wickedly put me up to stopping Don King and asking him a question. An enormous, portly, grizzled African-American flashing an oblong of diamonds on his finger the size of a mousemat, King is famous for having the vertical hairstyle of a man freshly released from a wind tunnel, for his beloved catch-phrase 'Only in America!', and for speaking at a volume that causes small buildings to fall over and helicopter pilots several miles away to wrestle with the controls. 'Do you know WHAT?' he yelled. 'This Saturday night they are calling a moratorium in KOSOVO and BOSNIA!' 'Really? Are you sure? Wouldn't that be quite difficult?' I wanted to say, but there wasn't a chance. 'I SAID to them,' he yelled, 'they got to call a MORATORIUM and watch the King's Crowning GLORY! NATO couldn't do it, but DON KING can do it! This way, if they DIE, they can die happy because they saw the fight of the millennium, and if they SURVIVE, they'll have SOMETHING TO TELL THEIR KIDS.

'Remember CYRANO DE BERGERAC?' he went on, without a pause for me to interrogate fully the concept of dying happy in Bosnia. 'Crossed enemy lines just to mail a letter to ROXANNE?' I nodded, confused, wondering what Cyrano de Bergerac had to do with Holyfield or Lewis, or indeed the war in the former Yugoslavia. The answer, intriguingly, was nothing. 'We had the Boston Tea Party in 1776, now we've got the FIGHT OF THE MILLENNIUM in 1999.' King evidently acquired all his scatter-gun erudition in a prison library, after being convicted of kicking a man to death – but tragically forgot afterwards all that other stuff they teach you in libraries about the importance of keeping your voice down.

'I went out SINGLE-HANDED and got this fight; I SLAUGHTERED the wild boar and dragged it HOME and drew its fangs and TORE ITS HORNS OUT, and I thank Britain for the Marquess of Queensberry who brought ORDER OUT OF CHAOS.' I wondered if I should ask a follow-up question. After all, I'd only said, 'So, Mr King, are many people signing up for the pay-per-view?' But I didn't get the chance. 'Will you do a little piece for us now?' piped up a telly producer, who had been waiting to one side for my one-to-one to finish. 'I'll do a BIG piece for you now,' said King, and just swivelled on the spot and started yelling in another direction.

All this occurred in my third year as a sports writer, and I apologise for starting, so bewilderingly, in the middle, but, as I hope this book will make clear, although I did the job for four years altogether, I felt bewildered and sort-of in the middle virtually all the time. I was permanently on an almost-vertical learning curve, clinging for life. For four years, week after week, at football stadiums, golf courses and race tracks, I would gaze around me – equipped with binoculars, pencil, notebook and enigmatic smile – and think, afresh, 'Lynne, what the fuck are you doing here?' Unfortunately, there was no point asking anyone else this question, because they couldn't tell me. My colleagues in the press box, notably, were actually asking themselves the same question – i.e., 'What the fuck is she doing here?' – while inwardly snarling at the fact that this know-nothing middle-aged female (who sat chuckling over her laptop when she wasn't complaining about the elbow-room or fainting for want of a half-time cheese roll) regularly deprived proper sports writers of prime space in a newspaper. I could

5

genuinely sympathise with how irritating this was; but I did feel they should have been clever enough to work out that it wasn't my fault, and that I'd never asked for this job; it had been someone else's idea. However, I couldn't deny how it looked. I had a very large byline picture featuring myself with a Louisville Slugger baseball bat. I sometimes wrote the whole back page of *The Times*. I had been nominated for Sports Writer of the Year. For someone who likes, above all, to be popular with colleagues and not attract undue disdain, I might as well have slit my own throat.

The irony was, I had enormous respect for these chaps who were my colleagues. Sports writers not only take sport seriously; they also know all about it without ever seeming to check a fact, read a book, or even study unfolding events too closely. And they do it, valiantly, for years and years, and years, and years. 'I've recently worked out that, adding up the days, I've spent a full year of my life watching fights in Las Vegas,' one chap told me on this trip to the Garden. While they would rather die than complain about the intolerable amounts of discomfort, loneliness, pressure and aggravation they have to put up with, I do know how bad it is, and I salute them for their fortitude. My own response to the intense you-can't-park-here-and-you-can't-park-there-either aggravation of the sports writer's life never really fitted with anyone else's, though, I noticed. I tended to get worked up about how badly things were organised; the other sports writers, on the other hand, were inured to bad organisation, and simply looked after themselves. If there was no electricity in the press box (as when the Millennium Stadium opened for business in Cardiff, for example), I'd be dashing about raising the alarm, while the chaps would each discover a dead socket and then, shrugging, set about making makeshift arrangements on an individual, self-serving basis. I never got the hang of this I'm-all-right-Jack attitude. If there was no information about where to park during a football tournament, I'd berate the organisers – but when I appealed to my colleagues for back-up, they would be mystified by my passion, and a bit embarrassed by it. 'I found a place round the back,' they'd say, annoyingly, as if that solved anything.

Naturally, a world heavyweight title bout in America brought out the most macho of their macho qualities; but in interesting and quite unpredictable ways. That week in New York was notable mainly for an unusual pack mentality in some of the alpha-group 'chief' British sports writers: wherever the chap from the *Sun* went (in a broad-shouldered camel coat, like a gangster), so followed half a dozen of our top, white-haired veterans, in a tight formation, half a step behind. These quasi-feudal processions, with the tabloid man at the front and the 'qualities' bobbing along in his wake, were quite strange to observe, especially as the chap from the *Sun* was actually in trouble with the Lewis camp for asking the intriguingly androgynous Lennox in an exclusive interview whether he was gay – which the *Sun* editorial staff larkily chose to print alongside an outrageous appeal for any former girlfriends of Lewis to identify themselves, spill the beans, and thereby put an end to speculation.

So it is fair to say I was an anomaly among sports writers, which was both my personal tragedy and my writerly advantage. All the other journalists attending

Madison Square Garden for the Holyfield–Lewis fight had known for twenty-five years that Muhammad Ali beat George Foreman in Zaire back in 1974. They would be disgusted (though not a bit surprised) to learn that it was quite fresh news to me. Knowing this made me feel both good and bad at the same time. I understood that I was thoroughly deserving of my colleagues' contempt, yet I didn't really care, because – on the white-knuckle ride of my learning curve – I was patently having a much more interesting experience than they were.

What was this fight? Why was it such a big deal? Well, what was clear from the outset was that many hopes were being pinned on it as a once-and-for-all kind of confrontation, and that this was, in any case, the highest level of fight you could hope to see. People in Bosnia might not genuinely be observing a ceasefire for the sake of it, but in boxing terms it was huge, because (in the words of the excellent British sports writer James Lawton) it was 'transparently legitimate'. There was no contender involved, since both men were title-holders, the proud possessors of belts that tragically don't go with anything, but nevertheless represent the limit of achievement in the field. Someone would emerge from this fight the 'undisputed' champion of the world, and for Lennox Lewis – Olympic gold medallist with Jamaican/Canadian background but British nationality – here was his chance, at last, to refute his critics and prove himself. Significantly, he would do this largely on his own terms. The exquisitely dreadlocked Lewis was evidently a man of quiet intelligence, with excellent strategic skills, and a powerful self-preservation instinct. He was famous for his enjoyment of chess, which admittedly sometimes infuriated his trainer ('I hate that chess shit,' the trainer told the press. 'People think it's a joke with me but it's not. I'd like to take that chess set and burn the damn thing'). But if his sleepy demeanour and unconventional boxing-clever intellectual qualities had sometimes made him a frustrating fighter to watch ('Biff him, Lennox! You're twice his size, for God's sake!'), they had served him very well in other ways. Specifically, they had kept him, against all the odds, financially beyond the reach of Don King.

When I say I knew nothing about boxing before the Holyfield–Lewis summons, I mean that I knew nothing about *real* boxing, and had never wanted to. Like many a sensitive soul, I had a natural aversion to the whole idea of people suffering irreversible brain damage for the blood-lusting entertainment of others. This aversion was built, however, on information contained in any number of acclaimed and supposedly realistic boxing movies, in which it is made quite clear that boxing – beyond anything known in other organised sports – stinks to high heaven of corruption, criminality and playing Joe Public for a mug. Fights are fixed; managers are hoodlums; mobsters with flick-knives climb into the shower with the patsy who refused to go down in the third; contender wannabes cop a one-way ticket to Palookaville. There is rarely a happy ending. Films like *Golden Boy* (based on a play by Clifford Odets), *The Harder They Fall* (based on a novel by Budd Schulberg) or *Fat City* (based on a novel by Leonard Gardner) depict the sport of boxing pretty starkly as a system that thrives on individual greatness but also consumes and destroys all things noble as a matter of course. In less grandiose terms, a strong, half-naked man stands alone in the ring, taking the blows, while a bunch of venal weaklings in snazzy hats pocket all his dough and then sell his broken body down the river.

Compromise always wins over integrity in this eternal tragedy. In these movies, fighters never get the bouts they deserve, despite begging for shots at the title, because it serves no one else's skulduggery to set them up. They are often obliged to take strategic dives – and sometimes they boo-hoo afterwards at the ignominy of it, like Jake LaMotta (Robert De Niro) in *Raging Bull*, whom it is still incredibly hard to feel sorry for, incidentally, because he's such a git. Finally, but most important of all, these traditional movie boxers are completely dumb about money – as confirmed by their regular, fruitless cry, 'Give me my money.' 'I didn't fight for under a thousand for five years,' boasts a boxer in the original play of *Golden Boy*. 'I got a thousand bucks tonight, don't I?' His manager, reading a paper, looks up and says no, actually tonight he got twelve hundred. The fighter jumps to his feet, livid. 'What? I oughta bust your nose. How many times do I have to say I don't fight for under one thousand bucks?' The manager shrugs. 'Okay, you'll get your thousand,' he agrees.

What the movies don't tend to deal with (because it's so boring) is boxing's system of administration, which is so byzantine and preposterous that no one outside has a clue how to penetrate it, let alone challenge or dismantle it. But if you already have a suspicious nature and a sceptical attitude to boxing based on prolonged movie-watching, you can't hear about the WBO, IBO, IBF, WBU, et cetera without narrowing your eyes and making ironical harrumphing noises. The World Boxing Council, you see, has nothing to do with the World Boxing Association besides two shared initials; meanwhile there's the International Boxing Federation, the World Boxing Organisation, the World Boxing Union, the International Boxing Organisation, the World Boxing Federation, the International Boxing Council, and the International Boxing Association. In other words, if you can ingeniously contrive any original three-word combination of this limited range of nouns and adjectives, and can afford a big round bit of metal with some leather attached, you can set up your own legitimate boxing organisation in your downstairs lavatory for the price of a packet of stamps. All of these organisations are in the belt business, and at the time of the Holyfield–Lewis fight in 1999, Holyfield was IBF and WBA champion; Lewis was WBC. Or, quite honestly, it might have been the other way round.

Either way, the one thing I understood about this fight from the moment I arrived in New York was that toilers in the foetid world of boxing were hoping for a breath of fresh air to blow through the whole sport this coming weekend. Boxing's reputation was as low as it could get, and commentators had long since run out of synonyms for 'stink'. A recent fight arranged for Lewis had been against the American Oliver McCall – a man who may have looked, on paper, like a worthy opponent, since he had once knocked Lewis out at the Wembley Arena (in September 1994), but who was in such a bad mental state on the night of the second fight (in January 1997) that he was in tears in the ring. It was ghastly, apparently. All the

11

commentators who saw this fight quickly ran out of synonyms for 'sickened'. A recovering crack addict, McCall wandered around the ring avoiding Lewis, crying, talking to himself, and having a public nervous breakdown. Lewis held back, cautiously offering the occasional jab, like a cat testing a dead mouse. It was a confusing situation for a boxer trained to put himself on the line. To adapt the famous line from *Raging Bull* ('I didn't know whether to fuck him or fight him'), on this occasion, Lewis didn't know whether to fight McCall or offer him a nice cup of cocoa.

But now, come Saturday night, by a Herculean effort, a diverted river was going to gush through the Garden and wash all the blood off the ropes. Holyfield–Lewis was a very big deal. In fact, I was beginning to realise that nothing in the world – certainly not Bosnia – was as important as this contrived fight, for eight-figure money, between two men who (as yet) I didn't even know very much about. As I sat in my tiny hotel room in the evenings – listening to the exciting parp-parp of the wintry midtown traffic; leafing avidly through boxing magazines; pondering Norman Mailer's theory that boxing, like chess, is all about 'control of the centre' (how true); and occasionally jumping up to practise a combination of right to the kidney, followed by uppercut and left hook (quite difficult without falling over) – I started to share the palpable sense of destiny.

My first sight of Evander Holyfield was at a grim gym in lower Manhattan. It was a raw, freezing day, and I shared a cab with the chap from the *Telegraph*, who was staying at the same mid-town hotel (The Paramount). The co-incidence of our staying at the same hotel had really bucked me up, incidentally, because it seemed to me, during my four years in the business, that I was forever comparing travel arrangements with this particular chap, and coming out the loser by a knockout in the first round. 'Where are you staying, Lynne?' he would ask, when we met (say) at one of the earlier matches of the World Cup in Paris in 1998, and I would attempt to make light of the appalling truth. 'Well, it's quite interesting,' I'd say. 'They've put me in a hotel that costs a mere £24 a night – which must have taken quite some doing, don't you think? My room stinks of drains, doesn't have a television or a lavatory, and the phone has a big dial on it and is bolted to the wall, so I can't plug in my laptop. But heigh ho, what can you do? It's incredibly handy for the Musée d'Orsay, and I honestly haven't been attacked yet walking back up that dark street from the Metro dragging my big heavy laptop after midnight.' Then, with a huge generosity of spirit, I would ask, 'Where are you staying, then, Paul?' And it would always be somewhere stylish, bright, central, fully equipped, expensive, modem-friendly and (all-importantly) served door-to-door by media buses, that would make me want to saw my own head off.

Discovering that Paul and I were on the same flight to New York from Heathrow, therefore, we had gone through the usual routine on the plane – except, for once, I asked first. 'Oh, I'm staying at that Philippe Starck place off Times Square with all the funky furniture and the low lighting,' he said. 'Oh really?' I squeaked, trying not to betray my despair. 'I'm at some dump called The Paramount.'

And for heaven's sake, for once we were in the same place. It was a miracle. For once in my life, I was probably going to get a room with some basic bathroom fittings. Of course, when we arrived, Paul got himself upgraded to a better class of room immediately, while I had to argue for a couple of hours at check-in because the *Times* travel people had failed to confirm the reservation (this always happened). But still, to be in the same hotel in New York as the chap from the *Telegraph* for a whole week was really, really something, and I still feel quite proud.

Back at Holyfield's gym, I was keen to get a sight of a real boxer by now – which was a shame, because when we arrived (at the appointed time) real boxers were nowhere to be seen. It was a bleak spot, this gym: a high-ceilinged, whitewashed-brick kind of underground space filled with punch-bags and stale air, not to mention huddles of impatient hacks sipping take-out coffees. There were a couple of large murals of famous boxers on the side wall – they turned out to be Joe Louis and Jack Dempsey, so I'm glad I didn't guess. And as we all hung about, waiting to be summoned through a small door in the wall (like something from *Alice*) to an inner, warren-like place where Holyfield was said to be sparring in private, I think I had a bit of an epiphany. Making a puny fist, I tapped a punch-bag (which didn't move), and someone told me the interesting fact that Mike Tyson filled his punch-bags with water, so that hitting them was more like hitting the human body. I quipped, 'Does he cover them in human skin, too?' and then felt ashamed for being so flippant – especially as no one laughed.

Later, we would watch Lennox sparring in a much nicer

space at the Garden, but hanging about in that dank, unlovely gym brought things home to me in an important way, and at an important moment. Sometimes people come into my office and say, politely, 'So this is where it all happens?' and I get all uncomfortable, because, obviously, nothing happens here at all except a lot of impressive tea-drinking, and I assume they're just trying to avoid saying, 'Oh my God, what a mess' in any case. But anyway, my point is, you go into an old, battered, smelly Skid Row gym like that, and suddenly this upcoming fight is nothing to do with the HBO pay-per-view millions, or the international diplomacy success of the promoter, or the trading of hollow physical threats by besuited fighters on podiums with fireworks in the background. Because this is where it all happens. This is where men build defences, and learn by getting hurt. This is where they sweat and learn and concentrate, and – in Holyfield's case – acquire neck muscles like anchor chains. Of course, I knew that Holyfield didn't use this scuzzy gym every day of his life: a multimillionaire, he lived in considerable luxury in Texas, with a swimming pool shaped like a championship belt, and had fathered nine children by twelve women (or something like that), while also being strenuously devout, which some people saw as not quite adding up. Holyfield once said in an interview that all men had to get out of their trousers from time to time, and the interviewer said, 'But not as often as you.' But that's not the point. By the time I got my chance to go through the little door and see the sweating, shaven-headed and massively muscular Evander Holyfield – sparring energetically in a darker, smaller, and even sweatier space – I was so sensitised to the idea of

15

boxing's sheer physicality that I almost fainted at the sight of him.

I hadn't been prepared for this sudden powerful interest in these two men's bodies. It came as a shock after three years in the trade. Every week of my life, I routinely heard about injuries of one sort or another – footballers with fractured metatarsals; tennis players with strained hamstrings – and the information didn't impinge very much. The chaps' bodies were just the tools of their trade. One of my treasured football press conference questions was, on the subject of a chronically injured star player, 'Anything new on the groin?' (My next favourite was golfer Justin Leonard saying that he'd taken his bogeys with a pinch of salt.) I admit that casual mention of footballers, in multiples, 'on the treatment tables' conjured a too-vivid image sometimes, because I pictured them naked and at rest, face up, expectant, lightly oiled, under sheets describing suggestive contours; and I also remember with great clarity a moment when the then fabulously dreadlocked – and very beautiful – Henrik Larsson, playing for Celtic, celebrated a goal with his shirt off and took me completely by surprise with what was underneath. But by and large, I regarded sportsmen as hairy-kneed yeomen whose flesh, skin and muscle were their own affair, and certainly nothing to do with me.

It helped to be reading Joyce Carol Oates at this juncture – and there's a sentence I never thought I'd write. But her book *On Boxing* is a small masterpiece. A great fan of boxing, she is in love with the plain fact that it's not a metaphor for anything else. While organised games are metaphors for war, and tennis (say) is a metaphor for

16

hand-to-hand combat, boxing isn't. 'I can entertain the proposition that life is a metaphor for boxing,' is as far as she'll go (and is as funny as she gets, by the way). 'Boxing is only like boxing.' Boxers, she says, 'are there to establish an absolute experience, a public accounting of the outermost limits of their beings'. People who attend fights because they like seeing blood spray about probably don't think about it this deeply, perhaps; but that doesn't make it untrue. A fight is a culmination of training, a moment of truth, a supreme form of reckoning, and the bottom line is that most of us will never experience anything remotely as testing as a public accounting of the outermost limits of our being. I once went the full twelve rounds with John Lewis Online customer services, and I won't say I wasn't bruised by it, but I would never claim it was the real thing.

For these two men to measure up to one another in a ring on Saturday night was not just a contrivance for the sake of entertainment; it was a magnificent, if still horrifying, necessity. Their job, I now saw, was not so much to hurt each other as to protect themselves and emerge with honour. I didn't want to see it happen, but at the same time I couldn't miss it. If they were going to risk so much, the least I could do was watch. Oates makes one outstanding claim for boxing: 'It is the most tragic of all sports because, more than any human activity, it consumes the very excellence it displays – its drama is this very consumption.' Or, as everyone kept saying in relation to Holyfield (aged 37) in the week before the fight, 'Sometimes you see a boxer age in the ring, right there in front of you.'

17

However, at this point, Holyfield himself was not antici-pating such a transfiguration. He was predicting he would knock out Lewis in the third round. He said it at the gym, and he said it later. The American press were very grateful for this uncharacteristic prediction, as it supported their rather simplistic sales pitch on Holyfield, which was that he had tons of 'heart'. We heard an awful lot about Holyfield's heart in the week before the fight. I started to think we should demand to see an x-ray, or at least have it weighed in separately. Lewis, meanwhile, was charac-terised as a kind of cowardly lion because – by contrast to Holyfield – he made no bones about preferring not to be hit. The American press were very unfair to Lewis, but you could see why he confused them, with his languid, sleep-walking manner, his unblemished good looks, and his unhurried, unemotional common sense. Lewis said that everyone asked him, all the time, about his supposed in-feriority in the 'heart' department; meanwhile, he never saw a picture of himself in the American press that didn't have a question mark next to it.

So one man was symbolised by an oversized pumping vital organ; the other by a curly punctuation mark invented at the time of Charlemagne. You can see why Lewis felt this wasn't fair, and why he kept making the point – quite patiently – that having a reputation for 'heart' comes from foolishly getting into situations where 'heart' is desperately required. Lewis did not intend to get into such situations. His 'sweet science' would prevail; then he would 'reign supercilious'. 'At age fifty,' he said, 'I want to be able to get out of bed. At age fifty, Evander Holyfield won't be able to speak.'

Clearly there were significant differences between the fighting styles and capabilities of these men. And as the sparring-day passed, everyone talked about fighting on the 'outside' and the 'inside'. I was surprised at how open each camp was about their fighter's relative strengths and weaknesses, but I suppose such things are impossible to hide. Lewis, the taller and heavier man, with a much longer reach, could control the outside as a matter of course. In training with Emmanuel Steward (leader of a famous gym in Detroit, and trainer of umpteen champions, including Holyfield), he had been working on his left jab, and on blocking the kind of counter-punch that poor old Oliver McCall (in better days) had knocked him out with. When we watched him sparring later that day, though, I'm afraid I got distracted from the jab, being overwhelmed yet again by matters of sheer anatomy. It was like the moment Piglet gets all overcome at the sight of Christopher Robin's blue braces. I think I had my fingers in my mouth for most of the afternoon. 'Look. Look at that flesh,' I whispered to anyone who would listen. 'Admit it, wouldn't you like to give that a little push?' Later in the week, we would get all the comparative vital statistics (they call this pre-fight ritual 'The Tale of the Tape'), but basically, Lewis was just enormous, six foot five, over seventeen stone, with shoulders like beach balls and arms like young trees, and skin so richly velvety that it surely has to be lovingly brushed each morning in the same direction. The parading of these men like prize cattle may be a bit distasteful, but it's also honest. If you're going to see them get into a ring and try to beat the living daylights out of each other, you need to know precisely what they've got to lose.

As the day of the fight approached, I tried to keep track of things, and to remember what I formerly hated about boxing. It was getting difficult. There's that very funny thing in Douglas Adams's *The Hitch-Hiker's Guide to the Galaxy*, when Arthur Dent finds out how unpleasant it feels to be 'drunk' – and it turns out this doesn't mean what it feels like to be inebriated, it means what it feels like to be swallowed in liquid form, and it's very unpleasant indeed. Getting close to sporting events, I often felt drunk in exactly this Douglas Adams sense; it was extremely disorientating. The world beyond the event shrank to a dot; I felt my perceptions flipping inside out; time expanded so that a week seemed like a month; I got hotly impatient with loved ones at home who said on the phone, vaguely, 'Is it over? Did I miss it? Did anyone win?'; I danced in sidelong manner around my hotel bedroom practising my feeble left jab and making 'Toof, toof' noises; and most weirdly of all, I read the work of Norman Mailer, nodding wisely, and even underlined it with a pencil.

In short, I was a different person. A few weeks before, the name 'Lewis' would have made me think of maybe C.S. Lewis, Sinclair Lewis, the John Lewis Online customer services department (damn them), or Lewis Carroll. Now I wanted to chant that there was only one Lennox Lewis, and I wanted him to keep his hands up, use his jab, block Holyfield's left hook, keep breathing, protect that lovely skin, and above all remember what chess teaches you about controlling the centre. On the day before the fight, I did something completely out of character, and it makes my heart-rate accelerate just to recall it. I phoned the office in London from my mobile – furtively, outside on 34th

Street in the face-shrinking, slab-like cold – and said that, come what may, I must see this fight. I think they were a bit surprised by my vehemence, but the Garden had been prevaricating about press tickets; they kept promising and then delaying, and I had started to get very anxious. What if they gave *The Times* only two seats? There were three of us in New York! Oh no, not again, I said. Not this time, buddy. I'm not getting bumped this time. The problem was, the office always liked the sort of 'colour' piece I wrote about being banished to some nasty sports bar, to watch an event on TV with the locals. But they could whistle this time, I said; they could whistle up their god-damned *ass*. 'If we only get two tickets, you've got to send Rob to some bar, not me. He hates boxing. He keeps writing pieces about the death of Joe DiMaggio instead. He doesn't attend the press conferences. He's spending all his time with Pelé. His heart's not in this the way mine is!' (Rob was the chief sports writer, and he outranked me in every way. There was no possibility they would accede to this demand.)

Luckily they didn't quarrel with me; they just said, 'Why don't we wait and see what happens?' But had they taken issue, I fear I would have quoted Joyce Carol Oates at them: 'Like all extreme but perishable actions, boxing excites not only the writer's imagination, but also his instinct to bear witness.' What a genius this woman was. She was reading my mind. Because, yes, yes, I must bear witness to this extreme but also perishable action. I *must*. This fight might not be dedicated to women (or if it was, it was never mentioned again), but this woman was now totally dedi-cated to *it*. On the Thursday night, with the ticket situation still unresolved, I briefly entertained the idea of pushing

Rob under a cab, or paying someone to lure him to a lonely dock on the East River and blow him away. It also occurred to me that the lobby of my fashionable hotel was so absurdly dimly lit, Rob's lifeless body could lie undiscovered for quite some time amid the trendy Philippe Starck chairs, so the sleeping-with-the-fishes option might not be necessary. But on Friday, finally, I got my fight ticket, and so did he. We had seats together, as it happened, and we went on to have a very interesting and remarkable evening in each other's company, marred (for me) only by crippling feelings of guilt and shame. I never told Rob that, had it come right down to it, I'd have done anything to get him out of the picture, or that being present at the Holyfield–Lewis fight on March 13, 1999 now meant so much to me that I'd considered it worth committing murder for a ticket.

THE FIGHT

It turned out to be a famous night in the history of boxing, all right, although the atmosphere in this world-famous arena was, at first, profoundly disappointing for a girl who had relished the idea of a Saturday off from British football fans. All week, the news hounds in our midst had been telling us that 'six or seven thousand' British fans were travelling to New York to support Lennox Lewis, yet it somehow never occurred to me that this was a coded warning to make for the Adirondacks. I never guessed the British fans would bring their usual boorish British-fan manners with them to MSG. But here they were, many in England football shirts, and all in full-throated away-game mode, in an enclosed place of entertainment well past bedtime (the fight didn't start till after 11 p.m.), chanting that Don King was a 'fat bastard' – which was fair enough actually – and also roundly booing everything American in sight.

I had mixed feelings. These fans were funny, but they were also incredibly depressing. They booed the ringside celebrities; they booed 'The Star Spangled Banner'; they couldn't pipe down even for the tribute to the just-deceased

American hero Joe DiMaggio. All those old boxing movies had not prepared me for the reality of this particular fight crowd. True, I'd seen scenes of angry fight-goers jeering, whistling and throwing folded programmes, and sometimes even uprooting furniture and trampling defenceless well-dressed women underfoot – but that was usually after the fight, not before. Why such animus towards the inoffensive Paul Simon? *Bridge Over Troubled Water* was not only an enduring classic album, it included that sensitive song 'The Boxer' which we would surely all do well to remember this evening. 'Why do they hate Donald Trump so much?' I asked Rob. 'Do they even know who he is?' When the presence of Jack Nicholson was announced, however, they stopped booing and gave a big cheer. Perhaps they were scared of him. It was a mystery I never got to the bottom of.

On the plus side, however, it's a big arena, holding over 21,000 people, and there was plenty of salt popcorn. Rob and I had seats quite a long way back from the action, but we had taken our binoculars, and there were large screens suspended above the ring. I felt really, really bad about how I'd been planning to murder Rob and dispose of his body, but I won't go on about it. I was now quite glad he was there. And I have to say, the build-up was horribly prolonged for someone already near to a state of hyperventilation, privately fretting about what might unfold within the next hour. Boxers have been known to die in the ring, you know. They have also died in hospital afterwards, without recovering consciousness. The crowd goes crazy, I was informed, at the first sight of blood. Holyfield was predicting a knockout in the third. Although Joyce

Carol Oates insists in her book that boxing is statistically less dangerous than other mainstream sports such as horse-racing, motor-racing and American football (and that therefore liberal middle-class hand-wringing about boxing is less straightforward than it looks), it's still true that boxing is all about efficiently biffing someone on the head, which is the most violent thing you can do to another person without resorting to weaponry (or to crime).

It's all to do with how soft the brain is, and how little protection it has inside the brain box. If the boxing author-ities could only find a way of packing the fighters' cranial cavities with little polystyrene balls, or kapok, or feathers – just for the duration of a fight – a lot of squeamish people in the wider world would definitely relax more. But no one has ever come up with a suitable material (or indeed, even tried to), so the brain is left to slosh about inside a hard casing, which isn't such a good idea when organised biffing is going on. Basically, if you carefully place a nice wobbly milk jelly inside a biscuit tin and then kick it against a wall for half an hour, you get a fair idea of what happens to the human brain during a heavyweight fight. A well-aimed blow from a professional heavyweight carries the equivalent force of 10,000 pounds, says Oates – and you can't help wondering whether boxers themselves are deliberately cushioned from this kind of information.

As an *ersatz* sports writer, I loved the drama of all occa-sions. I never felt it was my job to testify to greatness, as some sportswriters do; it was my job to see how an unwritten story ineluctably formed itself, in front of my very eyes, from quite unpromising basic ingredients – such as a flat rectangle of grass with lines on it and twenty-two men in shorts; or an undulating landscape with flags and sand pits at intervals, and dozens of individual men, dressed in natty knitwear, each with a small white ball and a bag of sticks. Waiting for the start of my first heavyweight fight was a moment of reckoning. The basic ingredients here were a spot-lit ring with ropes, and two very large men wearing padded gloves, with designs on each other's sense of physical well-being. A heavyweight fight was completely different from all other sporting occasions I'd encountered because this ineluctable drama contained in it the potential for ineluctable tragedy, and this was the first time I'd ever had to address anything quite so serious. As Joyce Carol Oates kept reminding me, this was not a metaphor for something else.

I still wished they would get on with it, though. Even when the fighters finally made their appearance in the arena the suspense was terrible, because it took them such a bloody long time to reach the ring. The Lewis entrance (first) was a shambles, with his ragged entourage having to shove its way through a crowd that appeared to be shoving back. Laid-back reggae was the incongruous accompaniment to this disgraceful near-riot, involving Garden security staff, fans, bodyguards, and a chap with a flag, and it would have been quite funny if it hadn't been so dreadful. 'Whose fault is this?' I wanted to know – but then I've already established how I feel about things being badly organised. Still, Lennox looked focused and unfazed by the turmoil holding up his progress, possibly because the mellow music was working so well for him, but also possibly because he towered literally head and shoulders above everyone else, and all the aggro was taking place about a foot below his eye-line. I ought to mention that in the thick of the mêlée was the tiny figure of Frank Maloney, Lewis's boxing manager, tastefully dressed up as a parody of the Artful Dodger in a Union Jack suit with a Union Jack cap. This fact alone, perhaps, kept Lewis's eyes fixed resolutely on the middle distance.

Holyfield entered – with considerably more ease – to a warm gospel song that was probably about how incredibly big his heart was, but I couldn't tell, there was so much cheering. And then, with just enough time for me to get used to the almighty size of the shorts they were both wearing ('What enormous shorts!'), there was the announcement of the two men, the belts they already held, the three ringside judges (one from South Africa, one from Atlantic City, and one from London), mention of the referee being the son of another referee, twelve rounds of three minutes, and ding-ding, blimey, before I could worry too much about how many synonyms for 'horrified' I was going to require before the night was out, it had started, amid roars from the crowd, and thousands of cameras flashing at once. Lewis came out very positively, left arm horizontal, left fist level with Holyfield's face, delivering smart, straight-arm jabs every few seconds, with Holyfield largely back-pedalling and evidently trying to figure out some way of getting to the 'inside'. Lewis was clearly in control, as Rob and I sagely agreed. We had decided to keep personal point scores according to the proper system – i.e., 10 points to the winner of a round and nine to the loser, unless there's a knock-down (then it's 10–8), or a draw (10–10). In the event of a knockout, it's still technically a win on points, apparently, but I never quite mastered the maths of that. I merely knew, as everyone does, that a knockout means it's all over. Meanwhile marks out of six for artistic interpretation and technical merit don't come into it at all, which was a shame because, by my calculations, Lennox was doing quite well on those counts as well.

At the end of round one, I felt pretty good. True, I needed a spongeful of water on the back of my neck, and a respite from the gum-shield, but I wasn't out for the count. Lennox also looked as if he felt OK. Holyfield was mainly looking a bit thoughtful, like someone who's been punched in the face non-stop for three minutes while concentrating on walking backwards. At the end of the round he had suddenly lowered his head between Lewis's legs and, bizarrely, lifted him off his feet rather in the manner of a trainee fireman – an unconventional, not to say desperate-looking and ungainly move that had earned them both a reminder from the ref about keeping it clean. In the second round, Lewis again efficiently kept Holyfield at arm's length, but also landed a couple of classy blows with his right. But Holyfield's prediction that he would knock out Lewis in the third was probably uppermost in both their minds during those first two rounds; it was certainly uppermost in mine. The fight would be won or lost, surely, in that third round – and if the drama were to be cranked up a bit now, to be frank, most people wouldn't complain.

Although I felt guilty about it, I had begun to see what people moaned about in Lewis's fighting style, and why his trainer got so short-tempered with that travelling chess set of his. Even when in control, you see, Lewis had the air of someone manifestly *thinking*, pondering his options, eyes narrowed, as if deliberating whether the Budapest Gambit would leave him too exposed, eight moves down the line, to the classic Schleswig-Holstein Defence. Holyfield, by contrast, with his head forward and sweat pouring off him, seemed to be simply more engaged in a bout of fisticuffs (as seemed fitting in the circumstances). Finding himself on the back foot in the more explosive third round, Lewis did stop calculating for a little while – Holyfield had charged out of his corner at the bell and started throwing serious blows, including two solid rights to the side of Lewis's head. But a temporary shifting of Lewis's rock-like centre of gravity was all that Holyfield had achieved by the end of a heroic and exhausting three minutes, and Holyfield walked back to his corner with his shoulders down, and his head down, too – or, at least, his head bent forward as far as it would go, given how firmly his prodigious neck muscles are attached like splints to the back of it. Was it all over for Holyfield? Lewis seemed to have been shaken, though, because the fourth was quite even. Only in the fifth did Lewis look back in control again.

Obviously, I've watched this fight again recently. By an absolute fluke, while I was researching and making notes for this book, I ransacked the house for my video of *Raging Bull*, and found at the back of a drawer a forgotten tape with 'Lewis fight' written on it in small letters. I couldn't believe my luck. It was in among my Jeff Bridges collection, behind such unforgettable classics as *Tucker: The Man and His Dream* (1988) and *Thunderbolt and Lightfoot* (1974). I turned it over in my hands, wiped off a layer of dust, and thought, this is exactly the sort of invaluable resource that usually turns up just after you've finished your book, or just after it's gone to press. So what a miracle. The week after my return from New York, it turns out, Sky Sports had re-shown the fight, in full, with in-studio analysis, and I'd recorded it (and then, for whatever reason, hidden it to be found after my death by the house-clearers). If I had found this tape at any other moment in the intervening eight years, by the way, I would undoubtedly have recorded *University Challenge*, *Pet Rescue* or an even lesser-known Jeff Bridges film on top of it. I still can't get over this domestic miracle, as you can tell.

What I had remembered from the fateful night was that Lewis had a good fifth round and that thereafter he seemed to be coasting, confident of winning on points. What the tape showed was that the first half of the fifth round had some terrific boxing from Lewis, but that old fight hands (including Lewis's animated trainer) were in despair that he didn't finish off Holyfield there and then. Later, Don King would say, 'When you have a man on the ropes, you're supposed to finish him, not play chess with him.' Lewis would reply, as always, that there was no sense in exposing himself unnecessarily to counter-attack, which is a perfectly defensible point of view. As far as Lewis was concerned, he was winning this fight and doing it his own way, by anticipating and frustrating Holyfield's moves, while landing a huge number of blows. Holyfield was bruised, puffy and in manifest need of a long lie-down (with his trousers on). My own impression at the time was that, 'While working Holyfield relentlessly with the famous left jab and openly dominating him, Lewis was like an angler teasing a fish on his line. Just because he didn't bang the fish on the head with a mallet doesn't mean he didn't catch him.'

But now I don't know. The rest of the fight was, in reality, not so one-sided as it seemed on the night. Lewis landed vastly more punches than Holyfield, but he didn't have a clearly brilliant winning round again until the last, while Holyfield rallied in the tenth. At the arena, however, we had stopped scoring quite a long time ago, and were convinced Lewis had won it comfortably, and won it in style. When the final bell sounded, Lewis raised his arms in triumph, and Holyfield just breathed heavily. It had been a thrilling fight, and the great thing for me was that there had been no excessive violence to be sickened by. The sense of relief was fabulous. The jellies were largely safe in their biscuit tins, after all – and at no point had I jumped up and screamed, 'Stop it! Stop it! Stop it! Stop it! Stop it!' (which was what I had secretly feared). Everyone in the ring congratulated Lewis on his brilliant fight. Rob and I congratulated each other on our outstanding profession-alism in the face of this historic triumph. Because it *was* historic, by the way: not only because it temporarily united the titles, but because no British man had held the un-disputed heavyweight championship of the world in the whole of the 20th century until this moment, in 1999, in the very last tickings of the millennium. From Lewis's point of view, his wait was over, he had silenced his critics, and his question mark could be changed forthwith to an exclamation point. A transparently legitimate fight had been transparently won. Lastly, those world-weary boxing commentators could at last start reaching for synonyms for 'hallelujah' and 'coming up smelling of roses'.

But then the scores of the judges were announced, so we all listened carefully – with smiles turning quizzical, and eyes narrowing, and heads shaking, and (finally) hackles rising. Because this is the part of the proceedings that the night is actually famous for. The American judge (a woman called Eugenia Williams) had scored it 115 points to 113, apparently, which seemed a bit close, but never mind. Except, hang on, she had scored 115–113 in favour of Holyfield! Good heavens. Only in America, right? But she was only one judge, after all. The second judge, the South African (Stanley Christodoulou) had scored it 116–113 to Lewis, which was a bit more like it, although still surprisingly close. And finally, the British judge (Larry O'Connell) had scored it 115–115, a draw. Both fighters therefore retained their belts and the contest was announced to have no winner, thank you and good night, drive home safe everybody, see you next time, just be careful on the stairs. 'What?' we all said. '*What?*' The place was full of bewilderment, disbelief and booing. We blinked, confused. Could they run that past us again? There must be some mistake. By most calculations, Holyfield had won three rounds at most. Such a decision was impossible, unless – unless, well, I mean, listen, buddy; do I need to spell it out for ya?

As, one by one, we saw how Lewis had been robbed, the temptation was to burst into tears. How *could* we have been taken in? Didn't they have us all fooled this time, eh? I found myself not bothering to think of synonyms for 'stinks'. I was too upset. I had been completely wrung dry for a full week for *this*? 'This stinks,' I kept saying, as disbelief turned swiftly to disgust. 'It stinks. It really stinks.

Oh, poor Lennox. Someone should say to him, this absolutely stinks.'

The astonishing thing was that the crowd didn't riot. Footage of Lewis's reaction in the ring shows him, vertiginously puzzled, looking around him and mouthing a short, one-word exclamation beginning with the letter 'M' (presumably 'Man!') and not beginning with 'F', which is remarkable in the circumstances. Then the fighters left the ring, and the crowd dispersed, and the next thing on this long, wearisome night was a rolling boil of a badly-organised press conference full of seethingly indignant men – and not just the British press, either; the American press was livid as well. The most significant outcome of the draw decision was that the American press was so outraged on Lewis's behalf that it forgot all about its previous assessment of him as a negligible fighter with a small squeaking hand-pump where his true boxer's heart ought to be. In fact, on ESPN (the sports channel), the bearded pundit who had spent all week rubbishing Lewis picked up the judgement and tore it in half on screen. Next day, the *New York Post* wrote: 'The fight plan may have been drawn up by the Lord, but the scorecards bore the mark of the devil. It was a night in which the glory and honour of boxing was supposed to return to its former home; instead, the stink returned to the air over the ring.' 'They robbed Lennox Lewis of the championship he won in the ring,' wrote the *Washington Post*. 'They damaged the sport they love. They called a fight a draw when it had been no such thing.' Meanwhile the *New York Times* said the decision resembled 'a Brinks truck heist perpetrated in front of 21,284 fans'.

We arrived at the post-fight press conference clutching the statistics, which had been released immediately, just to rub it in. Evidently these numbers had meant nothing to the judges, but they looked very persuasive to most of the people now assembled. Lewis had connected 348 punches (from 613 thrown) as against Holyfield's 130 connected (out of 385). As for jabs, Lewis had connected with 187 (from 364 thrown); Holyfield had connected with 52 (from 171). When you consider that a fight of 12 three-minute rounds totals 36 minutes, these statistics meant that Holyfield had been successfully hit, on average, 10 times a minute, and had been jabbed in the face five times a minute as well. No wonder, when he turned up for the press conference, he looked puffy and pained and had to keep leaning on the table for support. Meanwhile Lennox, with just a couple of Elastoplasts on small cuts, stood tall in his sunshades and FCUK hat (he was sponsored by French Connection UK, with its charmless acronym), and looked – relatively – fresh as a daisy.

The sense of let-down was almost unendurable. Had it all been a fix, after all? The bout that was supposed to settle everything had settled nothing – except, perhaps, that you can fool all of the people all of the time. Sensitive as ever, Don King tried to smooth the situation by summing up: 'Some are BORN GREAT, some ACHIEVE GREATNESS, and some have greatness THRUST UPON THEM. Tonight, Lennox Lewis had greatness THRUST UPON HIM!' – which was a characteristically perverse application of the Bard, I'd say, since Lennox's greatness had been very much achieved on this occasion, and then blatantly stolen from him in full view of millions of people around the world, some of whom had been persuaded to suspend warfare for the privilege. When you consider the murderous mood of the assembled press, the almighty nerve of Don King on this occasion was breathtaking. He started to plan a re-match. 'What this is, is MORE EXCITE-MENT!' he urged us, as if we were missing the bigger picture. 'It ain't over yet, this is so great! What do you do when you got a DISPUTE? You resolve it! So let's do it again! Let's do it AGAIN! Hey, judge NOT that YE be not JUDGED!' Lewis's camp walked out when they couldn't stand it any more, with Frank Maloney stating that the 'people's champion' was leaving the building. 'NOT a smart move,' King remarked.

Over the following week, conspiracy theorists tried to unpick the judging decision, convinced that there had been skulduggery. Nothing was ever proved. The American judge, Eugenia Williams, upheld that she scored the fight the way she saw it, even in giving Holyfield the fifth round. When shown the round again, she admitted she'd made a mistake, but argued that her view had been obscured by photographers. The British judge, Larry O'Connell, main-tained he had handed in his scores round by round, and was surprised that these agglomerated scores had amounted to a draw. Putting it in context, it seems that iffy judging decisions occur all the time in boxing, which is why trainers so strenuously urge chaps like Lewis to finish off oppon-ents when they get the chance, to put matters beyond dispute. But I will never accept that it was Lennox's fault that he didn't win at Madison Square Garden. If the draw decision wasn't downright corruption, then it was wilfully bad organisation. With so much at stake, they should have employed a more experienced judge than Mrs Williams. But hark at me. It wasn't Holyfield who turned into a crushed old man that night in Madison Square Garden: it was me. I muttered and railed. If I'd known how to do it, I'd have spat on the floor. I had fostered fond illusions about the nobility of boxing for only two or three days at the outside, but now those illusions had been shattered, I felt as cynical and embittered as the chaps who had inwardly wept about this stuff for years and years and years.

Rob and I walked back up 7th Avenue, discussing events and trying not to have our faces torn off by the freezing wind. I got to bed around 2.30 a.m., and went to sleep still clutching the fight stats, which turned out to be quite a good idea, as I was woken an hour later by a call from my boss in London, who had got up early to watch the fight (around 4 a.m. local time) and then gone straight to the office in Wapping in an excited state of mind. It was now only 8.30 a.m. in London, but he was raring to go, and already scheming to get the story on the front page of Monday's *Times*. So I read him the stats, made some coffee and started writing my column. It had been a comfortable week for the writing, by and large. The London first-edition deadline being 6.30 p.m., I had needed to file by 1.30 p.m. EST each day, which meant I could write (comfortably and in private) at the hotel in the morning, generally about things that had happened the day before. I had written about the sparrings, the weigh-in, Don King, and of course quite a lot of technical stuff about hooks, jabs and uppercuts in case the readers weren't quite sure of the difference. I had also taken an interest in an under-card fight between 'Ferocious' Fernando Vargas (from the us) and Howard Clarke (uk) – 'Ferocious' being the rather terrifying 21-year-old IBF junior middleweight champion, and Clarke a likeable 31-year-old Englishman from Dudley who was fighting – adorably – under the sponsorship of 'Fonz Leathers', the shop he worked in. Clarke's was the most heart-warming story on the night, as it happens. He went four rounds before being knocked out by Vargas, and I saw him having his dinner afterwards in a backstage area, fully dressed, evidently unharmed and completely thrilled to bits. He had earned £18,000 in a single night, and had acquitted himself better in the ring than he could ever have dreamed. His was the kind of benign boxing story not often made into a major motion picture, so it was all the more a privilege to hear about it.

As I started writing in the early hours of Sunday morning, I realised that this was to be not only my last piece about the fight, but possibly my last piece ever about boxing. This was strange and sad, but I tried not to dwell on it. Life would have to get back to normal – and very quickly indeed, as it happened. At the back of my mind I was trying to adjust to the peculiar fact that I had bought tickets (for me and a resolutely non-sporty New York friend) to see Sophocles' *Electra* at the Ethel Barrymore Theatre that afternoon, which I now saw required an absurdly large mental leap from one culture to another that might easily leave me falling short, scrabbling for a bit of vine to hold on to, and dangling over a bottomless ravine. As a person,

I am nothing if not efficiently compartmentalised, but this was ridiculous. My friend wouldn't even want to hear about Lewis and Holyfield. She was an art historian. And I was full of this fight. My ears were still ringing with it, and I was still hot with indignation. The only way I could smooth this transition was to remind myself that this particular Greek tragedy would be considerably more violent than the thing I had watched last night. It is noticeable in *Electra*, for example, that when the father-avenging Orestes gets his mother Clytemnestra against the ropes (so to speak), his bloodthirsty sister Electra does not call out, 'No need to finish her off, Orestes! You're winning on points. Any fool can see you're winning on points!'

I duly went to the theatre that afternoon, and it was as confusing for me as I had expected – especially when only one hour's sleep separated me from events at Madison Square Garden. Zoë Wanamaker was fantastic as Electra, I have to say; and with a very original haircut and Iron Curtain trench-coat to boot. The production was great, and I liked the translation. All in all, *Electra* very nearly succeeded in putting all thought of the Holyfield–Lewis stinkeroo decision out of my still-racing mind. But the audience was the trouble, ultimately: it was so damned quiet and inert compared to the fight crowd. I squirmed in my seat at how sedate it all was. Throughout the play, I sighed and harrumphed, clenching and re-clenching my leg muscles. How can people just sit here like lumps, with all this interesting and semi-justified slaughter going on? Did the ancient Greek audiences sit mute like statues? I'm sure they didn't. This lot didn't even boo when Clytemnestra appeared. They didn't even jump up and down when the first blood was shed (offstage, of course), or shout 'Stop it, stop it, stop it, stop it!' when the carnage was described. There were no half-naked showgirls coming on between scenes in stilettos, either, holding up bits of card – which wouldn't add much to the cost of the production, surely, and would really brighten things up. Blimey, was I in a strange perceptual state. I wanted to be back at the Garden, yelling 'Fix!' and 'Bastards!' and here I was, in a small, darkened auditorium, strenuously empathising with a crop-headed grudge-nurser who'd been crying vengeance for going on 3,000 years. The injustice of Holyfield–Lewis might not be of mythical proportions, but it happened only last night. If anyone should be wailing and demanding attention from the gods, surely, it was poor, poor Lennox Lewis?

As it happened, however, I had two further brushes with boxing. When 'Holyfield–Lewis II' duly took place eight months later in Las Vegas, I stayed up all night to watch it on TV. Lennox finally got his undisputed title, and I got fully re-animated in instant-know-all mode, especially when the commentators kept saying, 'Lennox has forgotten his left jab!' which really incensed me. 'What nonsense,' I kept saying. If Lennox wasn't using his left jab, and was mixing it more, it was because he knew that battering Holyfield's head at arm's length was a strategy that had failed to impress the judges on a previous occasion. 'Lewis knows what he's doing!' I started to yell at the telly. 'Is it likely that he has forgotten his left jab, sir, when you and I have not?'

Then, in July 2000, I was sent to see 'The Homecoming' – not the Pinter play, alas, but Lewis's triumphant return to the London Arena, in a fight against Frans (or Francois) Botha, a scared-looking South African who never stood a chance, quite honestly, and was knocked half out of the ring in the second round. Feeling remotely comfortable in fight surroundings was even more surreal than feeling like an alien, I discovered. I waved hello to the chap from the *Sun*. I recognised lots of boxers, all done up in tuxedoes and dicky-bow-ties. There was a moment before the fight when Garry Richardson (of Radio 4) tapped me on the shoulder and asked me to get the attention of boxing promoter Frank Warren (who was sporting a blood-filled eye at the time, rumoured to be the outcome of a disagreement with Mike Tyson). Anyway, I tapped Frank Warren on the shoulder and said, indicating behind me, 'Frank, sorry; Garry wants a word.' And I did feel very proud at that moment. Going up some stairs with the chap from the *Guardian*, we passed George Foreman going down. I think he even said 'Good evening.' But I decided not to stop him and say, 'I don't suppose you remember this, Mr Foreman, but in 1974 in Zaire, Muhammad Ali really took you by surprise.'

Yes, some people had paid £750 to be at this event, but it was just a day's work for Sports Writer Truss. Lewis entered the arena through a flame-licked portcullis flanked by skinny blondes done up like Beefeaters – and this time the lengthy procession to the stage was drawn out intentionally. Why Botha chose to wear a white fluffy bathmat for his own walk through the booing crowd at the London Arena, by the way, only the gods of comedy could tell us.

But from the moment he made his entrance, wearing the bathmat in jaunty poncho style with a black knitted bobble-hat to top the ensemble, Lennox's chances of knocking him out in the first round started to look extremely good. I assumed Botha intended to look like a white buffalo – this being his adopted soubriquet. But only if he had come out dressed as a rubber duck could the omens for a fifty–fifty contest have been worse. Not that Botha was an unworthy opponent in theory (or even on paper), but because from the moment they stood face to face, he had the look of someone whose torso might be packed to the neck with 'heart' (not that again), but whose brain was sending the message, 'Run! Run! Run for your life!'

This was a much less worrying occasion, as you can tell. I had a whale of a time. The battle between Botha's chief internal organs was quite as exciting to observe (by examining the look in his eyes) as the fight between Botha and Lewis.

HEART: Stay on your feet, Frans. Draw him in. You have very fast hands, don't forget, and a good right hook. Duck, reverse, footwork, come on. Just avoid his left jab, Frans, and you'll be dandy.

BRAIN: Run! Run for your life!

HEART: Don't listen to him, Frans. Listen to me. You're a good boxer. You took Tyson to five rounds –

BRAIN: But he's enormous! And he keeps punching the side of your head!

HEART: Don't listen.

BRAIN: Save yourself and flee!

HEART: Shut up.

41

BRAIN: No you shut up.

HEART: You shut up.

BRAIN: (AND CHORUS OF OTHER SENSES): Quick, Frans. Run! Run for your life!

The end was mercifully swift. Two minutes and 39 seconds into the second round, it was all over. Lewis jabbed Botha, then punched him with the right, and seeing Botha buckle, delivered two more immense blows to send the 'white buffalo' halfway through the ropes and out of the fight. It was the sort of undignified exit usually associated with two muscular nightclub bouncers with the benefit of a run-up. Lewis, however, delivered it with one punch from a position of rest, and if you've never seen power of such magnitude at close range, I can only report it's worth seeing. The only time I'd seen anything like it before would have been in *Popeye*.

When I stopped writing about sport later in 2000, it wasn't that I was finished with it. Mainly, I was finished with the lifestyle of the sports writer – or, at least, the lifestyle of the middle-aged female sports writer, which (as Alan Bennett once beautifully said of being Prince of Wales) is not so much a job as a predicament. But if I had mixed feelings about sport while I was fully submerged in it, I have even more mixed feelings now that I have been safely back on dry land for over half a decade, blocking my ears to Premiership transfers, refusing to look at points tables, and reading newspapers resolutely from the front to the back, instead of the other way round. My idea of myself is that I can now identify equally with both sports fanatics and sports agnostics – acting as a kind of human bridge – but it's not strictly true. There is more than a remnant of Moonie-style thinking still in me, so that when a sports agnostic says that he 'doesn't like' sport, I think, 'Ah, but you would if you just knew a little more about it.' There was a time when a man professing not to like football made him tons more attractive to me; now I receive the news with a polite smile and try not to blurt out, 'Blimey, were you born this negative, or did you have to work at it?' I am the agonised and restless result of a scientific experiment, like the poor, tortured creatures in *The Island of Dr Moreau*. I am neither one thing nor the other. Which is why I feel compelled to look back at those four years in sport and think, 'Was being persuaded to become a sports writer the best thing that ever happened to me, or should I consider suing the paper for the lasting damage it did me?'

I have certain cool feelings towards sport, of course. I have made up my mind about a few things. I feel, for example, from the fan's point of view, that it wastes one's life, colonises one's brain and wrings the emotions, all in unhelpful ways. It encourages the appalling know-all that abides within us all. It is sometimes stultifyingly dull, although you're not encouraged to say so. I have been all day at a Test match at Headingley and seen only 14 runs scored; I have been at Wimbledon and seen only two points played, leaving the game tantalisingly poised overnight at no sets to none, no games to none, 15 all. One night I paid £27 to see Chelsea at West Ham and the only exciting bit was when I dropped my pencil. It isn't remotely comfy, and the food is often dreadful – and as the chap famously said about the battle of Waterloo, 'The noise, my dear! And the people!' Even when it's good, it's agony. In fact, agony is very largely the point.

Yet I look back at Holyfield–Lewis and I am immensely glad I was there. It was a privilege to see this particular bit of history being made, and it doesn't matter to me that I subsequently never watched another fight after Lewis–Botha, and have only just found out for certain that Lewis retired – evidently with dignity and his brain still intact – exactly as he planned, while reigning champion. To many people, this battle between two overpaid and overgrown men in an artificial context counts for absolutely nothing. It is entirely trivial. In a world where real wars are going on, and people suffer under tyranny, what can it possibly matter that Lewis won the fight but didn't get the decision? To other people, the Holyfield–Lewis fight was a landmark event about which they cared deeply. No one keeps stuff in proportion; it's not human to do so. Sport's main claim to significance is that it acknowledges this great human failing, and provides an official outlet for it. Years ago, Boris Becker famously said, after losing at Wimbledon, 'Nobody died. I just lost a tennis match.' And while some people applauded him for his healthy sense of proportion, it didn't ring remotely true. While I was writing about sport, I was caught on the horns of this dilemma for the whole bloody time. I was like the poor confused jurors in *Alice's Adventures in Wonderland* who sit in their jury box, writing emphatically on their little slates, both 'important' and 'unimportant', because both words are equally valid.

Football and the Thrill of Knowing a Little Bit

Towards the end of May 1996, the sports editor of *The Times* asked me out to lunch, which was a bit weird. Sport was another country, as far as I was concerned. At the time, I was 41 years old, had been a columnist and TV critic on the paper for five years, and had once written a piece for it concerned specifically with women's apathetic attitude to sport, in which I'd confessed that I routinely tipped the second section of *The Times* (the bit with business at the front and sport at the back) into the bin each morning as it was quite clear that the basic qualification for a reader of this section was possession of a pair of testicles.

It had never occurred to me, by the way, that by expressing this viewpoint I might hurt anybody's feelings. It seemed like a harmless statement of fact. And, in mitigation, I did go on to explain that I was always obliged to retrieve the second section of the paper from the bin later on – with a squeal of annoyance and a pair of tongs – when I suddenly remembered that the arts pages were in there, too. Anyway, when I met sports editor David Chappell and his deputy Keith Blackmore, and they started off by helpfully reminding me of the column I'd written (Keith said one of his sub-editors was so outraged by it that he had cut it out of the paper and pinned it on a noticeboard), I didn't know what to say. I wondered briefly whether they had been appointed by their colleagues to take me out to a public place and there strike me about the face and neck with rolled-up copies of Section Two.

Whether what subsequently happened to me was an enormous and Machiavellian Grand Revenge on Miss Hoity Toity is a question that I still ask myself. Because, as things turned out, these chaps were to control my life for the next four years and change me for ever. At the time, however, our meeting merely seemed a bit odd, as we obviously had so little to talk about, professionally speaking. For example, they asked me what I knew about the forthcoming 'Euro 96', and I said, cheerfully, absolutely nothing, never heard of it, but probably something in the sporting line was my present guess. They seemed pleased by my unfeigned ignorance (and helpful attitude), but they nevertheless found it hard to believe. Had I really not noticed that England was about to host football's European Championships? That's honestly news to me, I said; and (no offence intended) not very interesting news at that.

I then politely asked whether this Euro thing took place every year – and it was at that point that Keith rubbed his hands together and ordered another bottle. What did I know about Terry Venables, then? 'Some sort of crook?' I ventured. Ever heard of Alan Shearer? Nope. Although, in an effort not to sound clueless, I think I mentioned a coach company called Shearings – which might not be strictly relevant (especially as it was, um, a different name).

How would I feel about going to some matches and writing about the championships from this blissfully innocent point of view, Keith said. And I said, well, I suppose I could. Journalists do all sorts of peculiar and unnatural things in the line of duty don't they? Personally, I had once undergone colonic irrigation for *Woman's Journal*. Football could hardly be worse than that.

I'm always glad that we had that conversation, those nice sports editors and I, because it fixes a moment for me perfectly: a moment when football was just a kind of noise that came from the television in other people's houses. I knew that some of my friends were married to men whose passion for football was indulged domestically (or so I believed), but it was something that took place behind closed doors; it was easy to turn a tactful blind eye. In those far-off days, football news was rarely in the headlines, or on the front of newspapers, and mainstream television critics such as I were rarely exposed to the game as a subject on the main channels. Reviewing telly since 1991, I had probably seen three significant pieces about football: the first was a very funny drama by Andy Hamilton called *Eleven Men Against Eleven* (with Timothy West as a club chairman); then there was a documentary about Diego Maradona, focusing on the 'hand of God' incident, the significance of which seemed to me to have been absurdly over-exaggerated, given that football was only a game. The third was the now famous 'Cutting Edge' documentary on Channel 4 (*An Impossible Job*) charting Graham Taylor's last year as England manager, with its hilarious touchline swearing, ghastly scenes of not-qualifying-for-the-1994-World-Cup, and the buffoonish and frustrated

Taylor exclaiming, 'Do I not like that!' and 'Can we not knock it?'

What else? I remember my female boss – the literary editor of an academic weekly – once on a Monday morning in the early 1980s saying that she had watched some football at the weekend, and that she had generally approved of what she saw. 'You're kidding,' I said. (Her usual leisure activities were playing tennis at a rather exclusive North London club and practising the clarinet.) 'No, it was quite balletic,' she said, her eyes wide in self-amazement. Apart from that, the footballing event that had impinged most on my consciousness was the Heysel disaster in 1985 – not because I understood how truly awful it was, but because I didn't. At this time I had a crush on a chap in the office who made a perversely big show of adoring football, especially Italian football; and for some reason I always felt that he was putting this on. I thought he carried copies of *La Gazzetta dello sport* around just to annoy me (or possibly – which was worse – to arouse the interest of other men). Either way, I did not respect, understand or believe in his passion for football, and I remember a couple of days after Heysel asking him why he was still depressed.

The Times's idea of sending an agnostic, literary, 41-year-old female survivor of colonic irrigation who'd always minded her own business to cover a bit of football in 1996 has to be set in context. And it's quite simple, looking back. In the mid-1990s, football was mounting its bid for total domination of British culture – a domination that it subsequently achieved. Nick Hornby's 1992 book *Fever Pitch* was responsible for making football respectably middle-class; Rupert Murdoch's Sky Sports channels (launched in 1990) for flogging football as a seemingly limitless source of home entertainment. Everyone could see that football was breaking out in unlikely places in the 1990s. In the *London Review of Books*, for example, Karl Miller (the Northcliffe Professor of English at University College London; not the German footballer) wrote a hyperbolic essay on Paul Gascoigne's World Cup performances in Italia 90, in which he described the flawed-heroic Gazza as, 'Fierce and comic, formidable and vulnerable . . . tense and upright, a priapic monolith in the Mediterranean sun.' At the other end of the mythologising scale, on Friday nights from 1994 to 1996, David Baddiel and Frank Skinner's laddish and brilliantly bathetic series *Fantasy Football League* (BBC2) placed football in the same friendly bracket as alternative comedy. Football's traditional associations – male, tribal, anti-intellectual, hairy-kneed, working-class, violent, humourless, misogynist, foulmouthed, unfashionable – were being undermined from all directions.

Given all these signs and portents, it was naturally felt – by clever *zeitgeist* specialists such as Keith and David – that Euro 96 might be a tipping point. Match attendances, which had sunk to terrible lows in the 1980s (Tottenham had been playing to crowds of around 10,000) were already recovering thanks to the formation of the Premier League and the investment from television – but, basically, *Après Euro 96, le deluge*. In the context of all this, I believe my own small journey into football for *The Times* was a clever editorial decision: I would be a trundling wooden horse freighting a few new readers into the sports section. It was also, however, a deliberate and rather rash mind-altering experiment, familiar from films such as *The Fly* and (more recently) *The Curse of the Were-Rabbit*, and I have sometimes wondered subsequently whether I ought to sue. No one thought about the consequences, least of all me. We merely thought: let's connect the brain of this apathetic 41-year-old literary woman to a big lot of football, maximise the voltage and then see what happens. If she starts getting up during matches to yell, 'Can we not knock it?' then the conclusion is clear: football can appeal to bloody anyone. If she starts describing Gazza as a priapic monolith, however, things have probably gone too far, and it may be necessary to reverse the polarity.

But I agreed to do it, so there you are. And my first act as special know-nothing Euro 96 correspondent for *The Times* was to go out and get a book. I acted on the advice of a child, which seemed appropriate. 'How should I prepare for Euro 96?' I said. And the child said, 'Get a sticker book.' So I bought a special Euro 96 sticker book in W.H. Smith's and the astonishing thing was: it was only a pound. Imagine my disappointment, however, when I took it home, shook it, and no stickers came out. Apparently you have to buy the stickers separately at considerable expense – something the child had neglected to tell me. But never mind. I was now committed to Euro 96. I had invested in it. And in the build-up to the event, I persevered with my research. I bought a magazine-sized glossy BBC guide to the championships, for example, which was packed with pictures of completely unfamiliar long-haired men doing historic things for their countries in very, very brightly coloured football shirts. Evidently, quite a few of these chaps played for English teams while artfully retaining their foreignness for international contests. I wondered how this could possibly work in practice. I also wondered, seriously, whether it ought to be allowed.

I also read every word in the supplement that came with *The Times*, bored to tears, and spent a long time studying the cover picture of Les Ferdinand with no shirt on, trying to memorise his chiselled features for later identification. (Since the injured Les played no part in England's Euro 96 games, this turned out to be a waste of time.) Having nothing else to do until the games began, I pored over the results tables waiting to be filled in, speculating on their use. There were columns headed 'w', 'd' and 'l', for example, which I immediately deduced were abbreviations. Win, Draw and Lose was my guess. However, after 'w', 'd' and 'l' came columns for 'f' and 'a', and here I drew a blank. I searched the page for a key, but there wasn't one. Damn. I couldn't work it out. f? a? Even if it was to do with the number of goals scored – which seemed likely – how did that get to be represented as two columns? Dear, oh dear, there was so much to learn.

The good news was that the opening match (to which I would be going) was England v Switzerland. Phew. What a good idea to start things off playing a nation known not only for its keen neutrality and cleanliness, but also for its extreme tardiness in giving women the vote. In all my years of not really listening to sports news, I had never heard of England fans having particular antagonistic feelings towards the Swiss – not even for their disgraceful suffrage record. Moreover, according to my Euro 96 guide, Switzerland were not one of the great teams of the world, either, so they would probably be an utter walkover on the field, thus ensuring a nice successful opening game for the home side. At this stage, it had not occurred to me that the 15 teams competing alongside England in Euro 96 had all needed to qualify for the event – or, indeed, noticed that many, many other European countries were not represented at all. I never asked, 'Shouldn't Sweden be playing in this?' or 'Where is the Republic of Ireland?'. I just thought it was fitting that small countries with no chance at all were playing alongside big footballing nations such as Germany, England and Italy. It seemed to have been nicely thought out; someone high up in football had obviously sat down in the winter with a yellow legal pad, a sharp pencil, a cup of coffee and a biscuit, and selected this bunch of interesting countries to play against each other – a bit like planning a really big dinner party, but with less at stake if it went wrong.

Meanwhile, I waited. At the last minute, *The Times* supplied me with an intriguing electronic device: a special BT pager decorated with the Euro 96 logo which would, they promised, thrillingly vibrate to inform me whenever anything important happened (in case I missed it, I suppose). For the time being, however, this gadget was inert, lifeless – even when prodded. I wrote an introductory piece explaining how I had achieved my pristine ignorance of football over a lifetime of loudly running the bath, boiling kettles and singing tunelessly to the cats ('La la la, What's for breakfast today, La la la, Spot of Whiskas, La la la') during the sports bit on the *Today* programme at 7.25 a.m. and/or 8.25 a.m. Then I finalised my preparations by asking my friend Robert to come with me to Wembley, knowing that he had an interest in football, and assuming he would snatch my arm off for a ticket. What a let-down, therefore, to discover that, while he would certainly be happy to escort me to England–Switzerland, Robert was a Sheffield Wednesday fan primarily, and not over-keen on international fixtures.

So that was it. On the fine morning of Saturday June 8, 1996, I set off for Wembley from Brighton station clutching a pair of tickets and a dormant pager, wondering whether I'd be able to recognise Les Ferdinand with his clothes on, imagining the tournament mainly in terms of social dining, and with a slightly under-excited friend in tow. Not great clues, any of them, to the fact that my world was about to be turned upside down.

I'll mainly skip over the England–Switzerland game. All I can say is that I was jolly pleased when Alan Shearer scored the opening goal halfway through the first half, partly because it made my pager go off with a very definite buzz (wow), and partly because everyone said he'd gone 21 months without scoring for his country, which seemed like a pretty good reason for him not to be selected for the team, actually, if you were being ruthlessly practical about it. When Switzerland equalised from a penalty in the second half, it was a bit confusing for spectators in the stadium, because we had no idea what had caused it (evidently a hand-ball from Stuart Pearce was the transgression), but the final 1–1 result – while apparently a great big downer for England fans – did not feel like any sort of injustice. England had been disorganised and had run out of ideas quite quickly; after the long-drawn-out palaver of the loosely-themed opening ceremony, and the excitement of the opening goal, the afternoon sort-of fizzled out, and there were long, yawning patches of pointless play that took place amid virtual silence, as if the whole event had suddenly been submerged under water.

Not that it was restful. I learned not to get settled too comfortably at football, because you were always having to jump up when anything faintly interesting happened. I also learned that, when a corner is taken, you don't stay standing up, but you don't sit down either: you assume a halfway position with a lateral twist which manifests the presence of hope, but is quite a strain on the buttocks. As for the England team, on this occasion I enjoyed them most when they had their backs to me – simply because this gave me a chance of identifying them. 'Turn round, for God's sake, so I can see who you are,' was my continual grumble. It was like the old days of watching *The Flowerpot Men*, with its teasing song, 'Was it Bill or was it Ben?' and the ritual infant response of, 'Don't know! Don't know! They're identical!'

But I remember that some of the players' individual footballing contributions started to stand out even in that first game of Euro 96: it seemed to me, for example, that there was no point in Steve McManaman running quite so fast with the ball up the sides if nobody else from his team could keep up. Screeching to a halt, he would realise his lonely predicament and then have to entertain the ball all by himself in the corner, where he was in clear danger of having it taken off him by a bunch of bigger boys. I wondered: should he be instructed to look round to check occasionally, or would this put him off his (considerable) stride? Thank goodness I wasn't in charge of the national team, with decisions like that to make. Meanwhile, I also noticed with interest that the crowd's high expectations of Paul Gascoigne – they stood up and made approving noises suggestive of 'This is it!' or 'We're off now!' or 'Yes, yes, yes!' whenever he got possession – were almost always doomed to early disappointment (groans all round, as he expertly passed to a nearby space with no one in it). Oddly, however, they never, ever learned from the experience.

I wrote a piece about the match, and I did not compare it (in any detail) to colonic irrigation, which I think was a relief to all concerned. But I did not start to love football at this moment. Over the following couple of days I watched umpteen group-stage matches on the TV, in fact, and lost the will to live. I found that I started doing other tasks at the same time as the footie – tasks which grew in complexity as the days went by. For example, during Germany v Czech Republic (on the Sunday) I did some dusting; during Romania v France (Monday) I made some curtains, and during Switzerland v The Netherlands (Thursday) I translated Kierkegaard from the Danish. It did not help that this was a particularly low-scoring tournament taking place in weirdly half-empty stadiums. Nor did it help that none of these foreign players was a household name in my particular household. When I now look at old footage of Euro 96, I see Dennis Bergkamp and the teenaged Patrick Kluivert, Luis Figo and Zinedane Zidane (with hair), Fabrizio Ravanelli and Gianfranco Zola, Jürgen Klinsmann and even Ally McCoist. Bliss was it in that dawn to be alive, and so on. But to me in 1996, all these blokes were just talented exotics, some of them with unexplained Elastoplasts stuck across their noses.

Meanwhile, the commentators said bizarre things like, 'That was a bread and butter ball,' and I'd get distracted thinking about types of open sandwich. The sound from my living room had become the sound from millions of other living rooms, of the droning, 'Here's Grumpy . . . to Dopey . . . back to Grumpy . . . good run from Sleepy, oh, Bashful's found some clearance!' All against the repeated background crowd noise of 'Ooh' (indicating a shot off target). I was wondering whether I should give up footie before it was too late. After all, I had a novel coming out in a month's time; I had a lovely regular job reviewing television; my nice boyfriend liked to see me happy but he really wasn't interested in football; my best friend actually preferred Sheffield Wednesday to this Euro stuff. Perhaps I should call it off.

So my bosses decided to get me out of the house again. Bizarrely, they sent me to Macclesfield to watch the Germans make peace with the local community – but it was nevertheless a clever move. As a television critic I led a life that rarely required me to put on outdoor shoes: the mere idea of stepping outside my front door and shutting it behind me twice in one week was alone enough to thrill my senses. Good heavens, I would have to catch a train and then reclaim the fare; indeed, I would have to find out where Macclesfield was. It was explained to me that the German team, under coach 'Bertie' Vogts, had been billeted to this Cheshire market town, you see (birthplace of the Hovis loaf), possibly as some sort of punishment for being too good at football. Naturally, they complained. In particular, they caused a local uproar by claiming that their practice pitch at the Moss Rose (nice name) had stones and bits of glass in it. By the time I got there, they had apologised for any distress caused, and the *Macclesfield Express Advertiser* carried the headline, 'VOGTS BACKS DOWN IN FACE OF FAN'S FURY' – the placing of the apostrophe suggesting, unfortunately, that Macclesfield Town FC had just the one fan.

The point of sending me, I think, was that the Germans had decided to do some open training, so the locals could watch, and I could get all excited seeing the charming and popular Klinsmann at close quarters; so it was a shame that I didn't know what he looked like – a Macclesfield teenager eating chips on a dismal concrete terrace had to point him out as a blond-headed dot in the distance. As a PR stunt, the whole thing did lack something. 'Are there going to be any autographs?' asked the kids. '*Nein,*' was the reply. As a way of deepening my interest in the tournament, the press conference (in German) wasn't much better. They gave me a T-shirt with 'Say no to drugs' in German on it, but I realised I couldn't wear it with any conviction. Drugs were starting to seem quite attractive, compared with Euro 96. I liked all this getting out and about, but the football? I watched a bunch of Germans in the distance play another bunch of Germans, with a German referee. I wondered if I was looking at the future. And the experience taught me something else: that the downside to travelling halfway up the country with a bit of footie hope in your heart is that, afterwards, you have to travel halfway down the country back again with nothing to console you for all those wasted hours.

So the only thing keeping me going, at this stage, was the BT pager, which had started off the tournament delivering quite terse and factual reports ('England 1, Switzerland 0, Shearer 22 mins'), but by midweek was employing interesting value judgements and adjectives. It was fascinating. I loved it. I hung on its every word. It described team performances as 'spirited', and so on. 'Dutch substitution de Kock for Seedorf (lucky not to be sent off)'. The worst thing was, I loved the way it went off at unexpected moments: it made me feel all connected and indispensable. I was at the checkout in Waitrose at 6.30 on the Thursday evening (packing cat food) when the balloon went up, and I had no choice: I stopped everything I was doing, grabbed the pager, and held it in front of my furrowed face, pressing its buttons. The checkout lady was impressed. She probably thought I'd be performing a kidney transplant within the hour. The message read, 'Please keep posted for tonight's crunch match between The Netherlands and the Swiss – goals, etc.' Unable to pass this on, I solemnly pursed my lips and waved a hand over the groceries as if to say, 'Well, it puts all this in perspective.' (Which was true.)

Then came England v Scotland. This time, the paper wanted me to watch footie in a local Brighton pub – and, as I write those words, I do start to think it was all a plot to destroy me, after all. They gave me some spending money in an envelope, and suggested a small, murky pub, forgetting to tell me that I needed to start camping out in front of its giant screen on Friday night if I wanted to have any chance of a seat for the match on Saturday afternoon. Robert and I arrived 90 minutes before the match, and the bar with the TV was already crowded with professional layabouts ordering beer in enormous pitchers and crisps by the box. All the seats were taken, and most of the floor space was taken, too. It was hard to see the attraction of watching footie in a pub – especially when the match was being broadcast on terrestrial television and therefore available in one's own home. The only interesting novelty in the experience, as far as I could tell, was the stickiness of the floor, which meant that, however roughly one was barged from the side, one could always regain the vertical. The screen was dreadful – a blurry, washed-out picture; meanwhile the half-light was a pickpockets' charter, the crowding was ghastly, the air was full of cigarette smoke, people were already quite rowdy, and worst of all, you couldn't hear the telly. How was I supposed to take detailed notes in these conditions? Someone really hadn't thought this through.

But there was something behind my grumbling, I realised. Something unexpected. I was tense about the football. A match was about to take place, the outcome of which might be decisive for England's progress through the tournament. Suddenly the previous Saturday's 1–1 result against Switzerland looked like a wasted opportunity: why hadn't England played better, tried harder, got more goals? Hadn't they understood what was at stake? Hadn't they had a couple of years to prepare for that match? With an hour to go before England v Scotland, I felt sick. The pager had sent me a message on the Friday with, 'Pressure on England and Scotland to win tomorrow', and I had thought this a bit superfluous, but now, as I waited grimly for kick-off at 3 p.m., I hated the fact that, yes, both teams really needed to win this if they were to survive the group stage of the competition. Scotland had only one point; England had only one point; The Netherlands had three. England was to meet The Netherlands the following Thursday at Wembley, and that was the last of the group matches. In less than a week's time, before the knockout stage started, England might actually be out. 'Come on, England!' someone shouted across the pub – and this was half an hour before the match, you understand. But it didn't seem such a banal thing to say, all of a sudden. 'Come on, England!' does sum up one's feelings in this situation pretty well. I tried to unclench my jaw, but it was hopeless. I tried to take an inhalation of breath without choking, but that was hopeless, too.

It turned out to be truly a game of two halves, that Scotland game. The first half, watched from that ghastly pub, was pure, goal-less misery; by the end of the 45 minutes, I'd had enough, and so had Robert. At half time we made a dash along the sea-front – all ozone, seagulls, energy and sunlight – and threw ourselves into a light, colonially decorated bar in one of the big hotels where the screens were of a normal TV size, and awkwardly bolted to the ceiling, but at least we could sit in upholstered white wicker chairs and hear the commentary. It was here that we saw the England team score its two goals against Scotland – and David Seaman save the penalty from Gary McAllister, don't forget, which was just as momentous (they said it was the first penalty saved by an English goalkeeper at Wembley since 1959). Gascoigne's tremendous, genius clincher – flipping the ball over Colin Hendry's head, dodging round him, and then volleying from some distance into the net – is one of the greatest ever moments of three-dimensional football, only slightly ruined by the way it's followed by him lying on the ground with his mouth open for the 'dentist's chair' goal celebration (a highly contrived reference to the England team's recent drinking excesses while on tour in the Far East). I'm always disappointed by that rush of Gazza's to assume the dentist's chair position. All that beauty and spontaneity followed immediately by something so yobby. It perfectly encapsulated Gazza's tragic misfortune: that the downside to having a foot like a brain is that you get a brain like a foot, to go with it.

The following Thursday, it was England v The Netherlands, the last of England's group games. The championships had been going for only 10 days. Against all expectations (and precedent), England beat The Netherlands 4–1. It was a historic night for English football. I watched the match from an airship circling Wembley Stadium. No one ever believes me when I tell them this. They think I am making it up.

It does sound suspicious, I admit. Why did the Fuji airship people offer *The Times* a place on board that evening? Well, who cares? My orders were to arrive in the early afternoon at a field near Woking, bringing a fearless friend if I wanted to. My friend Susan brought a straw hat and a pair of binoculars (clever). I brought the pager and some chocolate cake. A freelance photographer joined our party – but, aside from the pilot, that was it. Nice men from Fuji's German publicity operation met us and showed us the silvery airship as it rested in long, parched grass. A warm breeze rippled the tops of trees. All was peaceful. Susan and I asked intelligent questions about how the airship had flown here from Germany, what was its exact length, weight, age, mix of gases, pet name, number of flights, and so on – and basically tried ever so, ever so hard not to mention the *Hindenburg*.

In the end, sensing our English reticence, they mentioned it themselves. All thoughts of the *Hindenburg* were to be banished from our minds, they said; the canopy of a modern airship was emphatically non-flammable. The worst that could happen with a damaged modern airship was a very, very gentle descent, landing with a soft bump, probably somewhere open and safe and absolutely lovely like the middle of Richmond Park. Our American pilot, whose name was Corky (how marvellous), had flown airships round Superbowls hundreds of times; and so confident was he of the non-flammability of the vast, gas-filled canopy that he actually chain-smoked at the controls. The only thing we had to be prepared for, Corky said, was that being in an airship gondola was less like flying; more like sailing. Thermals made the ship both pitch and roll, especially in the full heat of a June day. He didn't add that, at the same time, there is a deafening noise from the propeller, and no bathroom. (We would find these things out soon enough.)

At 4.30 in the afternoon, a small team of German men in white boiler suits, four on each side, shouldered the nose ropes and solemnly walked our lighter-than-air dirigible to its launch position. It was a heart-stoppingly dignified operation. I felt there should be some Bach playing, and that they should be wearing powdered wigs. Then they let go of the ropes, Corky started the engine, and we lifted off. The instruments of an airship turn out to resemble those of H.G. Wells's time machine – a bicycle wheel for a rudder; cotton reels on bits of string for adjusting the mixture of gases; pedals for something or other (presumably not brakes). Reassuringly, however, Corky had state-of-the-art headphones with radio contact to air traffic control, and at no point took them off in order to change into a Phileas Fogg top hat.

'Move about if you like!' he shouted to us over the engine noise. 'Open windows!' I discovered that I felt instant nausea if I looked at the ropes hanging from the unseen canopy's nose in the middle distance – so I sensibly stopped doing it. The aforementioned pitching and rolling, as we made our way north-east, then north above such landmarks as Epsom, Croydon and Wimbledon, made moving about quite difficult, but we survived quite well in the circumstances, with our stomachs knocking against our ribs. An astonishing number of houses had identically-shaped swimming pools, by the way: if you were a swimming-pool salesman with the Surrey concession, the view would have made you very proud. Anyway, Susan firmly declined the chocky cake, but was otherwise OK, as was the photographer (who found the chocky cake very acceptable). Evidently a TV puppet called Otis the Aardvark had been copiously sick on a previous flight, which we all found completely hilarious.

We could see Wembley from miles away. There is a wonderful Dickensian passage at the beginning of Patrick Hamilton's novel *The Slaves of Solitude* describing wartime London as a great, breathing monster, sucking thousands of tiny people in through all the train terminals in the morning, and breathing them out again at the end of the day. This passage came to mind as we arrived over the great white stadium, which was drawing people towards it from far and wide on this light summer evening. Why doesn't TV use more aerial shots? It's such a missed opportunity. Of course, such shots would be easier to achieve if the airships could be stationary – which they can't: they have to keep circling, circling, circling, circling, otherwise they die, like sharks. But the view is phenomenal: 75,000 people assembling in one place for a sporting contest is a grand sight. The grass is incredibly green. The fans are (in this case) a beautiful white and a beautiful orange. Thousands of individual camera flashes make the scene sparkle. Once play starts, the 20 free-flowing outfield players spread and converge restlessly, like droplets of mercury being tipped about on a mirror – or like droplets of mercury all in mindful pursuit of a moving ball, anyway.

We were told we were flying at around 1,000 feet, but I don't know whether that was true. We could open the windows and lean out; we could see the players not quite well enough to identify them individually. And of course we had to keep re-orientating ourselves because of the non-stop circling. England are playing left to right. No, hang on, England are playing right to left. No, I was right the first time: England are playing left to right. But when the ball was destined to fly into the net (as it was four times for England in the course of that astonishing evening), seeing it from directly above was the best view you could possibly have.

What people tend to overlook about that generally well-remembered England–Netherlands match, actually, is how nice and varied the goals were for anyone watching from overhead. First, there was the penalty in the first half – which helpfully got us used to the sight of a white ball punching into the back of a white net and dancing there. A chap in white (Paul Ince, as it turned out) appeared to trip on the edge of the penalty box, and play was suspended. Players stood back to watch while another chap in white (Alan Shearer, as we later learned, courtesy of the pager) placed the ball on the spot. Up in the airship, we were bloody excited. Above the roar of the engine, we could hear the cheering from the stadium – but, truly, only just. It was like watching through the wrong end of a telescope. There was a run-up; the ball was smacked into the corner of the net, and the jubilant little ant-sized player ran off at top speed while we danced about in our little gondola, and Corky made his mind up to stay for the second half – which was a relief, as his instructions had been to leave Wembley at half time and get us back to Woking before dark.

The rest of the first half was highly absorbing, by which I really mean unbearable. The Dutch kept getting corners; players increasingly smacked into one another on purpose; the daylight started to give way to floodlight; cameras flashed; the score remained 1–0. Chocky cake was no longer of interest. The only thing that mattered was the puzzle of how to get that ball from one end to the other, using only white players, and finally knocking it past the chap guarding the net. Tactics were wonderfully clear from the air: you could see how a goal attempt was made; how a defence could be divided and defeated. The picture that eventually appeared with my piece, incidentally, was one of the first taken that night – about an hour before the match even started. It was in black and white, and showed the stadium half-full. The novelty was that the photographer was sending his pictures digitally from the airship via his computer and mobile phone, which was pioneer technology in 1996. The battery on his computer allowed him to send about three pictures before it ran down. It was such a shame. The picture did nothing to capture the thrill of being in a small but very airy room with a view of that glowing arena surrounded by eerily deserted – and ever-darkening – parks and gardens and streets.

The three England goals in the second half were all as fabulous from an aerial perspective as I'm sure they were from the ground. The first came from a corner: Gascoigne (it turned out) delivering a high, high ball into the thick of the English heads in front of goal, and then – bang! It was in the net. Having no access to replays, we didn't quite believe what we'd seen; it was so very quick and efficient. But we heard the cheers, and then the pager told us it was Teddy Sheringham who'd scored, and it was now 2–0, and I explained to Susan why it was a nice thing that Sheringham had done it, as this was his first goal in the competition, and she patiently put up with this bizarre instant-expertise stuff because she could tell I was excited. By this time Corky was on borrowed time, and we knew it, but we kept very quiet as we didn't want to jog him out of the circling – which I ought to mention had momentously reversed direction at half time.

What of the third goal? Well, it was marvellous in, again, a different way. This one was all about (yes!) getting the ball from one end of the field to the other using only white players and resisting the temptation to just knock it a long way forward and hope the right chap got to it first. It was a glorious bit of dynamic teamwork, magical to see, and it culminated in three attackers ranged in a line across the goal, with Gascoigne (as I now know) passing it immediately right to Sheringham; and then Sheringham tricking everyone by neatly side-footing it right again to Shearer, who had a clear shot at goal. Even the photographer started to get excited at this point. England had never beaten the Netherlands in any European Championships before, or in any World Cup either, apparently. The score now stood at 3–0, and we couldn't help wondering, if you dropped a piece of chocky cake onto the pitch from this height by way of celebration, what would happen? How soon would it reach terminal velocity? Would it disintegrate? Or maybe form itself into a perfect sphere, on the same physical principle used in the manufacture of lead-shot? Or, if it landed – whump! – on Dennis Bergkamp's head, could it possibly knock him out? After all, by the time the police could work out what had happened, we could be miles away, possibly over the Channel.

I will always be grateful to Corky that we saw the fourth England goal before we had to tear ourselves away that night. Again it was different; again it was beautiful, and somehow pre-ordained. A great surge from England culminated in the somewhat useless Darren Anderton taking a running shot at goal, which was deflected by the hapless Dutch keeper (Edwin van der Sar, whose name, at the time, meant nothing). The loose ball was picked up with lightning speed by Sheringham and there it was again – bam – back of the net, 4–0, glorious. Now we could hear the cheering, all right. But we really needed to get going, as there is a quite sensible law about flying airships over London after dark, and we had to get back to Surrey rather sharpish. Corky put on an astonishing lick of speed, shooting us back across London, across the river, over Putney Heath and Richmond Park, down the A3. We were all exhausted but extremely happy as we watched the darkening – and somewhat misty – landscape pass beneath us, and realised with a certain alarm that we were keeping pace with cars on the A3 travelling at 50 miles an hour. But it had been magical. I found myself humming 'Lift Up Your Hearts' for the first time since school, and waiting for the inevitable show of emotion from the pager, to see if it matched my own.

We landed back at Woking and were greeted by the chaps in boiler suits. When the engine was finally switched off, it was like having someone take a nail out of your head: for the next few days I was so sensitive to motor noise that I jumped in the air whenever the fridge started up. But what a great night to be converted – finally – to football. Three weeks earlier, I hadn't heard of Alan Shearer. Now I wanted to have his babies. Three weeks earlier, the mind-altering experiment had seemed quite harmless and (at worst) reversible. Now the damage was done. I had learned to cheer and grumble, love and loathe. During the England–Spain quarter-final a couple of days later, I stood there at Wembley wringing my hands in misery at how badly England played. 'Why are you passing it to Gascoigne?' I yelled (he was on terrible, dozy form that day). 'You might as well pass it to the cat, son! You might as well dig your own grave and jump in it!' England survived that quarter-final, although we all knew they didn't deserve to. But the following Wednesday, when England lost on penalties to Germany in the semi-final, I was all the more blank with grief, all the more inconsolable. I felt that I had been with our boys, in some sort of spiritual, eternal way, through the extremes of thick and thin.

It was impossible to imagine how Euro 96 might have passed entirely over my head, had I never had that lunch with Keith and David. Might I have heard the news of England's defeat with complete unconcern? God knows. Plenty of my friends certainly took no notice of Euro 96 and were blithely unaffected by its outcome. All I know is that, on the morning after England–Germany, I slung the food into the cat bowls and went back to bed to stare at the ceiling. No light-hearted songs today, kitties. No bath-running or kettle-boiling during the sports bits at twenty-five past the hour, either. On the contrary: I turned up the volume for Garry Richardson and cried softly onto the pillow, while desperately figuring whether – if I rigged it up to the mains and stood in a bucket of water – I could use the pager to kill myself.

THE MATCH

Less than a year later, by the time of the FA Cup semi-final at Old Trafford between Chesterfield and Middlesbrough in April 1997, I had come on a bit, footie-wise. In fact, it was terrifying how quickly I became a football bore after such a brief initiation. Many friends simply stopped talking to me, because all my stories seemed to involve either the manager of Wolverhampton Wanderers or balls grazing crossbars in the 89th minute. 'Come round and watch the Newcastle match,' I would say, and then wonder why they always had alternative plans. My boyfriend took me on a romantic weekend to a nice hotel in the New Forest which I spoiled by exclaiming, as we passed the bar on the way up to our room, 'Oh, thank God, they've got Sky Sports.'

The thing was, I was now attending football every week, as part of my arrangement with *The Times*. Possibly acting from a sense of guilt when they saw how much Euro 96 had disturbed my normal equilibrium, my masters gently suggested I go once a week to a football match, sit in the stands with the supporters, and write a column about it. They did publish this column, I hasten to add. It wasn't a considerate plot to help me through a difficult patch. And in a way, of course, it was a continuation of the experiment. Let's see if this woman *really* likes football, then, when she finds out it normally takes place firmly at ground level, out of doors in gritty northern stadiums in the freezing rain, and involves watching everyday league players run around banging into each other (in the absence of such advanced international features as steering, acceleration or brakes).

Thus, one week I might go to watch Division Three Brighton and Hove Albion against Torquay United at the local Goldstone ground; the next I'd be at the Premiership match between Southampton and Middlesbrough at the Dell; then it would be England v Poland (World Cup qualifier) at Wembley. They called the column 'Kicking and Screaming' but it was quite clear to anyone reading it that I was having a high old time, and didn't need to be dragged anywhere against my will. In fact, on weeks when there was no Saturday football (international call-ups being to blame), I would kiss the cats goodbye in the morning and then stand with my coat on at the front door, clutching my car key and rolled-up umbrella, just sort-of refusing to accept that I had no match to go to.

And it was a pretty good season, 1996–97, if you leave aside the fact that Manchester United ultimately won the league for the second year running. To the casual onlooker, this was a season notable mainly for the burgeoning practice of pinning outlandish hopes on foreign players, whose presence not only lent all kinds of new glamour to the game, but finally legitimised the hair band as a masculine fashion accoutrement. I remember a fanzine at Anfield highlighting

71

the difference – in terms of allure – between Liverpool's own Patrik Berger and United's Karel Poborsky. 'We've got a Czech; they've got a Czech,' it said, alongside unkindly contrasting illustrative photos. 'Ours has got a hair band; theirs has got a hair band.' The cruel point was, alas, that Berger resembled a rock star while Poborsky – well, Poborsky didn't. Poborsky was so old-crone-like in appearance that he evoked childhood terrors of the witch Baba Yaga in her house built on chicken legs.

Reaction to foreign players was bound to be mixed, given the proud xenophobic traditions of the game. But mainly, supporters needed a lot of reassurance that managers had not been out squandering their club's precious Eurocheque facility on the footballing equivalent of pigs in pokes. At a Rangers–Hibernian match at Ibrox, the man sitting next to me indicated the tall blond figure of Erik Bo Andersen (a Dane, as the name suggests), and said, wearily, 'See that man? Number 16? Really a heating engineer. Not many people know that. Can't play football at all, just a mix-up.' Andersen promptly made the worst unforced error I had ever seen. Standing a few yards in front of an open goal, he knocked the ball wide, to a general gasp of horror. 'That was terrible,' I said. 'Uh-huh,' said the Rangers supporter, taking his head from his hands. 'But he's a very good plumber.'

To a neophyte, however, the foreign players were extremely attractive and evoked no mixed feelings at all. Put simply, I was always on their side. This was the year Kevin Keegan deserted Newcastle without explanation, and left his dazzling foreign players David Ginola and Tino Asprilla in the hands of Kenny Dalglish, which was a bit like hiring Cruella de Vil as your puppy-walker. The consistent wronging of David Ginola (which continued when he moved to Spurs) became quite a theme of my weekly pieces, and I staunchly voted for him as man of the match week after week, even on occasions when he wasn't playing. But the more the xenophobic crowds hooted the fancy dans, the more I personally rooted for them. When Chelsea's handsome all-star international team took the pitch at Blackburn (it was one of Gianfranco Zola's first outings), I heard shouts of 'Go back to Spain!' which annoyed me so much that I got out my notebook and wrote it down. When I was sent to see Middlesbrough at Southampton at the beginning of the season, it was principally to report back on the expensive foreigners that Middlesbrough's manager Bryan Robson had just recruited: the Brazilians Emerson and Juninho, and the Italian Fabrizio Ravanelli. On that memorably golden autumn afternoon, Middlesbrough were roundly beaten 4–0 by the red-and-white British foot soldiers of Southampton FC, which was absolutely hilarious, of course. 'What – a waste – amunny!' was the gleeful chorus from the stands.

For me, 1996–97 was a time of all sorts of assimilation. I'd never bothered to find out before how football was organised, with leagues and so on. Was the Premiership a legitimate division, or was it just made up of clubs with TV contracts? As far as fixtures were concerned, I'd always assumed, given how much football there appeared to be every week, that the question of who-played-who was probably just everyone plays absolutely everyone else as many times as possible until the whole torrid business has to start all over again. Cup-wise, I didn't know there was more than one cup. Meanwhile, I'd never wondered where the notorious Hillsborough stadium was, or whether it was attached to any particular club; and I had no idea about the system of promotion and relegation, either: I assumed that, if a team was in the Second Division (say), that was where it had always been, and always would be. Finally, I didn't know that teams had nicknames like 'The Crazy Gang' or 'The Owls', or suspected that you only had to know:

a) the name of a club's ground
b) the name of the manager
c) the name of the chairman, and
d) the nickname

– and then you would be able to decode Des Lynam's script on *Match of the Day*. It was all quite easy really. 'Now,' Des might say, waggling his moustache, 'Ewood Park had a visit from Ruud Gullit's blue army,' and I'd sit there, happily translating, 'He means Chelsea went to Blackburn Rovers.' Twice in the season, incidentally, I saw West Ham (The Hammers) in opposition to Sheffield Wednesday (The Owls), a fixture I found too rich in unfortunate imagery. I didn't mind foxes beating magpies, or gunners beating spurs, but the idea of owls being beaten by hammers still affects me to this day.

What was most exciting about learning the language of football, however, was the discovery that an enormous number of my (male) friends had been speaking football for years, and I hadn't been able to tune my ear to what they were saying. Suddenly, I could. Instead of a loud 'ffffffffffffffff' noise, I could pick out quite a lot of words that made sense. This did not mean I could practise my own footie lingo freely in mixed company, though; oh no. I quickly discovered that, in footie conversations in social contexts, my female opinion counted for nothing, even though I'd probably seen more live football in six months than most men see in a lifetime (and was paid good money to write about it). If I asked questions, on the other hand, I was jolly popular. So that's what I mainly did. I found it touching that chaps who knew about football were so generous about sharing their encyclopaedic knowledge. 'So what is end-to-end play, then?' I would ask. 'Why do they call Tony Adams "Donkey"?' 'Which year did Brighton and Hove Albion get to the Cup final?' And they would be more than happy to tell me. No one in the literary world would be so forbearing in an equivalent situation, it seemed to me. Rude scoffing noises would be the entire response if you went about asking, 'So who's this A.S. Byatt, then?' or 'What's the difference between a foreword and a preface?' or 'Did you ever meet Charles Dickens, or was he before your time?'

Not having a team to support was a problem, but I realised I couldn't manufacture loyalty by buying a scarf. However, I did quickly adopt quite powerful likes and dislikes both for certain clubs and for individual players, and this was perfectly acceptable because if there is one quality cherished and indulged by all true football supporters, it is baseless prejudice. I discovered that it is really important to allow small flickering doubts about a player's ability to grow as quickly as possible into a deeply-held conviction ('He's useless! He's fucking useless!'), and for that conviction to fester until it's a kind of mental illness ('Why can't they *see* he's useless? Can't *you* see how useless he is?'). For example, I decided quite early on that Darren Anderton (of Spurs and England) was rubbish, and I still think I was right, actually, despite the fact that, when I consult my old *Footballers Fact File 1997–8*, I find that it describes him as a 'quick, intelligent winger who made a terrific contribution to England's Euro 96 campaign', and goes on to call him 'not only a pleasure to watch, but a must for inclusion at club and international level'.

Mm. Is it possible I was wrong about Anderton? Was it just his floppy haircut and vacant expression, really, that used to get up my nose? Surely he was always missing goals at key moments? But hang on, does it matter? We're talking about football logic here, and the normal rules don't apply. Thinking Anderton was rubbish was a perfectly legitim-ate standpoint, and (after all) was more about my right to an opinion than about his true abilities as a player. Thus, when Anderton failed to score in any match, a rational or disinterested onlooker might think, 'Oh, what a shame, he missed it. Wouldn't it have been nice if that had gone in?' But I had given myself permission to think something else: something along the lines of, 'Fuck that Darren Anderton! He's so fucking useless! And why doesn't he get a fucking haircut?' Even when he did something undeniably good, such as score a winning goal, there was no need to re-consider this extreme position, either. No, if Anderton suddenly displayed talent in some incontrovertible way, I could fall back on that grudging, concessionary attitude of oh-all-right-I'll-give-him-that-*but-it-makes-a-fucking-change-mate* ('It makes a fucking *change!*').

Other people did have clubs to support, though, and this made me very sorry for them, the lifelong misery of the football fan having been so vividly expounded in Nick Hornby's *Fever Pitch*. I do often wonder, however, whether it was the almighty scope for grumbling that truly attracted me to the game in the first place. I am terribly skilled at grumbling, personally; yet I still spend many hours perfecting it. Ask any of my friends. I am also an utter natural at whingeing and whining; and you should hear my railing – it's world class. No wonder those grandstands felt like home. Sit with fans and you'll find that they don't happily wave a hand at their team, saying, 'Aren't they marvellous?' No, despite being stoutly loyal through all the vicissitudes a cruel footballing destiny can chuck at them, they reserve the right to be permanently incensed, frustrated, fed up, and generally at their tether's end. Loyalty is expressed almost entirely through abuse. At my first game (the Brighton one), I sat next to a man who said, flatly, 'I've been coming to the Goldstone since 1958, and this is the worst team we've ever had.' A few weeks later, at Selhurst Park, I explained to a Crystal Palace season-ticket holder that I didn't know much about football, and he quipped, 'You've come to the right place, then. This lot doesn't know much about football either.' On a moonlit night in Monaco in March 1997, after Newcastle had been publicly humiliated by a team that incidentally included the 19-year-old Thierry Henry (by three goals to nil in the second leg of the UEFA Cup semi-final), I saw a Newcastle fan sum up his feelings about his noble team in tearful, regretful franglais. 'You, vous, Monaco – très good,' he told a surprised passer-by. 'We, Newcastle – shite.'

I always felt sorry for the fans. What exploitation. Their loyalty clearly meant a lot to them, but it was worth so much more (in lovely heaps of fifty-pound notes) to the clubs that it was like witnessing tiny helpless infants being mugged for their Cheesy Wotsits, over and over again. Purely in terms of value for money, football is shocking. I mean, what did fans get for their money at an average match? A cold, hard place to sit in the draughty outdoors, surrounded by mouthy maniacs, with the possibility of a thin beaker of scalding tea with lumps in it. True, they got a football match, but football obeys no known laws of entertainment, so there's no promise of anything worth seeing. Obviously, when I pleaded in print for the urgent invention of heated seats, I wasn't completely serious. I got quite accustomed to the frozen-bottom sensation, and eventually learned to wipe rain off the seat before sitting down. People also explained to me that no one goes to football for the culinary experience, either. But I still felt weekly outrage at how badly the punters were catered for. Seat ticket prices might be the same as for West End theatre, but the 'Food' information in my *Football Fan's Guide* covered only such matters as whether the pies were hot or cold, what the cost of pies was, how many pies were tested, where to buy pies, and how much filling the pies had got. The highest praise was reserved for drinks with lids on. True, there was usually a burger van, but I've never been able to eat from a burger van since seeing that incident in one of the Roddy Doyle films of someone being served a deep-fried nappy with chips. I suppose I could have packed a Tupperware box with sandwiches and salads and a nice green apple to eat on arrival at the ground, but

I never did, because – well, because it would have been entirely out of character, that's why. So, instead, I often drove literally hundreds of miles to football stadiums ('Here we are! Elland Road! And it only took five hours!') only to realise I was, yet again, in the middle of nowhere with only the crumbs in the seams of my coat pocket to prevent me from keeling over.

At this stage of my professional sports writing, I never questioned my instructions. My editors would say, 'We think you should see Wolverhampton v Port Vale at Molineux next Saturday.' And I'd say, 'Okey dokey. That sounds like an old-established ground.' And they'd say, 'Yes, it does, doesn't it? But in fact it's quite big and new, and it's even got big screens, and we think you'll have a field day.' It seemed to me that it was all experience, you see. I had no way of knowing whether a game would be good or not, so I didn't try. And, until you've actually been to Molineux (say), you can't possibly know that a game at Wolverhampton on a wet Saturday against Port Vale operates precisely like the Dementors in the *Harry Potter* books, sucking all the hope out of you by means of a stringy black cyclone coming out of your face, and leaving you afterwards a mere crumpled husk of gibbering despair. So I always said 'Okey dokey': to trips to Blackburn Rovers, Nottingham Forest, Liverpool, Bristol City, Coventry, Leicester, Aston Villa and so on. I would set off at dawn from Brighton, to allow plenty of time for getting lost (stadiums are rarely signposted), and for figuring out a way to leave the car somewhere unpleasant, unlit and dangerous in the surrounding streets, guarded by enterprising junior extortionists who charged you £5 to let you walk away alive. Such logistical issues loom large in the life of sports writers, I'm afraid. By the end of my first season, someone might tell me innocently that they saw the game of the bloody century at White Hart Lane, and I wouldn't enquire about match details: instead, I'd say, hysterically, 'White Hart Lane? On Tottenham High Road? Where did you park? Where the *fuck* did you park?'

Anyway, I mention all this naïve okey-dokeyness because, on my way to Old Trafford for the semi-final of the FA Cup between Chesterfield and Middlesbrough, it suddenly occurred to me, somewhere on the M6, that I might have drawn the short straw. Hang on, I thought. Two hundred miles back down the road, at Highbury, the other semi-final was taking place between Wimbledon and Chelsea. Damn. That could be a great match! True, I'd seen Middlesbrough a couple of times in the season (once in March at their magnificent Riverside Stadium, where they beat Derby in a Premiership match by a spectacular 6–1), but I'd formed all sorts of attachments to both the London teams which would surely make their semi-final the right one for me to see. For the first time in my sports writer career (but not the last), I actually felt quite hard done by. Why was I driving all the way to Manchester to see Middlesbrough demolish itsy-bitsy Chesterfield, a Second-Division Derbyshire side who should never, by rights, have got this far in the competition? I knew only three things about Chesterfield: Tony Benn was its MP for a very long time; it had a church with a curiously wonky spire; and it was where the sofas came from. Evidently

25,000 Chesterfield fans were making for Old Trafford today, leaving the town virtually deserted. It occurred to me that a visit to Chesterfield on this semi-final day might be a much more interesting proposition than covering the match. The population is only about 70,000 at the best of times. Imagine those empty streets. Imagine the poor lame lonely Derbyshire-accented child left behind because he couldn't keep up with the fans racing for the buses (I was thinking of *The Pied Piper* here). And above all, imagine the enormous opportunity for criminal chesterfield-rustling while the entire populace was elsewhere: out-of-town desperadoes herding thousands of deeply-studded, high-backed leather sofas, mooing and slipping, into the backs of vans.

What I hadn't really noticed, despite reading nothing but footie journalism for the past six months, was that Chesterfield's Cup run had been one of the most romantic Roy-of-the-Rovers affairs. The Spireites (nickname of Chesterfield) had conceded only two goals along the way to this semi-final, and had beaten Bury, Scarborough, Bristol City, Bolton Wanderers, Nottingham Forest and Wrexham. The fifth-round 1–0 victory over Forest had been a particularly glorious and notable occasion, at Chesterfield's small home ground, Saltergate: referee David Elleray had sent off Forest's goalkeeper for rugby-tackling a Chesterfield player. Blimey. There had been a red card, a burst of protest, and a firmly pointed arm. Unsurprisingly, passions ran very high indeed. In particular, Stuart Pearce (player-manager of Forest) was seriously peeved, despite the clear justice involved. Tom Curtis then scored elegantly with the ensuing penalty – for which there was a substitute goalkeeper, you will be relieved to hear, but only a rather dazed one who probably wished he hadn't got up that morning. I rattle off these names now, don't I? But when I perused the programme before the match, none of the Chesterfield personnel meant anything to me. No, no, never heard of any of them. There was a Jamie Hewitt listed, which briefly piqued my interest. Was this the notorious love rat who broke the heart of Princess Diana? On balance, given that he played in defence for Chesterfield, probably not.

One thing I had learned over the course of the season was that you can never trust a programme, in any case. I still always bought them, but I was wary. The team listed on the back is never the team that plays, which is fair enough, since selection tends to take place quite late in the day. But there is an additional sod's law applying to football programmes, called The Curse of the Programme Overtaken by Events, by which the player featured on the cover will almost certainly be crying with pain on a treatment table on the day of the match; if he gets a double-page feature, moreover, he will probably have either already left the club under a terrible cloud, or died. The programme for England's appalling World Cup qualifier against Italy in February had illustrated the point pretty well: the cover showed David Seaman diving for a save (this was the night weedy Ian Walker, as next-choice goalkeeper, became one of the most reviled men in England); inside were features on Paul Gascoigne and Gianluca Vialli (neither of whom played) and on that over-optimistic World Cup bid 'England 2006' (which was never going to happen). The only time I experienced an exception to The Curse of the Programme Overtaken by Events was at a twice-postponed third-round Cup tie between Brentford and Manchester City at Griffin Park. True, by the time the match was played, only five of Man City's original line-up were playing (and most had changed numbers). But a wonderful thing had happened. Players who got personal write-ups for the original date (but hadn't played) were actually fit again when the day finally arrived. One of them had even recovered from a broken leg. I found that incredibly cheering. Wait long enough in life, you see, and it all comes right. It reminded me of Lewis Carroll's excellent philosophical point about a stopped clock being better than a slow one, because twice in every 24 hours, it tells the right time.

Back at Old Trafford, though, I am neglecting the pre-match atmosphere, which was sensational. This was my first time inside this stadium (at that date it held over 55,000), and I loved it. My immediate surroundings I wasn't too keen on, as they were dominated by a small, violently fanatical Middlesbrough child supporter determined to poke me in the eye with his red flag; but the 'Blue army! Blue army!' chanting from the Chesterfield supporters was very uplifting. Blue-and-white face paint, blue-and-white curly wigs, blue-and-white shirts, loads and loads of blue-and-white balloons: gosh, someone in the Spireites' club shop had really risen to the occasion kitting this lot out. It did occur to me that the whole contingent of 25,000 could not really call themselves hard-core regulars, incidentally, since Saltergate holds fewer than 9,000 – but then I realised that this was what made them all so happy: these were johnny-come-lately, fancy-free, over-excited fans (a bit like me supporting England at Euro 96) who had known only glory, success, and the fluke-ish sending-off of other people's goalkeepers. They were programmed for joyous victory, because it was all they had known. Any other result was beyond their comprehension.

Compare the grim, tense and punch-drunk emotions of the Middlesbrough fans who had seen their team get to the late stages of both the FA Cup and the Coca-Cola Cup this year, but were at the same time facing relegation from the Premiership. 'If you love Boro, stand up!' was significantly the chant of the day, because it exhorted the fans not to lie down on the ground in a foetal position, moaning and sobbing. The previous Sunday, a last-minute equaliser from Leicester's Emile Heskey in the Coca-Cola Cup final had meant there would have to be a replay – which was, in itself, pretty demoralising. However, much worse was the fact that Middlesbrough had been penalised earlier in the year for not turning up for a match against Blackburn. Evidently, manager Bryan Robson hadn't given sufficient warning, or adequate reason (or something), and the upshot was, three points had been taken away. Now, having been to Blackburn myself, I personally didn't blame Robson for not wanting to go, but the Football Association saw it differently, and never reconsidered its position, despite a lot of pleading, sulking and threatening. Fans had been seething for months about the deduction of the three points, which would prove to seal their fate. When the time came for a line to be drawn under the 17th team in the table, three clubs would wave a reluctant goodbye and drop through the trapdoor down to Division One – and Middlesbrough was at No. 19.

As for Middlesbrough's high-profile fancy-dan players, the honeymoon period had long been over, on both sides. More foreign players had been brought in – the Italian Gianluca Festa, and the Slovakian Vladimir Kinder – but the policy had started to look a bit desperate. Ravanelli's problems with scoring were beginning to grate with any number of people ('Why can't Ravanelli find the goal?' I harrumphed, one week. 'No one moves it, do they?'). Meanwhile the saga of Emerson's repeated attempts at escape from Middlesbrough was a more-or-less constant source of hilarity to anyone unconnected to his employers. The twinkle-toed, raven-ringletted midfielder had the lightness and grace of a Gene Kelly, and there was a lovely shot of him in the *Match of the Day* opening titles doing a fond kissy-kissy at the camera – but this warm-blooded young black man kept flying down to Rio and neglecting to come back.

His preference for Brazil probably had something to do with the contrasting number of sunshine hours of Teesside and South America, but no one knew for sure. Anyway, 'Emerson goes AWOL' seemed to be the story every couple of weeks, especially in the grey depths of the winter. His fellow Brazilian Juninho was another matter, however. Totally committed, totally tireless, he flogged his heart out for Middlesbrough – and the more he did, the more tragic his situation appeared. The great Marc Overmars (who would join Arsenal just a couple of months later) had the same keen, doggy quality, I always thought. Throw a ball whatever distance and he would apparently really enjoy tearing off after it on all fours with his ears flapping behind him.

What a build-up. What an occasion. Both sides had so much to win, so much to lose. 'Blue army, blue army, blue army!' chanted the ecstatic Spireite supporters. Or, to be more precise, 'Blwami, blwami, blwami.' It occurred to me that, should Chesterfield meet Chelsea in the final, the meeting would have to be called a 'blwamiad', and the two sets of fans would have to agree in advance not to chant the same thing. But at this stage, the idea of Chesterfield winning this match was absurdly far-fetched. Great occasions do not generally go with great football games, unfortunately; usually the reverse. This was so fabulous and uplifting an occasion that I braced myself for the inevitable let-down once play commenced. Middlesbrough would probably score two in the first half, then kill the game. The Chesterfield balloons would gradually deflate. The tackling would get desperate and nasty. The boy with the flag would either successfully take my eye out or get the clip round the ear he was asking for. Tempers would fray. And I would pass out through lack of anything to eat since breakfast and also through fretting about the safety of the car, which was doubtless already wheel-less, before kick-off, resting on bricks with its engine removed.

But it was the highlight of my year, that semi-final. I had not drawn the short straw. If football does not obey the laws of entertainment, the point is that sometimes, gloriously, a great story writes itself right there in front of you on a piece of historic turf with an enormous number of interested people present – and you really know it when you see it.

The first half was notable at the outset mainly for its gusto, and for the pleasant surprise of Chesterfield's classiness in defence and downright nerve in attack. This was clearly going to be a free-flowing and dynamic game, with accurate long balls and intelligent strategies on both sides (as opposed to most football, on most days). Annoyingly, Chesterfield's shirts didn't have the players' names on, but apart from that, it was easy to see what was going on. A clear shot from Middlesbrough's Craig Hignett was blocked and caught by goalkeeper Billy Mercer (big groans; big cheers); another shot by Steve Vickers went wide. Meanwhile, Chesterfield's forwards seemed to make easy work of out-running Middlesbrough's defenders – to the evident frustration of Vladimir Kinder, who got booked for a late tackle, and then, just minutes later, committed a gross act of shirt-pulling in plain view of the entire crowd. The whistle blew, and referee David Elleray raced towards him with his hand in his top pocket. 'Hasn't Kinder already been booked?' I asked, unable to believe my eyes. 'Yes, he has,' said the fan beside me – and sure enough, oh blimey, Elleray showed Kinder a second yellow card, then a red one, and sent him off. Middlesbrough quickly re-organised themselves, with the ineffectual Mikkel Beck taken off and a new defender, Clayton Blackmore, brought on as a substitute. But this was a situation. It is not unknown for ten men to outplay eleven, of course; but nobody opts for that ratio voluntarily, especially in the semi-final of the FA Cup, unless they are raving mad.

At half time, despite the goalless scoreline, I was feeling quite strung out with excitement. Supporting both sides equally in such a match feels wrong, but it certainly doesn't make you indifferent. Mixed emotions can be just as powerful as the straightforward kind. Faint from hunger, and ready to snap a certain child's flag in half over my knee in a minute, I was absolutely desperate for more of this stuff. I scanned the programme for information about Chesterfield. They were the fourth oldest club in the Football League, apparently. Not long ago, they had been in the old Fourth Division. In fact, they'd got into the Second Division just two years ago. They all appeared to be English: Jamie Hewitt was even born in Chesterfield. Their shirt sponsor was North Derbyshire Health, which seemed rather wholesome by comparison with the Premiership's assorted mobile phone companies, electrical goods manufacturers and brewers. On the whole, they seemed like a very good thing. Unearned self-satisfaction is the besetting sin of sports writers, and I felt it now. 'Here am I,' I thought, smugly, 'at this terrific game. A lot of people would like to be in my shoes.' And then I remembered that I'd been quite fed up about it in the car, expecting only a wasted afternoon, so felt jolly ashamed of myself.

Nine minutes into the second half, this great match got even better, with the introduction of goals to the story. A long ball from midfield was picked up by Chesterfield's Jonathan Howard on the right wing. He beat his defender, and passed the ball goalwards to his accelerating team-mate Kevin Davies, who stretched and shot towards the bottom left-hand corner. Middlesbrough's goalkeeper Ben Roberts (with girlie hair band, as it happens) threw himself down to stop the ball, but deflected it directly to the feet of the immensely tall Chesterfield striker Andy Morris, who happened to be loitering with intent at the far post. Morris looked down, saw the ball, gave it a little kick into the back of the net, and sort-of strolled off, evidently thinking, 'Well, that was easy.' One hardly had time to absorb this thrilling development when, a few minutes later, Morris was sprinting towards goal, holding off Festa. Inside the 18-yard box, Roberts threw himself down again as a human barricade, and Morris rather elegantly tripped over him, the result being a penalty to Chesterfield. Were the underdogs to go 2–0 up? No, surely not. But captain Sean Dyche drilled the ball into the middle of the net, so yes, yes, yes. No one was dreaming. Suddenly, Chesterfield were winning the FA Cup semi-final.

Sensing the game getting away from them somewhat in this second half, Middlesbrough made an effort to pull themselves together, and constructed an extremely businesslike goal in reply, with Emerson lofting a beautiful long ball to the unmarked Blackmore on the left, who raced forward and crossed it so perfectly into a knot of defenders surrounding Ravanelli right in front of the goal that it almost couldn't fail to go in. While getting one back was a bit of a relief, it was evidently no cause for time-wasting celebrations, as far as Ravanelli was concerned. He smartly collected the ball from the back of the net and made a big show of grimly waving his team-mates back to their starting positions. 'No time! No time!' Could Chesterfield maintain their lead? Well, yes. They actually scored again – a great shot from Jonathan Howard ricocheting from the crossbar almost vertically into the goal and being knocked clear. But although the linesman gave the goal, the referee disallowed it. In the stadium, we had no way of telling whether this was a good decision (it wasn't). All we knew was that within five minutes Juninho had collided with Sean Dyche in the penalty box at the other end and contrived to win a penalty for Middlesbrough. Hignett took it and scored. It was 2–2. I had vowed at the moment I took up watching football that I would never, ever say, 'If we'd scored just now, we'd be one-up!' because it's such a stupid remark. However, on this occasion, the temptation was too great. If that goal had not been disallowed, I reckoned, Chesterfield would have led 3–1. But now it was 2–2, and the 90 minutes were nearly up, and the whistle blew, and we were heading for 30 minutes of gut-wrenching extra time.

God almighty. A lesser person honestly could not have taken the emotional knocking I was taking here. A lesser person would have crumpled. But I think what I mainly felt was grateful to be here; grateful to see something so good. There were afternoons at football, I'm not kidding, when the action on the pitch provided roughly the same excitement as watching week-old kittens failing to get out of paper bags. Players in lower divisions sometimes just chased the ball, like little boys, instead of constructing anything; sometimes they crowded so badly, there appeared to be about forty of them on the pitch at once. Sometimes every pass seemed to go to an opposing player. Sometimes, the football just wasn't very good. This was not one of those afternoons.

Extra time saw no letting up of commitment from either side. In the first period, Middlesbrough got corner after corner, and made shot after shot. I believe I started to knit my hands in front of my eyes, as one does in wildlife films when the injured antelope is brought down by persistent hyenas who are fed up with being made fools of. 'Keep running, Chesterfield! Keep running! They haven't got you yet!' But in the end, it happened: Steve Vickers took a shot at goal that hit the crossbar and bounced back over the head of Juninho, falling near enough to Festa for him to score. Middlesbrough thereby took the lead for the first time in the match, and their fans went wild. But could they increase this lead? Could they hold on to it till the whistle? The answer, unbelievably, was no, and no. In the 119th minute of the match, Chesterfield equalised. Oh my goodness. Jamie Hewitt – the man who was not a famous love rat and who, astonishingly, hailed from the very town he played for – headed the ball in a high arc over Roberts into the goal and saved the day. If only Hollywood cared tuppence for football, this could have been described as a Hollywood moment. Time stood still. It was the most beautiful and death-defying ball I'd ever seen. It was clean. It was unstoppable. It curved just under the lip of the bar. And it happened in the very last minute of the game. On the field of play, the stars of Middlesbrough lay down in despair. Maybe it was finally time to face facts: this really wasn't going to be their year.

I was at the Cup final on May 17. Middlesbrough had beaten Chesterfield in the replay, but they lost at Wembley to Chelsea (2–0) and took away from their heroic season precisely nothing. I felt so sorry for Juninho that I cried. As is often the way with finals, it wasn't a patch on the semi. An Australian chap sitting next to me, high up in the stadium, had paid £400 to a tout for his ticket, and had never seen live football before, which made me all the more conscious of the lack of real dramatic interest. He didn't even enjoy seeing Sir Cliff Richard in the pre-match entertainment, or the marching band of the Royal Marines. After Di Matteo's amazing opening goal (which took place after 45 seconds), there were long periods of nothing much, which made me impatient on the Australian's behalf. 'Give us another goal!' I wanted to yell. 'This man only works in a pub!'

Looking back on my first season, I had loved it, but I was seriously worried about its effect on my brain. My understanding of the geography of England had been completely warped by football. Coventry was no longer a cathedral city of car manufacture with a terrible history of war-time bombing: it was principally a place where little Gordon Strachan jumped up and down on the touchline. Nottingham, which had once meant D.H. Lawrence and Boots the Chemist, was only the dismal Trent-side area of Meadow Lane (Notts County) and the City Ground (Nottingham Forest). Manchester, famed for its progressive 19th-century politics and modern metrosexual night-life, was represented by the industrial complexes of Trafford Park Road. Wimbledon had meant the novels of Nigel Williams and shortbread at the Windmill tea-room on Wimbledon Common; now it meant an image of Vinnie Jones reaching behind him to hold a young Paul Gascoigne by the scrotum, while threatening to tear someone else's ear off and spit in the hole. A few years later, I did a tour of England doing talks in bookshops, and I found myself saying things like, 'If you turn off here, you get to Villa Park' – as if anyone was interested. I had been to Anfield, but not to Liverpool, and that was fine. It was as if Liverpool was a city attached, peripherally, to a very important football stadium, rather than the other way round.

I now read newspapers starting at the back, and had incredibly strong opinions about a lot of things that were utterly unimportant. I had started to get exasperated with Emerson, for example, in these last two FA Cup games. Having watched him any number of times during the season, and sympathised with his homesickness, I still found it annoying that he pulled out of tackles nine times out of ten. Was this another Anderton-type prejudice on my part? Probably. But I had eyes in my head and it seemed to me that Emerson, in his rather crucial central position, had perfected an infuriating form of missing-the-bus football, whereby he would spot the ball nearby and accelerate towards it ('Wait for me!') and then realise the bus was drawing away ('Ding, ding!'), so give up instantly, and stop expending unnecessary effort. Swinging his arms, he would slow to a contented strolling pace, as if to say, 'Oh well. There'll be another one along in a minute.'

But what worried me most was the way these footballers had started to displace other knowledge. Emerson had previously been an influential transcendentalist philosopher whose house I had visited in Concord, Massachusetts. Well, not any more. Similarly, the name Zola had been a straightforward matter for me until a year ago, as a French realist novelist of the late 19th century who dealt with dark subjects and got mixed up in the Dreyfus affair. Where was that Emile Zola now, in my brain? I searched about, but he was hiding in some dark recess, supplanted by a small, brilliantly gifted Italian goalscorer whose kit looked as if it had been hand-sewn by his mum for a slightly bigger boy. Looking just at the Chelsea team list for the Cup final, Hughes had been Poet Laureate, Newton a great scientist,

Wise the short fat hairy-legged half of a great comedy duo, and Sinclair the inventor of a small motorised vehicle that never caught on except as an object of derision. Now they were all, emphatically, these other chaps in blue shirts, about whose day-to-day adventures I was absurdly over-interested. One day I saw the headline 'Adams in Talks' on the front page of a newspaper, and was disappointed when I discovered this was a reference to Gerry Adams and that the talks were about bringing peace to Northern Ireland. I had naturally jumped to the conclusion that this was a story about the much more important Tony Adams (of Arsenal and England) doing some sort of contract renewal.

The best thing was that I'd met a lot of fans, most of whom were nice people with a pretty innocent enthusiasm for a sport that had a lot of merit. Of course I was scared from time to time, usually after the match, as I scuttled back to the car (or, occasionally, to the station, which was worse). I've always been fearful of crowds, so it was a big effort to propel myself, week after week, to places where tens of thousands of other people would also turn up. As for football-fan behaviour, a drunken man shouting foul abuse from the seat behind could certainly ruin any match for me, and it happened several times, but I was generally more interested in the less clichéd behaviour that no one had told me about. At Southampton, for example, I heard a couple of fans chatting learnedly at half time about the photography of Robert Mapplethorpe, and I certainly wasn't prepared for that. Then, at Selhurst Park, the man on my right had been supporting Crystal Palace since the 1930s, and occasionally rasped an exasperated 'Leave ORF!', while the much younger fan in front brooded like a human volcano and at intervals erupted with the shout, 'NOTHING HAPPENED!' At Brentford (which I loved), the fans yelled encouragement to their individual boys ('Come on Marcus; come on Nicky') – but one man in particular was evidently convinced that the players and the ref could hear him, which was a bit worrying. 'Ref!' he shouted officiously. 'Three minutes left!' And he held up three fingers to prove it. As for the chanting, it was sometimes funny, sometimes crass. I particularly enjoyed 'You'll never beat Des Walker,' chanted by the Sheffield Wednesday fans – which, OK, isn't that interesting, except that for a long time I thought they were singing, 'You'll never *meet* Des Walker,' which seemed like a really useful philosophical point to make, because most of us never will.

Obviously, after a year of this, it was time to stop this pretence of sports writing and re-enter the real world, before it was too late. With any luck, I'd be able to get my Zolas back into perspective in a year or two if I did a lot of deep breathing with my eyes closed. But then my bosses suggested I expand my sports portfolio to take in tennis, golf, motor-racing, rowing, cricket, horse-racing and rugby, so I had to think again. And I'm afraid I pictured Emile and I pictured Gianfranco, and I thought, in a genuinely befuddled way, 'Real world? Which of these represents the real world?' Before me stood the shade of a great French writer whose stories were already written, and a lively, brilliant and engaging football player who made new stories every time he set foot on a football pitch. Emile would always be there. Gianfranco wouldn't. I wanted to be in the real world, apparently, so I signed up to be a sports writer. I signed up to be one of the boys.

Tennis and the Value
of Sports Writing

Funny occupation, though, sports writing. People have been known to go a bit mad in the cause, and it's hardly surprising, given the artificiality of the lifestyle and the demands of the work. Also, one's status is very hard to get into perspective: sport is big and important, but does that make a sports writer big and important, too? There are people who can't quite cope with this question. While I was doing the job myself, I wrote a deranged sports writer character into a comic novel: a man who said things like, 'Seve Ballesteros gave me this sombrero' and 'I taught Jack Charlton how to fish' – and colleagues who read it said they definitely recognised the type. My fictional sports writer's entire family was emotionally scarred by his confusion. On his deathbed, when the phone rang, he rallied himself to say, with his final breath, 'If that's bloody Alex Ferguson again, tell him to – [*cough, cough*] – sod off.'

Why is sports writing a kind of byword for alienation? Well, it's a pretty lonely job. But, looking at it from the outside, you might imagine that what would nag at the professional sports writer was simply the essential triviality of the subject. 'Perhaps I'm wasting my life on something that doesn't matter,' he would think, on sleepless nights. 'After all, if all sport stopped tomorrow, nothing bad would happen, would it? God gave me gifts and I am using them to monitor the growing animosity between the French-born manager of a very successful north London football club and the Spanish-born manager of a different very successful football club, based on Merseyside – an animosity which may be of no interest whatsoever by this time next year.'

But, astonishingly, this is not a problem. No one involved in sports journalism worries that sport isn't worth writing about, or entertains for a moment the 'if all sport stopped tomorrow' scenario with which I personally entertained myself on many a long break-neck drive back down the M6 (while also light-headedly debating whether to stop for motorway service food or just carry on risking a blackout at the wheel). The world-without-sport was my favourite fantasy on those journeys. I liked to picture football stadiums dug over for allotments, and so on. I liked to imagine how the complete cessation of sport would release an enormous amount of weekend time for men (in particular) to spend reading improving novels, growing courgettes as thick as your wrist, or taking their children on lovely long walks beside canals.

It would make an interesting dystopian novel, too – this world without sport. So easy to imagine: a future, library-quiet world in which suppressed sports followers had to pursue their faith underground, with secret meetings, always begun with a ritual hushed singing of 'Football's Coming Home'. What a market in illegal relics there would be. When the Goldstone ground in Brighton was deconsecrated (or whatever the word is) in 1997, the true followers of Brighton and Hove Albion dug up bits of the pitch to keep as little shrines, and there was an item in the local paper about a man who was keeping the centre spot alive in a bucket – I remember hoping he realised he had to repaint the spot as it grew, otherwise he would end up with just a bit of grass. And now I come to think of it, there had been another item in the local paper about a woman with a damp patch on her wall that miraculously resembled the boxer Chris Eubank, who lives in Hove. The headline said, 'I've Got Chris Eubank Coming Through My Wall.' Imagine the power of that in a world from which all sport had been banned. A small basement flat in Hove would become an object of clandestine pilgrimage. Alternatively, however (and looking on the bright side), perhaps no one would recognise the Miracle of the Damp Patch Eubank in this brave new world, and the wall would be painted over.

But even if you accept that sport has huge significance in itself, surely a sports writer will still anxiously ask himself: what is the value of writing about it? How much is there to say, really? Isn't some of the day-to-day busi-ness of sport too unimportant to deal with? And what of that mainstay of sports writing, the match report? What is the point of writing a 600-word first-hand next-day report of, say, a quarter-final match at Wimbledon? For one thing, you can't possibly do justice to the action. And for another, at the same time as you are writing your piece, millions of tennis fans are actually watching it for themselves on television – and they are doing this with the additional benefits (unavailable to the poor mug sitting in the press box) of continuous commentary, regular analysis, pertinent running statistics and instant, slow-motion replays.

I pick on Wimbledon for three reasons. First, because it was my first assignment as an accredited sports writer: i.e. working from a press room, and sitting in a press seat. (Or, rather, *not* sitting in a press seat, because there were three allocated desks for each paper in the old Wimbledon press room, and *The Times* had six writers, so I ended up, on my first day, writing miserably in a smokers' enclosure in the press canteen.) The second reason is that tennis is famously quite hard to bring to life on the page. It is noticeable that, whereas there are many great books about boxing, horse-racing, football, cricket, baseball and golf, there are few even halfway readable books about tennis. And third, tennis was the first sport I ever tried to read about in a newspaper before I was called to the profession; and the experiment was so profoundly unsatisfactory that it put me off trying again.

This occurred in 1991, when Andre Agassi made his first real mark at Wimbledon. He had competed there once before, in 1987, and was knocked out in the first round by Henri Leconte – but, to be fair, most Wimbledon watchers have no recollection of this. Anyway, hoping to find expert background information about this phenomenal player who, seemingly from nowhere, was making it to the quarter-finals in 1991, I opened the sports pages and was simply bewildered by the cool, haughty, long-distance, from-our-own-correspondent-in-Bechuanaland attitude I found there – especially as the precious who-is-this-bloke-then background info I sought was not on offer, either. I was quite perplexed. I had gone to the paper to enhance my appreciation of an interesting sportsman. I felt I had been prepared to meet sports journalism halfway. What I found was a toffee-nosed dismissal of him, based on his haircut and his eye-catching two-tiered shorts. Most confusingly of all, the tennis writers evidently believed that their mere physical presence on the spot conferred an almost divine authority on their accounts of proceedings – and on their judgements concerning Agassi's 'silly trousers', too.

This was extremely odd. Weren't these chaps aware that a lot of people watched Wimbledon at home? Had no one ever mentioned it to them? It was as if they loftily surveyed those neat grassy oblongs in south-west London from a balcony somewhere, and had no idea what all those little TV cameras and commentary boxes were for. 'You may have heard a few rumours about this chap Agassi,' was the tenor of the reports – transmitted, one imagined, by way of a humble cockney telegraph operator in a pith-helmet, kneeling on the floor of a makeshift tent, while the writer paced about and dictated, pipe in hand. 'Well, take no notice of those jungle drums, dear readers. This comically dressed young man will never achieve the stature of Ivan Lendl.'

In short, the air of complacent self-importance was a bit shocking. But I was glad, when I started having to give thought to all this in the summer of 1997, that I could remember those unfavourable first impressions. Because it took no time at all to discover where at least some of these sports writers' extraordinary sense of entitlement came from. First of all, there is the accreditation business, which makes a sports writer shake his head at the jostling, holiday-mood crowds and think, 'You may be here to enjoy this; I am here to understand it. You are here for the Pimm's and strawberries; I am here to work.' (Which is fair enough, actually.) But more importantly, from the professional point of view, there is the wonderful, deeply unfair, but utterly incontrovertible fact that sport sells newspapers, which means that anyone who writes about sport for a newspaper is conscious of the fact that he has already – without necessarily writing a single word that's worth reading – won the double rollover jackpot in the lottery of life.

To join the sport department was, simply, to join the winning team. And my main reaction when I realised this was: why had no one ever told me this before? Why was I 42 before I found out? For twenty arduous and quite inky years, as an editor and a writer, I had toiled in the fields of literary criticism and arts features, thinking it was a life worth leading. And now, completely unexpectedly, by simply having the word 'Sportswriter' embossed on my new *Times* business card, I had received the biggest hike in status of my entire career.

I had never known what I was missing, you see. I had loved those windowless, dusty, demoralised and half-starved books and arts departments. I had run a couple of them myself, and had assumed it was normal to live in a constant state of flinching apprehension that one's meagre page allocation – and indeed one's meagre office space, and meagre job – would at any moment be savagely halved, or subsumed into lifestyle, or snatched away completely. In my youth I had edited a single, measly, once-a-month arts page on a weekly newspaper which, every single time, the editor would neglect to include in the page-plan. 'Don't forget my arts page, Peter,' I would remind him, helpfully, from the doorway, when I noticed him working on the schedule, with ball-point and ruler. 'All right, all right, don't go on about it,' he would say, shooing me away with the back of his hand. But it was always the same. 'You forgot my arts page, Peter,' I would have to point out when the plan arrived, and he would silently clench his jaw, and get up from his desk, roll his eyes, and then personally lumber around the news room gathering back all the page plans that had been distributed – and all the time I knew he was cursing me, but he was also cursing the arts.

But now here I was on the winning team on a newspaper, and it was wonderful. No one forgot to include the sports pages. Goodbye Doncaster Rovers; hello Real Madrid. Not only that, though. Suddenly, I was on the winning team in the culture as a whole as well. Having a job that involves reading long books with a pencil counts for relatively little these days in the UK, I find, even if you read them before they are in the shops. Getting free tickets to the FA Cup final, the British Grand Prix, as well as (oh yes) the World Darts Championship at Frimley Green, on the other hand, makes you a kind of god. On the rare occasions when sports writers interface with non-journalists, therefore, the experience does absolutely nothing to help keep things real for them, ego-wise. To a vast number of people (who admittedly don't think about it very deeply), sports writing is simply the best job in the world. 'Ooh, can I carry your suitcase?' people always say. Or sometimes it's the variant: 'Can I come with you – in your suitcase?' For some reason, luggage is always mentioned, which is one of those baffling facts in life that it's just not worth stopping to question. So I was never judgemental about the suitcase-carrying offer. I just wish I'd had the nerve occasionally to laugh politely and then say, 'Blimey, absolutely, suitcase, what a brilliant idea, it's that blue one actually; listen, I'm off to Stoke on Saturday, you couldn't do the driving as well?'

The symbiosis of sport and newspapers is actually quite a lovely thing to behold. The wonderful thing is, despite the fact that a fan can watch sport on telly till his eyes fall out, he still wants to pay to read more about it the next day. And the result is that sport has traditionally been very well covered by the British press, so there's a certain circularity to the matter, because the quality of the journalism then draws the fans in to read it. Is it an accident that sport is the right-sized subject for newspapers? I think Darwin would have a few things to say about that, if he were around today. Anyway, somehow it is possible for each newspaper, each day, to fill between eight and twenty-four pages on sport, with reports, interviews, previews – and above all, pictures. Meanwhile the appeal is obvious. As a subject, sport is a complete parallel world, but a manageably small one, with reassuring overtones: nothing that happens in sport is ever so bad that it even momentarily disrupts the endless cycle of tournaments, leagues, championships and race programmes. Individual players and teams may suffer terrible disasters, but usually they can start again the following week, or the following season, with a fresh outlook and a clean slate. It is now pretty well established that the human brain needs to think about something beyond itself – something fairly complex and open-ended, ideally involving lots of characters who need to be kept straight in one's head, and regular exciting landmark events. On the one hand, *The Archers* evolved to fill this need – and, on the other hand, so did sport.

All sports fans are avid for news. Avidity for news is the thing that defines them. Loving sport and not wanting to know that (say) the owner of Manchester City has lost confidence in Sven-Goran Eriksson after quite good league results is not only unthinkable; it's philosophically untenable. And no wonder, therefore, that the journalists are rather good, because they are fans as well as professional communicators, so the urge to convey the smallest item of fact is automatically multiplied. There was a very well-informed chap who used to join the *Times* team at the Open (golf) every July, and he had a kind-of roaming brief. He would come to the desk a few times a day and say, in a low confidential whisper (even to me), things such as, 'Don't mention this to anyone else, but if Mark O'Meara breaks 70 today, I've worked out he'll be the first Masters winner over the age of 40 since Jack Nicklaus to follow up a missed cut at the PGA with success on the first day at an Open held in Scotland on the west coast.' And I would say, hypocritically, 'Really? How fascinating. Do you know, I think there's a piece in that. I can't wait to see what happens.' But then, when he'd gone away again, I would see what he was getting at, and worry about my reaction. *The readers would want to know this O'Meara fact, Lynne. This is the sort of thing that readers want to know.* And then I would counter-argue that I was already 400 words into a piece about the joy of owning waterproof trousers, so it was a bit late to change track now.

So, what is sports journalism, really? Take away the mystique created by the fact that it's all highly-excluding gobbledegook to people who don't care, and it's pure, basic journalism: stories concern exceptional people doing stuff, exceptional people talking about stuff they've done, and the very same set of exceptional people being quizzed about stuff they might do in the future. As an exercise recently, I bought all the broadsheet newspapers every day for a week and cut out all the sport. Then I left the pages in a heap on the floor of my office for a number of months, so that their news value could mature, or ferment, or – whatever. My rather feeble idea was that, once the spurious next-day interest had safely passed, I could analyse (or at least measure and add up) the coverage of everything in them, from football to bowls, and see how stories developed from day to day. The gathered pages weighed 1.4 kilos, and my first impression was that it wasn't a particularly interesting week, so they wouldn't take long to read. But once I started, I was compelled to revise the original plan. Studying just the first day's coverage – on the arbitrarily-chosen start date of Thursday January 24, 2008 – took me two days, and was utterly, utterly absorbing. At the end of it, I admit that I still didn't care much that James Toseland (motorcycling) had come 11th in Sepang (Malaysian Grand Prix), or that a strange breeze off the south-east coast of Australia (some sort of sailing event) had made a race go funny, but I was satisfied that not a single crumb of sport-related news had been ignored.

The night before January 24 had seen a fairly big

football match: Everton v Chelsea in the second leg of the Carling Cup semi-final (Chelsea won 3–1 on aggregate, and by 1–0 on the night). The one, solitary goal of the match was scored by Joe Cole in the 69th minute (i.e. well into the second half) – and by all accounts it was a well-executed one-touch drive from a long ball from Florent Malouda, a gravity-defying volley which made the main picture in all the papers (in fact, it was exactly the same Reuters picture in all of them). Now, 156 column inches of print were, in total, devoted to this game, with each paper running at least two pieces: usually, a match report and a more reflective piece, plus lots of pictures. Martin Samuel in *The Times* was alone in mentioning what a dull evening it was at Goodison Park – 'The game was tired and tame

.

.

.

the occasion was muted' – but it was obvious to anyone that this game was a considerable let-down after the other, far more action-packed semi-final second leg the previous night between Arsenal and Tottenham (not only six goals scored, but a punch-up between Arsenal team-mates).

Elsewhere, in the *Independent*, from an extremely detailed match report from Ian Herbert we learned not only that the occasion pitched the 'flash fluorescence of Chelsea . . . against sheer Evertonian spirit', but such minute-by-minute information as that, at one point, Shaun Wright-Phillips's movement flummoxed Lee Carsley and led to an ugly challenge on the midfielder for which Carsley was booked on 24 minutes. I have no idea, by the way, how anyone's brain can retain such details of footballing action when events have moved on – retain them, that is, long enough to set them down in words. I mean, this stuff does all happen very quickly. In my experience of trying to keep up with football matches while writing at the same time, you would have time only to say, at most, 'Why did he do that?' or, 'Would you say Carsley was flummoxed there?' or (more likely in my case), 'What happened? Did anyone see what happened?' before play resumed, and another foul took place, and the whole original incident was wiped from one's mind.

This is the skill of match reporting – a skill I never even attempted to acquire. 'It was left to [Mikel] Arteta to carve out the best chance of the game when he delivered another perfect ball for Andrew Johnson who reversed and span with the ball in his path before taking it into the penalty area, only to find the side netting,' writes Herbert. Good heavens. What a good description. I once worked alongside a football correspondent at the World Cup in France who, while watching – and presumably mentally noting – such ball-by-ball detail at the start of the second half of England v Argentina, was dictating from memory a report of the action in the first. And I could hardly contain my admiration for either his *sang froid* or the capacity and flexibility of his brain. I eavesdropped openly on what he was saying, by the way, and everything he described – chaps reversing and spinning, or flummoxing other chaps – I could not remember seeing.

How was the match-reporting space filled, then, on January 24, 2008, if not by the drama of the occasion at Goodison Park? Well, despite the dullness of the evening and the paucity of goals (or even chances), there was still a huge amount to say about Everton losing to Chelsea in the second leg of a Carling Cup semi-final – because, quite frankly, look at any match and there always is. For one thing, this was a rare silverware opportunity for Everton, whose last excitement on such a scale was back in 1995. What a crushing blow for the fans, then. David Moyes, the Everton manager, said afterwards that it was a brilliant effort by the lads, 'but we need to find that extra ingredient that gets us to Cup finals and wins Cup finals' – which, like most such inadequate post-match statements by managers would hardly give hope to the thousands of miserable supporters who already knew all about Everton lacking the magic 'winning' ingredient. They had woken up each day knowing this, and gone to bed each night knowing it, year after year.

Meanwhile, Nicolas Anelka – who, at this point, had been on the Chelsea strength for less than two weeks, having just transferred from Bolton at a cost of £15 million – had hit the bar in the second minute of the second half, but maybe had not contributed as much to the Chelsea victory as some had wished for. But on the other hand, how much could a man whose cumulative transfer fees now totalled £80 million really care about the Carling Cup? New-ish England manager Fabio Capello had watched the match from the directors' box, so there was speculation that he would be including Joe Cole in his immediate England team-selection plans. And what else can I tell you; what else? Captain of Chelsea John Terry wasn't playing, but – rather excitedly – one of the match reporters tells us that 'it was reported' (so he didn't see it himself) that Capello and Terry actually 'spoke at half time'!

Astonishingly (I'm sorry), there is yet more of incidental interest to be gleaned from this game. Oh yes. Don't forget we are talking about 156 column inches here. Chelsea goalkeeper Peter Cech (who saved a header from Joleon Lescott) had become a father for the first time earlier that day. Although both teams had lost players to the African Cup of Nations competition, Everton missed theirs more, for the obvious reason that they couldn't afford to just go out and buy Nicolas Anelka. Some of the Chelsea fans had come all the way from Cyprus. Of historical note was the fact that Frank Lampard's father (also called Frank Lampard) was responsible, nearly thirty years ago, for the goal that deprived Everton of a place in the 1980 Cup final – a fact so incredibly interesting that the *Telegraph* man put it in, even though neither of the illustrious Frank Lampards was on the pitch for the game under consideration. A victory for Chelsea at Wembley (against Tottenham) would give them their sixth trophy in four seasons. The din from the Everton crowd 'lacked some of the poetic soul of Anfield, but it was raw and raucous and fitted the occasion perfectly' – which I have no doubt is true, but is surely a bit of an additional insult to the Everton fans. They can't even *shout* as well as Liverpool? And Avram Grant, Chelsea's manager, was (possibly) finally emerging from the daunting shadow of his glamorous, smouldering, dog-smuggling predecessor Jose Mourinho.

Besides the match report, there is a raft of football news. Jonathan Woodgate, playing for Middlesbrough, might be going to Newcastle. In fact all four papers report the fact that Kevin Keegan, managing Newcastle, is keen to bid for Woodgate – although other clubs are keen, too. (In fact,

Woodgate signed for Tottenham four days later.) Emmanuel Adebayor, the starry Arsenal striker who head-butted a team-mate during the other Carling Cup semi-final, has made a statement saying that it was all down to his zeal – his 'passion' for the game getting regrettably out of hand. The victim of the assault, the young Danish international Nicklas Bendtner, is reported to be unpopular with his team-mates, and it is recalled that Arsenal are not good losers in any case (something quite similar happened last season). The *Guardian* notes that Arsenal's manager Arsène Wenger is furious, which, for obvious reasons, doesn't have much impact as news. Arsène Wenger is always furious. The *Guardian* also suggests that Bendtner 'raked Adebayor's achilles' (no one else says this, and there is no evidence), and offers a fabulous little picture feature entitled 'When Team Mates Attack', with famous incidents such as John Hartson kicking Eyal Berkovic in the head at West Ham's training ground in 1998. (I seem to remember this was put down to over-excitement, too.)

The remaining big football stories are similarly teeny-weeny (you might think) but of considerable interest. For example, Sir Alex Ferguson (speaking in Riyadh, where Manchester United are having a little holiday) sympathises publicly with Liverpool's manager Rafael Benitez over the lack of support he seems to get from the owners of the club. This is a massive story in three of the papers. Meanwhile there is speculation about who will take over as manager at Southampton, now that George Burley has been cleared to take the job of managing the Scottish national team. Front-runners are generally agreed to be Glenn Hoddle (pictured), Alan Shearer, Kevin Blackwell and Billy Davies. (Three weeks later, Nigel Pearson was appointed.) Following up from the Tottenham victory on Tuesday night, there are stories on manager Juande Ramos, and the reassuring news for Tottenham fans that the Bulgarian striker Dimitar Berbatov is not going anywhere. 'I look happy, don't I?' Berbatov is quoted as saying. 'This club can challenge for trophies.' (In the Carling Cup final a month later, Berbatov scored an equalising penalty, helping Tottenham to win 2–1. Two months after that, in April, he is quoted as saying he quite fancies playing for Milan. In September he completes a move to Manchester United for a fee of £30.75 million.)

Such is the football coverage for one very average day. The rest of the pages are similarly thorough – and just as unmissable for anyone interested in sport. In tennis, it's getting to the closing stages of the Australian Open, and all eyes are on the 20-year-old Serbian, Novak Djokovic, who is about to meet the world number one Roger Federer in the semi-final of the men's singles (and go on to win the tournament, as it happens). It is generally agreed that Djokovic is now right up there with Federer and Nadal, and that this is exciting. Mark Hodgkinson in the *Daily Telegraph* describes Djokovic as having 'an all-round air of self-confidence that makes Russell Brand look shy and retiring'. Neil Harman in *The Times* describes how Djokovic lost concentration in the last game of his quarter-final: 'He frittered away serve after serve, while having to deal with taunts from his own supporters.' Meanwhile Steve Bierley in the *Guardian* is all praise: 'He has achieved a level of controlled excellence, combined with an unbending mental fortitude, that has lifted him to an undisputed third place in the world, behind Nadal and Federer.'

Alongside all this news there are opinion pieces and celebrity columns, the most bizarre of which is a very defensive and strongly worded piece in *The Times* about it being perfectly all right for men to ogle women tennis players, especially when they look like the four hottie singles semi-finalists in Melbourne: *viz*, Jankovic, Hantuchovna, Ivanovic and Sharapova – all of whom are pictured in red-carpet evening dress mode, with their long hair down, one of them in a very, very, very short skirt. 'There has always been a soft-porn dimension to women's tennis,' states Matthew Syed – and having worked on the sports pages myself, I know that this view is not a new one, and that the idea for this piece may have originated quite high up in the paper. Syed argues that, since women are allowed to ogle male rugby players (and clearly do, to his annoyance, all the time), it's hypocrisy to criticise the red-blooded male custom of seeing female tennis players as sex objects. Besides (he goes on), don't these female tennis players pose provocatively for photographs all the time? Don't they trade on it? 'That we have not, as a society, reached a place where heterosexual men can acknowledge the occasional erotic dimension of watching women's sport without being dismissed as deviant tells us everything we need to know about contemporary sexual neuroses.'

All this explains, I think, why my dipping into the sports pages in 1991 was such a disaster. It was me. I simply wasn't up to speed, was I? I didn't know that sport – as a subject for newspaper coverage – was so earnest, so involved, and so aware of itself as a continually unfolding story. When I now look at the *Times* coverage of Agassi at Wimbledon in 1991, I find it well-informed, often spot-on in terms of his talents and potential, and even funny. The background information I wanted is there, after all; just deftly included in the match reports. All my other objections melt away, too. The idea that a newspaper account of a match should be some sort of adjunct to yesterday's television coverage strikes me as silly (and even offensively so); meanwhile, the Bechuanaland posture of our-man-on-the-spot is delightful and the main appeal of the report. The authority that comes with being present at an event is the cornerstone of sports journalism. Not being present at an event you write about is, I think, the only automatic sacking offence. It's just a shame that so few writers do anything to remind you of their presence – no mention of the cold and dark at the Goodison match, for example. Was it raining, perhaps? Did a sharp wind blow from the end where the church is? What state was the pitch in? Did Chelsea wear yellow? Did Everton wear blue? Was there that special football-ground smell of fried onions mixed with fresh manure (from the police horses)? Unfortunately, such namby-pamby descriptive stuff is sniffily classed as 'colour', and is left to soft old literary types like me.

Of course, no one would want to read, in a match report, about the conditions the writers work under – the narrow tip-up desk at the halfway-line, where you sit trying to write 900 words for delivery 'on the whistle', surrounded by other reporters doing the same thing, tightly shoulder to shoulder, some of them calling the office, others broadcasting on club radio, and all of them wonderfully stolid in their refusal to get involved, in any way whatsoever, in crowd behaviour – especially Mexican waves. This bah-humbug attitude to crowd self-entertainment makes the press a bit unpopular sometimes, but that's tough. 'Oh God, no,' the reporters groan, when some bright spark starts one of these tedious group celebrations. 'Whoooaaa!' goes the wave, round one end of the stadium; 'WHOOOAAAA' it goes round the other. Then the wave slops up against the press box, where the occupants remain seated. Then, perfectly on cue, it starts up again the other side of the obstacle, 'Whoooaaa!' And off it goes again. As someone who hasn't been in a press box for a while, I like to watch Mexican waves whenever they're reported on the telly, just so that I can see where the hiatus takes place, and send telepathic killjoy support to all my suffering killjoy chums.

When I first heard about the 'press box', by the way, I naïvely assumed that the term implied enclosing walls, and even a ceiling and floor. I expected comfy seats and a picture window. Possibly cups of tea with saucers. What I soon learned, however, was that where press boxes actually *were* enclosed, they were ghastly; the benefits (of warmth, and safety from missiles) were easily outweighed by the fact that you can't hear properly, have to combat claustrophobia, and get much more distracted by your colleagues, who might be chatting, eating, smoking, or loudly dictating dismayingly unrecognisable descriptions of the footie you've just been watching. At cricket grounds – where the matches last considerably longer than 90 minutes, of course – the reporters do sit indoors, behind glass, and are completely cut off from the atmosphere. At Lord's, the famous space-ship press centre (on stilts) is fronted by sound-proofed tinted windows, and on the one occasion I worked in it, I hated it. I kept having to shake off the sensation that I had suddenly gone deaf.

In addition to the outdoor 'press box' at football stadiums, there is usually a dingy lounge of some description, with a TV in it, bolted to the wall. In my day, this lounge would sometimes offer the luxury of electrical sockets, but there was no guarantee. Oh, the misery of those footie press lounges. All the charm of a working man's club at ten in the morning. The lounge at Coventry City's Highfield Road had been cunningly adapted from some sort of airless subterranean cupboard, half of it taken up by a flight of carpeted stairs, with only five chairs for 28 people, and when you said, 'Any chance of a cup of tea?' they looked at you in disgust and snapped (as if it was reasonable), 'Not until *half time*!' I remember turning up there one day when the match was sponsored in some way by Yorkie bars. I think I was the first to arrive, and I watched with interest as a man with a box of Yorkies distributed about two dozen bars around the place. That ought to keep a few spirits up, I thought, innocently. A few minutes later, a couple of local sports writers arrived, and one of them said, 'Oh good,' and put the full two dozen in his bag. 'Kids' lunches,' he explained – as if that made it all right, then. 'The wife went nuts when she found out I didn't get them all last time.'

When football writers talk about the relative merits of various grounds, it's the food they will probably talk about. Nowadays, I hear that Arsenal (at the Emirates) lays on a tasty spread of hot dishes for the journos, so perhaps things generally have improved. I certainly hope so. In my day the same club (at Highbury) gave us tasteless carrot sandwiches – and not many to go round, either. All it needed was for one fat bloke from a tabloid to get a whole tray to himself, and you were done for. Meanwhile, I couldn't wait to go to Leicester's Filbert Street, once I heard about the cream buns. And I liked the spacious, smoky press lounge in a corner room at Aston Villa, where there was quite a spread, although the lady pouring the teas once put me right off the footie by telling me a horrific story about how her mother had been murdered by a next-door neighbour (who got away with it), and she'd had to clear up the blood by herself.

Back at Wimbledon on my first assignment, it was a big deal just to meet other sports writers. Aside from one or two trips to Wembley, my first year had been about sitting in the stands with the regular punters and writing at home a couple of days later. Now I not only had colleagues, but I had to deliver my 900 words by 6 p.m. using a mid-1990s uncooperative bastard of a laptop that combined immense weight with no beauty and a hair-trigger intolerance of error – and do it while exiled to the far corner of a smokers' den, don't forget, because a nasty old man with a red face (with some official authority over the photographers) had shouted at me, 'This is an eating area! Not a writing area!' when I set myself up at a regular table in the restaurant.

Good God, it was such an appalling day, my first day

at Wimbledon, and I'm afraid my bitter memories of it have for ever changed my opinion of the place and made me uncomfortable (not to say chippy) about working there. The posh people in the press office – who made a big show of welcoming their posh old friends ('Julian! Hello!') through a hatch arrangement – seemed not to like the look of me at all. Having handed me my badge and a heavy complimentary Wimbledon equipment bag full of programmes, maps and so on, they seemed to disapprove of the fact that I didn't know where to go next. The day was hot. I had a heavy bag with a computer in it, and now I had another heavy bag. I had a jacket that was now surplus to requirements. Was there anywhere to leave stuff? Certainly not. Can I take all this lot with me on court, then? No, of course you can't. Where would my colleagues be? No idea; go and look. But not that way: that's the way to Centre Court. I was told at the end of my first Wimbledon fortnight, by the way, that the obstructive and hoity-toity personnel of the press office could be easily got round by sending bottles of scotch as a thank-you gift – and this news incensed me so much that I nearly went straight round to their fancy hatch and hit someone.

What I was learning quickly on my first day, however, is that sports writing means never getting any help from anyone. Not even your own colleagues, initially. I mean, fair enough, they didn't know me. I'd met only one of them before, at football. When I reported for duty, I didn't even know the name of the tennis correspondent. I turn up in their territory, huffing and puffing with heavy bags, demanding 'Where do I sit, then?' and they quite naturally say that these three desks are taken; have you tried in the foreign press area upstairs? So I go up there, dragging these fucking bags, and am told by a hoity-toity obstructive person that this area is for *foreign* press (am I stupid?), and I get hotter and more emotional, which naturally makes everyone all the more keen to get rid of me. Luckily, ahead of me is a very gentle day, tennis-wise. I am to watch a British hopeful on an outside court, and I'll have a couple of hours to turn the piece round, assuming I can find somewhere to settle long enough to do it. I recognise that, by giving me such a soft assignment, the office is thinking tactically: my piece is dispensable. If I screw this up, no one will miss the report on the British hopeful, and the story can be covered quite easily with a picture.

Were there any positives to this day? Well, I loved the fact that the crowds were so quiet at tennis – as contrasted to football – that the chap sitting next to me on Court 17 waited patiently with a small stick of carrot in his hand until the change of ends, for fear that chomping on it might distract the players. (He then masticated it very carefully, with no sound.) I think I got to meet our photographers Marc and Gill, who were great; and I gradually realised that the other chaps on the desk were pleasant and funny, and that it had been my job to get off on the right foot with them, rather than the other way round. It had never occurred to me (in fact it's occurred to me only now, really) that my months of prominently-displayed stuff in the sports pages might have prejudiced my colleagues in any way against me; on the contrary, I assumed they wouldn't know who I was.

I did get a small buzz out of the fact that this was Wimbledon – a tournament I've watched on TV all my life

– and that great players were preparing to do great things there over the next two weeks. But watching Wimbledon on TV is quite different from being on the spot, and the crowds were tiring, and the distances were quite big, and there were some confusing one-way paths, and I turned up successfully at Court Number One for an opening ceremony only to find out that a special ticket was required, so I went all the way back to the press-office hatch to get one, and they said I couldn't have one because I wasn't Dutch (I think); and I kept going the wrong way round Centre Court, and I couldn't believe no one told you anything – *you have to find everything out for yourself* – and basically I was close to tears for the entire day – sometimes tears of frustration at having my way barred by people pointing a firm arm in the opposite direction, sometimes tears of discomfort and self-pity, but mostly tears of realistic anxiety that my unfamiliar laptop would crash (as it duly did) when I was three quarters of the way through writing my piece, fifteen minutes before deadline.

I was staying with my mum for that Wimbledon fortnight in 1997, and I returned to her after the first day such an emotional wreck that she encouraged me to resign at once and go back to reviewing television. But I'm glad I persevered. As the two weeks went by, I learned that, just as other people pushed me off the desk, I could do the same to them – by simply waiting until they went to the lavatory and then lifting all their stuff onto a handy shelf and sitting down. The sports writers turned out to be great company; in fact, the best company in the world. I came to grips with Copymaster – the system installed on all our laptops, by which we wrote and filed. I learned the ropes about getting onto Centre Court – although the idea that this privilege was in the gift of a hoity-toity obstructive person who guarded the steps like a three-headed dog made my blood boil at the time, and still does. We had a number of rain days, so I went off and ingeniously extracted enormous amounts of 'colour' from sod all. And sometimes I was scheduled to cover a match that, through rain delays (or by design), didn't come on court until five o'clock – so I'd have to watch some of it live, and then go back to the press room and follow it with half an eye on the TV screen, and file a piece for the first edition at 7 p.m., and then revise it for later editions as the match progressed. Which is how sports writing is always done.

The easiest thing about the job, always, was the business of writing to deadline about stuff that was (often) still going on. I never thought, 'I won't be able to do that.' I always thought, 'I am really lucky to be doing this, because this is great.' I used to imagine how theatre critics would manage if they had to work under the same conditions, all jammed up next to each other. They don't know they're born, those people. Imagine them all tapping away with their reviews of *The Seagull*, which they had started at the interval, before they knew whether anything of special tragic note was ever going to happen. 'The evening holds no dramatic moments,' they would be confidently writing, in their intros, with five minutes to go; 'If one expects a tragedy, it is not forthcoming.' At which point, 'Bang!' comes the shot from offstage. All stop typing, and some are heard to whisper, 'Konstantin may have shot himself.' All scan their pieces in alarm, and scroll back quietly to the top, check their watches, chew their lips, and then sit poised for confirmation from the stage. 'Which one's Konstantin?' pipes a small voice from the end. The doctor comes in and says that it was just a bottle of something exploding in his bag – at which Konstantin's mother is visibly relieved, and some of the theatre critics, satisfied with this innocent explanation, press 'Send' and start packing their bags. Then the doctor confides to Trigorin, 'Get Arkadina out of here. The thing is, Konstantin has shot himself.' At which, there is a thunder of keyboard pounding as all the critics start again, with, 'Sensationally, in the 134th minute of *The Seagull* last night, one young man's destiny was tragically fulfilled . . .'

THE PLAYER

The 1999 men's final at Wimbledon is remembered by historians of tennis as one of the great matches of the modern era. On Sunday July 4, 1999, Pete Sampras beat Andre Agassi in three sets, and in the course of it raised his game to heights few tennis-observers had ever seen before. Sampras was 27 years old, and already the holder of five Wimbledon singles titles; he went into the championships as the number one seed – as he had for five out of the six previous years. Agassi, aged 29, had been champion at Wimbledon only once (in 1992, beating Goran Ivanišević in a tense five-setter), but had by now managed to win all four of the Grand Slam championships – the Australian, the French, Wimbledon and the US Open – which meant he was likewise a giant of the game. For those with hazy memories, Sampras v Agassi at Wimbledon may seem like something that happened all the time in the 1990s ('Not Pete and Andre *again?*'), but in fact it had happened only once before, in the quarter-finals in 1993, when Sampras took the first two sets against an apparently sleep-walking Agassi, then conceded two sets, then polished him off in the fifth.

Theirs was indeed the great rivalry of that period, however – or, at least, it was marketed as such by Nike, famously in the sexy 'Just Do It' TV ad in 1995, in which the two players jump out of a cab in a busy downtown area, stretch a tennis net across an intersection, and start walloping a ball at each other, with orgasmic grunts, until a horn-honking bus ploughs into the net and the excited onlookers scatter. The idea behind this ad, obviously, was that these two hormonally-charged young American alpha-males couldn't contain their volcanic feelings of spontaneous wallop for each other – and that they there-fore carried tennis court accoutrements with them at all times, so that they were always ready to try each other out on new and exciting surfaces. One wonders whether the Nike ad-men ever suggested a naked-wrestling-on-the-carpet-by-firelight sequence as well, but possibly my mind is wandering into dangerous territory. Anyway, it was definitely a head-to-head between these two that was engineered as often as possible at all tournaments, so it was doubtless a real bummer for Wimbledon that, after the 1993 quarter-final, however hard the seeding committee tried to contrive it, Sampras and Agassi did not meet again across a competitive grass court in SW19 for another six whole years.

On the Sunday morning of the match, I knew I wouldn't be watching it – and I wouldn't be seeing the delayed women's singles final between Lindsay Davenport and Steffi Graf either. Never reliable at the best of times, my Centre Court access had been withdrawn midweek, for the simple, common-sense reason that the press box on Centre Court had a finite capacity, and proper sports writers from all round the world obviously needed the seats to put their bums on. I bore this blow quite well, I think. This was my second time at Wimbledon, and in terms of my dealings with the press office I had largely stopped (in that lovely phrase, not used half enough these days) kicking against the pricks. Also, in terms of seniority on the sports pages, I knew my place. On hearing that my chum Simon Barnes had been held up on a dicky train from Mortlake that morning, I helpfully – one might even say nobly – collected the *Times* Centre Court accreditation on his behalf.

Speaking to the office at the start of the day, I had found out that they had quite definite views about the outcome they wanted from the upcoming events: Steffi to win the women's; Andre to win the men's. Such a result would guarantee sales next day, you see – since Steffi and Andre were both extremely popular old-timer type players, and they had both just won the French (although nobody knew they were an item yet). I thought this was fair enough. I then asked them what they wanted from me, and they suggested (what else?) that I spend yet another day roaming the grounds and reporting the atmosphere – which is how I happen to know that, at the moment when Sampras started to get transcendental, breaking Agassi's service game at the start of the second set, the people in the queue for pizza didn't give a toss. I wondered, miserably, what on earth these people were doing here – paying money to get in, and then not bothering with the tennis. I was reminded of stories of the crucifixion (ordinary Jerusalem people going about their daily business and just putting the lights on when it got dark in the afternoon), but tried really hard to drive these thoughts from my mind. The power of association is all very well, but it's best not to rely on it totally – especially when it leads you down the road to casual blasphemy.

So I didn't see the matches, but I watched the scoreboard obsessively. And, well, as it turned out, *The Times* was unlucky that day. Lindsay Davenport won the women's in two sets; Pete Sampras won the men's in three. Dear, oh dear. At the end of play, I went back into the press centre and sat down next to Simon Barnes, who was literally rubbing his hands with glee at the thought of all the lovely, lovely tennis greatness to which he would soon expertly attest. I opened my laptop, took a sip of a cup of tea. And then, thinking I ought to show that I had at least followed the results while on my humble trudging duty, I did a foolish thing. I made the innocent and light-hearted remark, 'So. The wrong ones won.'

I regret this now, of course. But if it's any consolation, I also regretted it instantly, because this was not the thing to say to a sports writer in a state of rapture. 'People who can't appreciate fucking genius should fuck off,' was Simon's memorably hot reply – and I'm fairly certain (as Wodehouse might have added) that he meant it to sting. But feelings were running high, deadlines were pressing, and Simon was among the few sports writers who'd been friendly towards me from the start. So, while he then went on to write a heavily ironic opening about exactly how and why Steffi and Andre had lost to 'the *wrong ones*', I, feeling a bit shaken, went on to write a speculative, space-filling 900 words of drivel asking whether the folks on Henman Hill were 'the true fans' (as the TV commentators evidently liked to think), or in fact drunken layabouts with no homes to go to. While I was doing this, I kept wondering, 'Should I interrupt Simon to explain? Does he really think I should fuck off? Isn't that a bit unfair?' But I make it a policy not to argue with people who are angry with me already, especially when I have a deadline impending (and nothing to write about), so I didn't.

The fact that I hadn't been allowed to see a single point of the Sampras–Agassi match and therefore couldn't possibly be accused of not appreciating fucking genius was immaterial, in any case. Simon has always felt (and enjoyed feeling) that he is specially qualified to appreciate the talents of great sportsmen such as Sampras; and of course it is essential to this belief that the rest of the world can't see it at all. In 2003, when it finally became clear that Sampras had quietly retired, Simon wrote a farewell song of praise to his hero, pinpointing the 1999 Wimbledon final as the day when anyone who had 'put in the hours and covered the hard yards of sport' spotted the emergence of true greatness. The fact that no one – *no one* – disagrees with him about Sampras cuts no ice at all. Recalling that day in 1999, he wrote four years later, 'Those who felt that yet another Sampras win was a bit of a bore were entitled to their view.'

The only thing I would now argue with in this, is that July 4, 1999 was a pretty interesting moment for Andre Agassi too – and that this has been rather overlooked in all the lovely Sampras myth-making associated with that day. I know this seems an odd thing to say. How could anyone 'overlook' Andre Agassi, you ask. Surely he was in the limelight constantly for two decades? Didn't he work at it? Wasn't he adored everywhere? After Muhammad Ali and Tiger Woods, he is probably the most universally recognised American sportsman. Well, I can see what you mean by that. I just think Agassi is an interesting case of where sports writing doesn't quite cope, and that the reasons are worth exploring. If Pete Sampras was a gift to sports writing, Andre Agassi exposed its shortcomings. You could watch Andre play, week after week and year after year; you could write about it a thousand times for the next day's paper; you could comment amusingly on his latest body-hair choices; but still you could never get a handle on the man. He wins when he's supposed to lose; he loses when he's supposed to win. Is he a flake or what? What sort of perspective can you get on Andre bloody Agassi, and how could it be worth the effort? What does he care what anyone in the tennis world thinks of him, when he's so rich and popular, and stars all the time in TV ads? In 1989, when he was already a contender in Grand Slam finals, a columnist in the American magazine *Sports Illustrated* woundingly asked whether Agassi was 'the game's new savior or just another infantile twerp'. And the headings 'SAVIOUR' and 'TWERP' were probably at the top of most sports writers' notepads (with a line down the middle) whenever they thought about him ever after – or until he finally retired, an impressive 17 years later, in September 2006.

In my experience, Agassi would generally elicit a shiver of impatience, a frisson of distaste, in people who write about sport, largely because of his sheer wealth and rock-star popularity, but also because – in so many ways other than the literal – he didn't play the game. A wilful shape-shifter, evidently with a lot to prove and a pair of equally-matched demons tussling inside him for his tennis-playing soul, he found a simple way of clouding the issue of his inner torment: he dressed up in eye-catching clothes. Looking back, this strategy seems a bit obvious – but it wasn't obvious at all to the people paid to watch. When Agassi played Andrei Chesnokov in the first round of Wimbledon in 1992 – having reached the final of three Grand Slam events in the preceding 12 months – John Barratt did not say, 'Looks a bit tense and haunted to me, this talented young man; personally, I blame the way his tennis-mad father brought him up. And call me simplistic, but I also wonder whether this look-at-me long blond ponytail is a classic example of psychological double-bluff, because actually he doesn't want people to penetrate what's inside.' No, Barratt did not say that. Instead he chuckled, 'He looks a bit like a pony, doesn't he?' And when Agassi had completely mysteriously chucked away the second set (6–1), but then regained himself to polish off Chesnokov in the fourth, Barratt commented, 'A showman to the last, the Las Vegas kid goes off to the kind of applause we usually give to pop stars.'

'A man of contradictions' goes nowhere near to accounting for Andre Agassi. Perceived as an obnoxious lightweight who couldn't decide whether he was serious or not about his sport, he became, in the long run, in 2003, the oldest man ever (at 33) to hold the number 1 spot in the world rankings. In 1998, he staged the biggest come-back that had ever happened: from 141st to 6th, in a single year. At the start of 1999, the British Davis Cup captain David Lloyd flatly declared, 'He couldn't beat my mum now. He's finished.' Agassi then went on to win the French Open and the US Open in 1999, and the Australian Open the following year. The effort was heroic. The achievement was extremely improbable. In fact, though, one might see Agassi's amazing mid-career comeback as a magnified version of what happened in so many of his matches. Win two sets easily, then drop the third and fourth spectacularly, and then – having made sure you've drawn all the crowd's anxiety to your cause ('Come on, Andre! Come on, Andre! We love you, Andre! It *can't* be all over!') – fight back and win by 10 games to 8 in a gut-buckling fifth. But it was no less remarkable for that. In July 1999, therefore, he was not only on glorious form; it was a perfect mid-point in his Wimbledon career. Seven years earlier, he had become champion – in a field that still included John McEnroe, Stefan Edberg, Ivan Lendl and Boris Becker. A full seven years later, Agassi would finally retire from Wimbledon, when beaten in the third round by Rafael Nadal – a man who was so far his junior that he was, literally, *in the womb* when the 16-year-old Andre Agassi turned professional in May 1986.

Didn't Andre Agassi present a far greater (and more interesting) challenge to sports journalism than Pete Sampras? So why was he so hard, or unrewarding, to write about? Well, it didn't help, probably, that his entire motivation in life seemed to be to prove everybody wrong, all the time. You might also argue that the unconventional, not to say amorphous, shape of Agassi's tennis career was impossible to assess while it was still going on: his roller-coaster form was probably a truly tiresome phenomenon to observe at close hand. But if it was pointless to try, I'm sure he very much wanted it that way. He often skipped press conferences, preferring to pay the tiddly fine instead. Asked once at a Melbourne press conference to distinguish the latest comeback from the one before, he said, smilingly but unhelpfully: 'Well, that was my new, new attitude. This is my new, new, *new* attitude.' He has now been paid $5 million by a New York publisher to write his memoirs – a fact that suggests he hasn't lost the knack of getting top dollar (John McEnroe got a measly *one* million for his excellent book *Serious*). It's just a bit worrying that no one in publishing has noticed Andre Agassi's career-long propensity for creating false expectations ('He's going to win!'/'He's going to lose!'/'He's going to write his memoirs!'), and then doing his utmost to defy them.

However, the big issue Agassi raises most uncomfortably for sports journalism is that of where sport meets entertainment. It is, you see, the main tenet of sports journalism that spectator sport is never to be confused with other spectator activities; other ways of paying professionals (actors, circus folk, rock musicians) to entertain you by doing what they're good at. For myself, sometimes I can see the distinction quite clearly, and I can even uphold it with gusto; at other times, something flips in my brain and the distinction just melts away, exposing sport as quite monstrously bogus in how seriously it takes itself. The vital difference between sport and theatre, or sport and opera, of course, is that sport is unwritten; it happens for real. No authorial brain devises it before it takes place. In the world of sport, if Konstantin shoots himself in the last minute of extra time, no one has told him to, and it gets listed under the heading of unforced error. But for all this absolute spontaneity on the field of play, the relationship between sport and 'reality' is obviously a bit tenuous, when you think about it. Wimbledon finals do not simply break out when two terribly well-matched young people can't suppress their competitive yearnings any longer. Sport is staged – at great expense, with great expertise, and at great profit, too. Spectators book their seats months in advance. And at home afterwards, the handsomely rewarded players pause only to light the gas with the top £50 note (from a handy foot-high stack of £50 notes) before turning the page on the calendar and looking forward to next week's tournament, excitedly humming that great showbiz curtain-raiser from *Kiss Me, Kate*, 'Another op'nin', another show!/In Philly, Boston or Baltimo'!/A chance for stage folks to say hello!/Another op'nin' of another show!'

The money thing is so tricky. No one would want the Wimbledon champion to be asked, after his victory, in front of the crowd, whether he has specific plans for the big cheque (new curtains, that kind of thing), or even, 'So, where will you be playing next week?' It would break a spell. But it is nevertheless quite strange that no one involved in sport ever acknowledges the truth of the matter: that without the existence of a paying public, professional sport would not take place. There is somehow an accepted belief that all these matches, races, heats, games, rounds, bouts, legs, chukkas, rallies, regattas and rubbers just happen because they have to. Sport occurs by some imperative law of nature, for its own sake, in a pure, self-sustaining and perpetual world of competition – a world to which avid spectators may be admitted, incidentally, but only if they are prepared to fight for the privilege, and don't demand too much by way of value for money. What sustains this idea is the genuine earnestness of the players. They really care whether they win or lose. It is their life. They put themselves on the line for reasons of personal pride. If they notice the adulation of the crowd at all, they consider it their sportsmanly duty not to let it distract them from the job in hand. As for the issue of the prize money – well, we are led to believe that any sum involved is a mere token. Look at a triumphant Wimbledon finalist and you certainly don't see a man thinking (or not primarily), 'Oh thank God. This means I don't have to sell the car.'

A similar topsy-turvydom characterises the relationship between sport and sports journalism. Sport takes the line that it's doing the media a huge favour by letting them in. The football grounds give you a nasty room to work in, and shout at you if you go the wrong way looking for the Ladies, or sit at the wrong sort of table in the canteen. Football managers give press conferences with extremely bad grace. The press is a nuisance that is barely tolerated – but no one objects that the boot is on the other foot; that without the keen and extensive publicity that professional sport receives from newspapers and other media, it would simply not exist. Again, it is the sheer seriousness with which the players take their job that elevates the enterprise. I wonder if this is why the rhetoric of sporting 'greatness' sticks in my craw as much as it does. True, the poetic tribute to an athlete has a great tradition, and can be stirring when it's well done. Two and a half thousand years ago, the great lyric poet Pindar (518–438 BC) was hymning the heroes who had won mule-cart races at the ancient games – and although we now don't know anything else about those garlanded winners, Pindar's words are still very lovely to read. 'Great deeds give choice of many tales,' he wrote in his 'Pythian IX' ('For Telesikrates of Kyrene, Winner of the Race in Armour' – translated by Maurice Bowra). 'Choose a slight tale, enrich it large, and then/Let wise men listen!' But it just seems to me that there's an element of credulousness in celebrating the greatness of these chaps, who are themselves the cat's paws of the system. Every time a journalist enriches a tale of 'great deeds' – deeds done quite unnecessarily, of course; and in artificially created conditions, for the profit of others – it sends the message to the sports organisers that their secret is safe, that no one will ever find them out.

Against this background, it's not surprising that Andre Agassi was not a darling of the press – or not until the second, humbler half of his career, when the screaming had died down and he was wearing a plain white sleeve-less woolly. How do you argue that sport is not a branch of entertainment when it's quite clear that thousands of people would pay good money just to watch this man knock a ball against a door? How do you insist it's not about money when he owns a customised Boeing 727? Asked once what he liked about Agassi, the famously laconic Sampras said, 'I like the way he travels' (referring to the jet). 'This child of Las Vegas' was how the BBC's Wimbledon commentators regularly described Agassi. 'He's a star, the boy,' said Des Lynam in 1991, just before Agassi's quarter-final against David Wheaton. 'What a showman,' everyone said, with a giveaway wrinkle of the nose. Disregarding the hoo-ha is something a sports writer is trained to do, because hoo-ha is irrelevant to the serious matter of bat and ball. But this was the problem with Agassi. You couldn't extract him from the hoo-ha, and you certainly couldn't take the hoo-ha out of him.

Why was he more popular with the crowds than Sampras? Was it because he was a shallow character with a large portfolio of advertising deals? The reason was actually a bit more respectable than that. What pleased the crowds was his miraculously quick and deep return of serve, which meant that (just in time) he single-handedly rescued men's tennis from being a monotonous display of one-sided power serving from a new breed of faceless middle Europeans who didn't appeal to anybody and who wore unpleasant socks. All right, the claim 'he rescued men's tennis' may be a bit of an over-statement; and the big servers didn't *all* have unpleasant socks; and all right, I know I also liked the way Agassi's shirt was cunningly cut short at the front so that it showed his hairy torso when he served. However, when I close my eyes I can picture him in the old ponytail days, standing behind the baseline, looking brave and small (at 5'11", he is shorter than a lot of the top players), and a bit worried and decidedly pigeon-toed. He frowns a bit. The crowd falls silent. He looks like a waif. At the other end, a man twelve feet tall with feet the size of doormats (and strange hosiery) winds himself up to launch a ball at 150 miles per hour, which goes faster than the human eye can see it.

Whap. Basically this is like watching a person catch bullets between his teeth. Except that Agassi returns the bullet! With a lightning reflex whip of the wrist, he flips the ball straight down the line, or whizzes it across the court, stranding the enormous, Neanderthal server mid-stride as he lumbers to the net. Does a crowd like to see this? Of course it bloody does. The ability to catch the ball on the rise and whack it back before anyone knew what was happening was what made Andre Agassi so popular with tennis fans from his very first appearance on the scene. The appeal was atavistic. It was David v Goliath. It was standing up to the big bully with the thick accent and the duelling scar. And above all, it was keeping the ball in play, for heaven's sake, which meant there was a chance some actual tennis might ensue. For all these reasons, plus the furry tum, beyond anything else you can see on a court, it made you cheer, 'Hooray!'

All the famous contrasts to Sampras doubtless show Sampras as the superior being, sportsman-wise. Agassi loved to talk and analyse; Sampras's favourite line in litera-ture was supposed to be 'Don't ever tell anybody anything' from *The Catcher in the Rye*. Andre was beloved by the crowd; Sampras was once asked whether he might ever drop his Borg-like cool, and he observed, 'It's worked so far.' Sampras served; Agassi returned. Sampras had the greatest forehand; Agassi's best shot was the backhand. Sampras had beautiful running shots; Agassi usually preferred to hit the ball with both feet firmly on the ground. In that 1999 final, Sampras dived for volleys twice, scraping his forearm quite badly in the process. Once it worked and once it didn't, but the abiding memory is of Andre's stunned, blank disbelief that such a brilliant drop shot could be reached. Andre never dived, did he? I can't remember him doing it. His movements were never so extravagant. He hardly seemed even to reach very far – all his shots took place quite near his body, neat and small and tight. In a joint profile of both players in the *New York Times* in 1995, Sampras rather meanly told the writer Peter de Jonge that Andre 'told me that if he ever dove for a ball, he'd look like a fool'.

But the main difference between them, always acknowledged by Agassi, was this huge psychological contrast: Pete Sampras knew he was good, while Andre Agassi was a mass of self-doubt. And again, crowds sensed this, and responded to it. Did it have a lot to do with their respective childhoods, you ask. Well, I'm hardly qualified to say, but I would suggest that if psychologists were hoping for a field day, they'd be disappointed here, if only because it's all so clear and straightforward. Sam Sampras, Pete's father, always took the view, 'Whatever makes Pete happy makes his mother and me happy.' And whenever I read that, it makes me sniff. The nightmarish Mike Agassi, on the other hand – who had started training Andre's hand–eye co-ordination in the cot, and who drove away Andre's older sister Rita with his appalling, trouble-making tennis-parent ways – greeted his 22-year-old son back from his Wimbledon triumph in 1992 with the barked question, 'Why did you lose the fourth set?' What chance did poor Andre have? 'My father put a lot of pressure on me to not accept losing,' Agassi said on CBS's *60 Minutes* in 1995. 'I never felt pressure to win. I felt pressured just to not accept losing.' As for the difference between him and Sampras, he said, 'The one thing that Pete has over me – or I shouldn't say over me – that I wish I had – is such a simple approach and raw belief that he is just better than everybody. With me, it's different. Even at the level of number one ... I still could convince myself that, Geez, maybe I'm just not as good as I think I am.'

It is probably clear from all this that I loved Andre Agassi. From start to finish, I knew I was being quite cynically taken in by something that wasn't strictly tennis-related, but I didn't care. 'Come on, Andre!' I yelled. His propensity for dropping sets at key moments simply made his matches more dramatic; the sense of a man conducting a desperate internal psychodrama made every match a drainingly cathartic experience (except when it inexplicably didn't). His unauthorised biographer Paul Bauman, in his 1997 book *Agassi and Ecstasy*, has a convincing explanation for some of those strange not-playing-any-more stretches in Agassi's matches: that if you deliberately don't play, you can tell yourself you weren't really beaten. This is the sort of immature and unprofessional attitude to one's sport that can really wear out the patience of the people paid to write about you. You fight your way to a quarter-final and then you piss it away? Why? The word 'tanking' comes up all the time in accounts of Agassi. I thought it might have connotations of chucking a game, but it seems to mean only losing when you shouldn't – which, I have to say, makes other people's annoyance with him for doing it all the more interesting. Whose business was it, besides his own, if he lost matches that appeared to be in the bag? Well, it seems as if it was everybody's. Early in his career, Agassi caught the attention of the American sports writer John Feinstein, who was then writing his book *Hard Courts*

(1991). 'He has become the most blatant tank artist in the game,' Feinstein wrote. In 1988, Agassi had infuriated John McEnroe by tanking; by dropping a set against him in a semi-final in Los Angeles. McEnroe called it 'insulting, immature, a cop-out'.

I would say that Agassi's whole career hinged this way and that on how he handled the flight or fight question. As a kid, he was always threatening to quit; as a young man on the tour he swore and spat at umpires; later, he was forever being fined for skipping press conferences and getting the hell out of there (by large private jet, with 'Air Agassi' on the tail fin). He pulled out of tournaments at the last minute. 'I don't have to do this,' was the obvious feeling behind it. He was famously addicted to junk food, and memorably quipped, 'You can never beat anyone too badly or go too far for a Taco Bell.' He dressed like a rebel, but was a born-again Christian. It is fascinating to me that his one championship win at Wimbledon should have been against Goran Ivaniševic, a man whose mental well-being was even more visibly on the line than Agassi's own, but who was at the other end of the scale in his commitment to the game. When Ivaniševic lost to Sampras in the final in 1998 (he had lost to him in 1994 as well), his despair was Miltonic. Instead of playing the role of plucky runner-up, he sat on his chair with a towel over his head for a very, very long time. Asked afterwards if he would be cheering Croatia in the World Cup, he said, 'I cannot cheer anybody now. I go kill myself.' By contrast, when Agassi was asked after his Wimbledon win whether his kneeling down in thanks had been a deliberate (or even

138

rehearsed) gesture to remind the crowds of Bjorn Borg, he was so insulted he said, 'If I find myself having to defend that, I'll leave the game.'

But by July 4, 1999, it seemed that the fight-or-flight question had been resolved in Andre Agassi. He had evidently decided to fight, after all. You might say this was his new, new, new, new, new, new attitude – and for once, you could believe it. In his personal life, divorce from Brooke Shields was safely behind him. The hair was gone. The clothes were conventional. Brad Gilbert – famous for preaching the philosophy of 'winning ugly' – had been Agassi's coach for five years, and their relationship was surprisingly firm considering how much unattractive losing Agassi had done under his guidance, especially in 1997–98. Gilbert's coaching is often contrasted with that which Sampras received first from Tim Gullikson (who died from a brain tumour in 1996) and then from Paul Annacone. While Sampras appreciated minimum intervention from his coaches, preferring to play instinctively and to practise in virtual silence, Agassi went on court with his head brimming with a zillion strategic instructions implanted directly from 'the best brain in tennis'. Gilbert's combative credo is that you must force your opponents to play 'shots they don't like from positions they don't want'. And by all accounts, he is not a man who keeps his ideas to himself. Sampras told the *New York Times* in 1995 that he could never work with Gilbert because, 'I couldn't take all that talking, discussing every angle, every shot. Whenever we used to practise together, I'd say, "Brad, would you just shut the fuck up for 30 minutes?"'

Tennis was glad to see Agassi back on form, but hadn't it been caught that way before? Well, here is one of the great strengths of sports journalism (and of sports fanhood in general, actually): while the memory for facts and figures may be fierce, foolproof and astonishing, the scars from even quite deep emotional wounds melt away instantly in the presence of the tiniest little flame of hope. Thus, Agassi was welcomed back to Wimbledon and seeded fourth as if nothing had happened. In the *Daily Telegraph*, the veteran tennis writer John Parsons was thrilled to bits when Agassi won the French Open in the month before Wimbledon. Without him on the scene, 'the game had lost its attractiveness', he wrote. Sampras was interestingly quoted as saying, 'I don't know where he's been.' Steve Bierley in the *Guardian* was equally generous, equally pleased for Agassi's historic win in Paris, which made him the first man to win all four Grand Slam titles on three different surfaces: grass, clay and hardcourt. 'The pity is that Agassi . . . has wasted so much of his career – one year on, one year off – and what might have been one of the great on-court rivalries with Sampras fizzled out almost before it began.'

I am putting off a description of the match itself, partly because I wasn't there, but partly because I know it is beyond me. I'm so sorry I didn't mention this earlier, but describing tennis in such a way that it is recreated in the mind of my reader is something I absolutely can't do, despite taking loads of notes and paying proper attention and everything. If you don't believe me, here is a taste of the 1999 Wimbledon final between Andre Agassi and Pete Sampras

– one of the great matches of my lifetime. 'Ace', I write, next to the score, 15–0. You can really see that, can't you? 'Baseline rally.' 'Ag lobs; S smashes.' 'Cross-court b'hand ret from Samp – *v shallow angle*.' When I write these daft things down, I do so in the belief that they will later transport me to a specific memory, that they will trigger some mysterious 'replay' mechanism in my head; but, well, I actually wrote these yesterday, while watching the match on tape, and I'm quite sure they will conjure up quite as much in the mind of the cat currently asleep on top of my printer as they do in mine. 'At net, *with bounce*' I see here, in my record of the seventh game of the first set, served by Sampras. Good grief. Skipping ahead I find, 'Volley, leap, smash', 'F'hand winner down line', 'Great half-volley!!', and (I think I do remember this one), 'Let cord (no apology).'

Luckily, I have also taken notes of what the BBC commentators said as they watched this match – stuff about how Sampras, in the first six games, hit more baseline winners than Agassi (which must have been demoralising), and how Sampras served 'three boomers in a row'. This is the best Sampras has played this summer, says John Barratt. Agassi is fighting; he's playing brilliantly. He has even improved his first-serve percentage. But Sampras has responded by raising his own game to unprecedented heights. He is now playing 'unbelievable tennis' and is 'in the zone'. The commentators point out that when Agassi serves down the middle, he stands a better chance of winning the point – but then Sampras notices, too, and does something about it. This is 'near faultless tennis from Sampras', they say, as he takes the second set. 'There's not a hope of Agassi breaking back,' they say in the third. And as Sampras wins with an ace (on a second serve) to gain his sixth Wimbledon title, they declare him, happily, 'the greatest grass court player of all time'.

Of course it was Sampras's day. And of course he won. In the years of their 'rivalry', the overall outcome was Sampras 20: Agassi 14, but when they met in Grand Slam finals, the ratio changed markedly. They played six of these in total, and Sampras won them all except the 1995 Australian Open – when it was quite clear to everyone that the hospitalisation of his coach Tim Gullikson had hit him very hard. Agassi said after that match that Pete's courage had been inspiring. 'He's a class act,' he said. 'I think he's shown these past couple of weeks why he is No 1 in the world.' But Agassi's determination to give Sampras a great game at Wimbledon in 1999 was quite classy, too. His new, new, new, new, new, new attitude was starting to be apparent. He was getting serious. On court, he had always been quick, but he was now quite alarmingly impatient to get on with it, serving ('Whack!') with minimum ceremony ('Whack!'), as if he had a car on a meter outside ('Whack! Whack!'). Just as he had always taken the ball disconcertingly early, now he was playing matches in the same way, not waiting for the normal number of breaths between points; catching everyone off-guard and bulldozing the game, not necessarily to his own advantage.

What Andre Agassi did, eventually, was try to turn his back on entertainment. For the next seven years, he stuck with grim determination to the bat-and-ball stuff. In some ways, this was quite sad; like watching Tigger being pitilessly de-bounced. But the alternative was unthinkable, obviously: it was being beaten by David Lloyd's mum. And the more seriously he took the tennis – and the balder he got – the more respectful the press were: he was playing the game, at last. In the past, he'd had various interesting exchanges with the press, which (as is the way of these things) he could never live down. Once, at Wimbledon, he was asked whether he knew his shorts were transparent, and he enjoyably riposted, 'No, but obviously you are.' In Peru, as a very young man, he asked, 'What's an Inca?' At a joint press conference with Jimmy Connors in 1993, a reporter reminded them both of a stupid remark Agassi had made about beating Connors years before, and he blew up: 'I *knew* one of you jerks would mention that. I was 18 and thrown into an environment. Let's put *your* life under a magnifying glass.' (As it happens, there was no need to get defensive on this matter, as Connors had already publicly, and hilariously, got his own back on Agassi by saying, 'I enjoy playing guys who could be my children. Maybe he's one of them. I spent a lot of time in Vegas.')

When Agassi retired from Wimbledon in 2006, I watched it on TV, and wept a bit. When he retired, for good, at the US Open on September 3, I was on holiday with friends on Cape Cod, paying no attention to sport any more – and only vaguely aware that the tournament was on. But on the day of his last ever match (against a low-ranked Benjamin Becker, in the third round) a spooky, tiny, vestigial bit of sports writer triggered the laboured train of thoughts, 'US Open . . . hang on . . . Agassi . . . retired from Wimbledon . . . hang on . . . *retired from Wimbledon* . . . this could mean . . . hang on . . . what day is this . . . I think I heard he beat Baghdatis, so that would

143

mean he's still . . . hang on . . . I wonder if I should . . . would anyone mind . . .' – and finally I thought 'Oh sod it' and put the TV on, and by amazing luck I caught the whole thing. It was a weird afternoon. From time to time, I would urge my uninterested friends to watch it with me: 'This could be history, you know. If he loses, this is it. No more Andre!' But this wasn't the sort of history they cared about, and besides, they had kayaks to row and bikes to ride (which is the point of being on Cape Cod, after all).

Of course, he lost that day. And he made a farewell speech designed to wring the heart, thanking the crowd for their support down the years. Arguably, it was the love of the crowd that had fatally undermined Agassi's career, distracting him from his main purpose; but, luckily for him, he was never going to see it that way. His speech at Flushing Meadow – in the context of a sensational ovation that went on for half an hour, with constant close-ups of that little tear-stained face with those deep brown puppy-dog eyes – was admittedly a bit sick-making, even for me, but it was exactly how you would have wanted it all to end, with this heart-felt tribute to the fans. 'The score-board said I lost today, but what the scoreboard doesn't say is what it is I have found. And over the last 21 years, I have found loyalty.' *Oh, Andre!* I sniffed. *I never deserted you! I mean, I did sort-of lose track a bit latterly, but I was always yours, you know that. Was it really 21 years, though? Didn't you turn pro in 1986? That makes it more like 20 years, surely?* 'You have pulled for me on court and also in life,' he went on. *And that was certainly true. I had pulled like mad for Andre. Without stint. At great personal expenditure of emotional energy. Drained, I was, sometimes. Drained.* 'You

144

have willed me to succeed sometimes even in my lowest moments.' *Yes, I have. Although to be fair you made that necessary a bit too often, didn't you, with all that tanking and stuff?*

But there was no point resisting this thing. It was going to get everybody in the end. *Oh Andre!* 'You have given me your shoulders to stand on to reach for my dreams,' *Oh, [sniff], that's too much, really, stop it, 'reach for my dreams', stop it.* 'Over the last 21 years, I have found you' – *Sob!* – 'and I will take you and the memory of you with me for the rest of my life.'

Afterwards, he was asked what he would remember about his last tournament. Would it be the amazingly tough second-round victory over Marcos Baghdatis (seeded eight)? Well, would it fanny. No, it would be the applause he would remember – 'the applause from the fans, the applause from my peers. That was [*sic*] the greatest memories I've ever had, memories I'll keep for ever.' Pete Sampras would never have said that, would he? He would never have thanked the fans for their support, or told them they had inspired him. If he even heard the applause of the people whose money made the whole shebang possible, he considered it completely irrelevant to what he was doing. When it came to Sampras's own time to retire, he didn't even make an occasion of it. He won the 2002 US Open (against Andre), then said no, he wasn't retiring yet, wasn't retiring yet, oh no, might play next month, no definite plans at all to retire – until finally the penny dropped the following spring that he'd retired already without mentioning it. Agassi was a great player of tennis, but he had to work twice as hard as Sampras to get the world to see him as a sportsman, just because he loved the applause so much – applause that is essential, but must never be acknowledged as such. 'Do you have any questions for us?' someone asked at that final press conference. And he said, 'Are you guys really going to miss me or are you just acting like that?' At which he got his last – and most hard-won ever – standing ovation.

Golf and the Basic Misogyny of Sport

The scene is a bunch of sports writers, who are all men, and who are all my friends. We are gathered to cover the Open (golf) at Royal Birkdale in July 2008, we're in a pub in Southport, and I am happier than I've been in ages. In this company I am able to forget all my everyday cares, and even to stop fretting about the play I should be writing. Most relaxing of all, there is no pressure on me to be entertaining, because these blokes are self-evidently a great deal more entertaining than I am. Bliss. The fact that I'm a woman, and the oldest person present, with an unflattering haircut and a regrettable reputation for grammatical correctness, seems not to be a matter for concern; for this I am genuinely grateful. So the night is going well, and will continue to do so, and I hate to bring this up really, because it makes me feel like a bastard. But at one point, one of these good guys decides to tell a joke about a man chatting up a woman in a nightclub. And the joke goes like this.

'Here,' he says to her, in a low voice. 'Can I smell your fanny?'

'Certainly not,' she says.

'Must be your feet then,' the man ripostes.

Now, I can appreciate this as a clever joke; but unfortunately, I can also see it (damn, damn, damn) as incredibly offensive. It is now some years since I gave up the sports writing game as a full-time profession, but the casual telling of this misogynist joke on this pleasant night is a vivid reminder of the sort of unprovoked stab-to-the-vitals that I used to endure all the bloody time with these men. What I most resent is the out-of-the-blue etiquette crisis it presents me with: quick, quick, what are you going to do? You can't just pretend you didn't hear! Or . . . can you? Oh Lynne, surely not. You're not really going to *pretend you didn't hear*? Well, sadly, yes, I am, because it's all I can manage. And so, while the others laugh, I gather to my face a faraway sort of expression, intended to convey curse-my-bad-luck-I-missed-your-punchline-but-look-everyone-else-is-enjoying-it. The idea that anyone's attention can wander before the end of a three-line joke isn't strictly plausible, I know; the idea that anyone can be struck stone deaf so inconveniently outside the world of a biblical story isn't likely, either. But pretending that a tragic combination of these two highly unlikely things has just happened to me has worked in the past, and it gets me through another sticky situation now – although I regret this unfortunate phrase, obviously, as soon as I have written it.

My main true feeling is shock; but it's a shock I know I must absorb with minimum fuss. Storming out of the bar is not an option. A political dissection of the joke is not to be recommended. Saying 'Ladies present' (even with heavy irony) would ensure no one ever spoke to me again. There is, in fact, no way out. The price of being a woman in a man's world is that, when you are treated as an honorary man, you can't complain that you aren't one. You can't have it both ways. If you are walking alone and scared down a dark street in a foreign city after a riotous football crowd has only partially dispersed, you can't say, 'I'm a woman. I shouldn't be in this position.' If your hotel is disgusting and full of leering salesmen talking loudly about their sexual conquests, you are bound to think, petulantly, 'Would my bosses want their wives or daughters to be exposed to stuff like this?' but you still cannot resort to special pleading. And if someone tells a joke that revolves around the stink of a woman's vagina, your main reaction should, in fact, be gratitude. After all, you are being credited (albeit mistakenly) with an all-forgiving sense of humour. And do you really think 'fanny' is the good old English term your friend usually uses when he tells this story? Good grief, woman. Can't you see that this chap is gallantly attempting to spare your feelings?

If you don't want to read about this gender stuff, believe me, I wish I didn't have to write about it either, but it's rather unavoidable in the circumstances. First of all, I should mention that I am not the only woman ever to write about sport (or, indeed, the only women to enter a male-dominated world), so please don't assume that I think I am. But I can't speak for other women sports writers, because they were (and still are) doing the job properly, competing directly with the men in terms of knowledge and expertise, and I was always meant to be a kind of novelty act, dancing on the sidelines, playing the part of the Martian sending a postcard home, which weakened my position in significant ways. I remember a senior sports

149

writer expressing to me his total bafflement at my value to the coverage of the Ryder Cup at Valderrama in 1997; and he wasn't being unkind, he was truly confused. Out on the crowded course, on one of the practice days, I had purchased a rather spiffing golf periscope, and had devoted a couple of paragraphs to the joy of being able to watch the fairway action, by way of cunningly-aligned angled mirrors, even when your view was blocked by a lot of big Americans in baseball caps. I also loved the idea that you could spend all day saying, 'Up, periscope' and 'Dive, dive, dive' without having to worry about that notorious submarine-captain hazard of getting your thumbs trapped in the handles. The office had so enjoyed this little flight of fancy that they demanded a picture to go with it, so our photographer took a shot of me holding my periscope – although the picture didn't make much sense, quite frankly, as I wasn't standing behind a crowd of tall people watching golf; I was standing in open ground. Anyway, no one believes this story about the pained senior sports writer, but I swear it's true. 'I mean, that periscope sort of thing,' he said to me, with a look of misery. 'That goes right over my head.'

The way I see it now, I was in a classic double-bind from the moment I said 'Yes, please' to this amazing job. On the one hand, having always resented being categorised as a woman, I adored the idea of doing something that women didn't normally do. What better way to escape the constraints? What better way to transgress? I was always uneasy about the women-only Orange Prize for fiction. It makes me fume that there's still a programme on the radio called, without irony, *Woman's Hour*, as if the other 23 belong by rights to someone else. By the same token, it used to drive me nuts that the *Guardian* had a 'woman's page'. I can't stand it that every woman in the world is supposed to be more interested in shoes and hair products than in the causes of the First World War. I once sat glumly on a panel of 'women humorists' and just stared at the floor, squirming, while the others wisecracked about the war between the sexes, and the uselessness of men, because I didn't think anything they said was funny, and I didn't understand any of the questions. When I wrote a series of half-hour radio monologues for men (I'd already done a series for women), I was completely horrified by the kind of thing newspapers wanted to commission from me. The assumption was that I had devoted months of my life not to creating good stories and arresting characters (played by brilliant actors), but to lobbing insults at the natural enemies of all womankind.

One interviewer actually asked, in an email, 'Did you speak to any men?' – and I didn't know whether to laugh or cry. Did she think men's mental and emotional workings were opaque to the rest of us? Hadn't she noticed that their voices and concerns were quite well represented in the culture? Was I supposed to say to my milkman in the morning, 'Look, you've got the appropriate chromosomes, so you'll probably understand this character better than I do, even though I invented his biography, his story, his voice, his range of emotions, the dilemma he's facing, and every single one of his attitudes.' *Did you speak to any men?* I remember I looked at this question for a long time. Was this person confusing 'men' with 'unicorns', perhaps? Did she think men were some shy, skittering, mythical species you only ever saw out of the corner of your eye? I felt like saying, 'Well, I dug a trap in the garden to see if it was true that men existed, and I have to report that, actually, *none fell in.*'

So I think it's clear that I don't like being categorised as a woman, and that writing about football offered a brilliant chance to dodge and weave, and keep them guessing. But this is where the double-bind comes in, because I soon had to face the totally galling fact that, as far as sports writing is concerned, I was valued almost entirely for having two xs and no ys. To which I could only say, 'Oh, fuck, fuck, fuckety-fuck.' But it was all too true: my gender was my usp. Had I woken up one morning with a smart new pair of testicles, it would have been curtains for me as a sports writer. Can you imagine how annoying to me it was that my gimmick – being a woman – was a biological accident common to over fifty per cent of the people on this earth? And that the premise – look, a woman writing about sport! – was at base quite sexist, anyway? Not much had changed, it seemed, since Dr Johnson made that unflattering comparison between a woman preaching and a dog walking on its hind legs. A woman reporting on a football match was clearly of the same order of curiosity as a horse calculating the cube root of 27 and tapping out the answer with a hoof. What's that, Neddy? Did you stamp three times? What's that, Lynne? Did you see the goal go in and switch on your laptop? Give that woman a sugar lump and a nose-bag.

I did try to be positive. Looking back, I see that I tied myself in knots trying to reconcile all this stuff. Where a more carefree and confident woman might have taken this happy-freak-of-nature status as a glorious gift, and used it splendidly to her advantage, I am neurotic, wary and apologetic by nature, so I didn't. I saw dangers and traps. I saw territorial men, blaming me for something that wasn't my fault. And so I made the mistake I've made in every other area of my life, sooner or later: I piously tried to place myself beyond reproach, in the pathetic belief that this would ensure me respect. I demanded no special treatment on account of being a woman: as far as possible, I pretended not to be one. As for my sexuality, well, it's a bit complicated. I was aware I might be accused of using it unfairly (by people who needed glasses), and I was also petrified of being sexually humiliated on account of my obvious unattractiveness, so I figured that the safest option was just to sublimate it. Knock it on the head completely. Switch it off at the mains. In retrospect, I think all these decisions were disastrous for my ultimate well-being; worse, however, they were based on a misunderstanding of how 'a man's world' actually works. Just for starters: *being undemanding earns you respect*? Good heavens, what planet was I living on? Looking round at my male colleagues, how could I fail to notice that they gained not only respect but regular hikes in status directly in proportion to the number of times they could be arsed to call up the office (on deadline, for maximum effect) and shout and swear at the very people who were in a supreme position to fire them?

Was there active misogyny in this world? Well, yes: loads. But I think it was more insidious than that. What I tended to think, when I first entered the press boxes, was that the culture of sports writing was a result of normal self-selection: logically, this profession was bound to be quite highly populated by blokes who were more comfortable in a world that contained no women. And I felt quite sorry that a handful of women sports writers were contaminating this lovely x-y paradise for them, freighting oestrogen into it without permission, neglecting to leave their irreligious hair, lipstick, fannies and breasts outside in a plastic bag, or something. Was there a passage in Leviticus covering this woman-in-press-box anathema? If not, those enlightened writers of the Old Testament had uncharacteristically missed a trick. At provincial football grounds, I would often find myself sitting next to some tired old codger in a damp belted coat who was obviously proud of having a regular tip-up seat, a regular pulse-dial bakelite phone on his desk, and a regular job of calling up some long-suffering woman in a warm city office every time a noteworthy event occurred on the freezing pitch below. He would never be interested in the social life of the press box, this old codger. He would never get excited by the action. He most certainly did not regard himself as a good-will ambassador for the game. So what made this man turn up? Easy. The chance to get away from his wife (who doubtless danced a jig the moment the sad old bastard left the house). It's not surprising that part of me should feel guilty for invading such men's special sanctuary. In my more fevered moments, I would wonder whether I ought to stand up and announce the current state of my menstrual flow ('The trouble is, they don't make pads big enough'), so that the chaps could make their own minds up about sitting anywhere near me, or killing me by means of public stoning.

Now, all-male worlds are quite interesting, and I don't

mind admitting that my favourite film of all time is Peter Weir's maritime epic *Master and Commander*, in which the only female character is a non-speaking black-eyed temptress with a parasol in a canoe off the east coast of South America, her presence in the film serving only to establish that the ponytailed Russell Crowe has heterosexual hot blood coursing through his veins, in case anyone was getting worried. But the more I saw of this particular all-male world of sports writing, the more I found it peculiar that it was even legally allowed to exist. Why is sports journalism considered a job that only a man can do? Why is it (generally) only men that are drawn to it? Is it a job *for a man*? I mean, it's not like going down a mine. It's not like rounding up mustangs, or rescuing people from towering infernos. The idea sometimes put forward by the old guard – that you have to be able to play football (say) before you can to write about it – is open to any number of rational objections, among which are:

a) quite a lot of women have played football;
b) many terribly good footballers have to sign their names with an X, and write extremely tedious copy, even when helped out by top sports writers;
c) no one says Michael Billington doesn't have a valid opinion of theatre because he has never directed *Tartuffe*.

Obviously sport is a macho world full of sexist attitudes, and anyone reporting on it needs to be one of the lads – for protective colouring, if nothing else. I mean, if Sir Alex Ferguson condescended to tell you that cunt joke, you'd be well advised to find it amusing. All I wonder is: are there any exclusively male reporting qualities that can fully account for men's complete – and continuing – dominance of this profession? I don't see how that can be possible. Oh well. An interesting sidelong perspective on all this was offered to me in Paris during the World Cup in 1998, when I met a be-scarfed woman football writer from Alexandria. I was as taken aback as anyone to see her accredited at the Stade de France – and slightly miffed that I was, outrageously, obliged for once to share my handsomely accoutred (and brand new) female toilet facilities. Anyway, she told me that in fact her newspaper in Egypt had sent an entirely female reporting team to the World Cup – and the reason was straightforward enough. They didn't trust the men not to get too involved.

Evidently there is research to show that watching football increases testosterone levels. And I'm highly inclined to believe it: the first time I read about this research, it was during a lengthy football tournament and – honest to God – I had just been staring into space, pondering the question 'I wonder how a carburettor works?' So maybe exposure to football will make us all hairy-knuckled and gravel-voiced in the end, and the problem of being a woman in a man's world will conveniently disappear. What has been fascinating in the past ten years is to see how, image-wise, the world of sport is every day tailored to a more politically correct inclusion of women. Broadcasting now has some terrific women sports presenters – although, controversially, a resistance to women football commentators. *Match of the Day* cameramen seem to have stopped picking out attractive women in the crowd, but you could see why they used to do it. First, it provided pleasant eye-candy for the viewers; and second, it gave the interesting (if misleading) impression that footie support was pretty evenly spread across the genders. I was once invited to watch *Match of the Day* being prepared and broadcast from the studio, and saw the highlights editors busily inserting shots of small boys with packets of crisps to signify half time, small boys eating pies, and so on. From their Highfield Road footage that day they had a Coventry–West Ham game with the ultimate Saturday-afternoon gift: a stocky young bride arriving in the stands, in white, straight from the church, completing her nuptial outfit with a Coventry scarf. Was this the 'something blue' she had chosen to wear to the ceremony itself? You couldn't rule it out. The chaps even had a later shot of her in the crowd lighting a half-time Rothmans; but big-heartedly, they decided not to use it. But does one woman in her wedding dress amount to the overthrow of sexist thinking in the world of sport? I am here to tell you it does not.

This section is supposed to be about golf; and it will be, I promise. I just needed to set the scene first; explain how I am too easily lured by the excitement of the transgressive, even when I am quite fully aware of the uncomfortable price I'll have to pay. Taking an interest in golf was one of the most transgressive things I've ever done, when I think about it: it required a massive dismantling of life-long prejudices – prejudices not only of gender, but also of class, culture, politics, and taste. To many people in my cohort group – university in the 1970s, fluffy left-wing politics, a career in the media, an interest in literary matters

157

– golf represents everything establishment, reactionary and anti-intellectual; everything smug, WASP, racist and male chauvinist; and (above all) everything offensively tartan-trousered. Come the revolution, most of my old chums will drive Centurion tanks across golf courses with red flags between their teeth, churning up the greens and firing twenty-pounders at the car parks and the clubhouses. Obviously I still feel sad about the friends I lost the instant I said excitedly on the phone, 'Well, I've been reading Ben Hogan's *Modern Fundamentals of Golf*, and it turns out, you see, that the plane for the downswing is not only less steeply inclined than the backswing plane, but is also oriented with the ball quite differently. This is the key to the whole mystery of the golf swing, I'm sure of it. Hello? Are you still there? My waggle is coming on enormously, by the way. Hello? Hello? Hello?' I'll never forget the sound of that dial tone in my ear. It wasn't just that I was being boring and obsessive, because they were used to that. It was that I was being boring and obsessive about golf.

The class thing is easily explained. I was a working-class girl, who knew nobody who played golf. However, I grew up in the 1960s on a newly built council estate in a green, leafy area of south-west London, which meant there was a notable golf club nearby (where it was rumoured Bruce Forsyth was a member), so I was aware it was a game played by rich men with Jaguar cars with whom it would always be impossible – no matter how long I lived – to have any fellow feeling. There was also a polo ground very near to our house, bizarrely. It was between us and the Thames. My mother sometimes washed up the dishes in its old wooden pavilion on scorching Sunday afternoons.

From across the small, airy copse which separated our house from the polo field, the rest of us – my dad, my nan, my sister and I – would hear the bells ringing romantically for the chukkas, carried to us on the breeze from the river; but we were immune to such calls from the outdoors: we turned up the volume on the telly and drew the curtains more securely to prevent reflections on the screen. We did occasionally go to watch the polo, but only if we first heard the tell-tale noise of a landing helicopter, which signified the arrival of the Duke of Edinburgh, or Prince Charles, or both. And even then, we usually preferred to watch Ingrid Bergman in *The Inn of the Sixth Happiness*, because you never knew when you would next get the chance, and we all liked that bit with the children singing 'Knick knack paddy-whack' as they marched their way to safety.

But occasionally, we did stroll down to the polo. Does anyone else remember 'Professor' Jimmy Edwards? A very keen polo player, he was. I remember his large stomach, trademark moustache and bug-eyed purple face as he galloped back and forth in his straining jodhpurs. Sitting on a dusty track outside the perimeter of the polo field, we unimpressed council-house kids would suck on Strawberry Mivvies from the ice cream van, and watch assorted energetic nobs in shiny long riding boots thunder past on chestnut steeds. What a noise. What a palaver. The chukka bells rang out. A posh male voice announced the score. Horses clashed with a clatter of sticks. Highborn people put themselves in the way of life-threatening injury. We didn't have a clue what was going on. But between chukkas we scruffy non-paying spectators were suddenly included in events: while the nobs and their great, sweaty horses took a lengthy breather in the green shade of tall, rustling trees, we were invited to contribute to the afternoon's entertainment by milling onto the field and treading the divots back into the turf.

I never knew what to think about this lowly divot-treading. After all, I was a helpful girl, as all my school reports kept saying. I also loved horses with a normal school-girl passion, and read about them in books called things like *Jill Enjoys Her Ponies*. I knew all about gymkhanas. Good heavens, I could even spell 'gymkhana'. But there was something about being asked to repair the damage done to the surface of the earth by galloping nobs that didn't sit comfortably with me, and it still doesn't. Fairly recently, I attended a charity polo match in Wiltshire, near Highgrove, in which Prince Charles played, as well as both of his sons; and it brought back a lot of bad memories, to be honest. For a start, I was 30 years older and I still didn't know what was going on. The most entertaining aspect of the match was the way the commentator couldn't identify his princes – 'That's Prince Harry – no, Prince William – no, Prince Harry!' and in the end yelled excitedly, 'And it's all princes now!' by way of covering himself. But the real challenge came with the bloody divot-treading. It made no differ-ence that, here in Wiltshire amongst the rich, I was able to observe women in high-heeled slingbacks and pastel-coloured Ascot outfits quite happily turning to turf-mending when asked. It still made me feel like an oik.

I got interested in golf entirely against my better judge-ment one glorious, sizzling summer when I was in my late thirties, writing a novel in a holiday flat on the Isle of Wight. By chance one evening at the village telephone box I met a nice, attractive local man called Peter who announced himself at once as a sports enthusiast, so of course my first thought was, 'That's that, then.' Nevertheless, I found myself sitting with him in a hotel bar at Freshwater Bay, asking politely about golf – about pars, birdies, woods, irons, the handicap system and so on – and I can only report that something twigged. Maybe it was a combination of him, the night, the lapping of the waves in the moonlight, and the sheer romance of being on the Isle of Wight, but I thought his enthusiasm was something I'd like to share; it occurred to me, too, that the only thing preventing me from crossing this significant divide was unexamined snobbery. So, one lovely warm evening, towards sunset, he borrowed his mother's clubs (and her car as well), and we drove up to the spectacular, blowy Freshwater Golf Course, with its westward view of the cliff-high Tennyson Down, and he watched and encouraged me while I happily topped some golf balls with a lofted club against a stiff wind from the sea.

I will never forget the exhilarating thrill of guilt I felt as these badly-struck balls scudded off to right and left – and occasionally, oh my God, took flight for a yard or so. Look at me here, bending my knees and keeping my head down, betraying everything I believe in! I felt sullied, but I felt liberated too. Never in my life had I followed a road sign that said 'Golf club this way'. Never in my life had I attempted to hit a tiny ball, smack on the meat, with the angled head of a long stick. I'd been too busy indoors, probably, shelving books in strict alphabetical order. When

Peter told me about the 14th at Freshwater (a par-three known as 'The Drop'), I desperately wanted to know what it felt like to drive a ball off the elevated tee and see it plummet down to the waiting green far, far below. I think he had to tear me away from the course when the sun finally went down. I was all for kipping in a bunker, so as to be ready to resume lessons, as soon as possible, at break of day.

Then came the truly life-changing experience. Spotting that golf was the unlikely route to my affections, Peter invited me to his mum's to watch the 1995 Open from St Andrews on the TV with his entire family. Abandoning my novel without a second thought, I signed up for the full four days, offered to contribute to the food, and had one of the happiest long weekends of my life learning to identify the players and to follow the counter-intuitive plus and minus scoring convention that comes so easily to golf's initiated. It was a revelation. Long before Costantino Rocca forced the famous play-off with John Daly on the Sunday night with that legendary, impossible long putt on the 18th (after his equally famous fluffed chip), I was captivated. For one thing, this game was dramatic. For another: what a lot of famous golfers there turned out to be. Before this, I had heard of Seve Ballesteros and maybe Gary Player. Now I discovered that Bernhard Langer was a world-famous and universally recognised born-again German recovering from the yips. Corey Pavin was a world-famous and universally recognised American whose legs were too short, who had once been extremely obnoxious at a place called Kiawah Island. Sam Torrance was a world-famous and universally recognised popular Scotsman who chain-smoked like Andy

Capp. Meanwhile the world-famous and universally recognised Colin Montgomerie had the interesting nickname 'Jennifer' (although I was later forced to accept that the amusing custom of calling him this was actually unique to Peter's mum).

The young Tiger Woods had played at the Scottish Open the previous week – as US Amateur Champion – and there had been quite a kerfuffle about him, but my new friends warned me to be suspicious of the hype when he turned up at St Andrews. They reckoned he might be a flash in the pan, and that the big-boned British amateur Gordon Sherry would probably amount to more than Woods in the long run. (I still have hopes this might come true.) The big news was that John Daly won the Open that year. We would have preferred to see Rocca triumph, but the mega-hitting Daly was undeniably exciting to watch. We all went 'Ooooh!' like an old-fashioned advert for fireworks whenever Big John slugged the ball. As someone who had so far managed to knock the ball along the ground a maximum of twenty-five yards (using a driver), I was naturally lost in admiration for Daly's crack-whizz 300-yard shots. I couldn't wait to get out there again, to grip it and rip it just like Big John. Which is why, when I got home to Brighton, I immediately called up a local golf course and arranged to have some lessons.

And that was when I was forced to accept that all those old prejudices of mine did have some foundation in reality, after all. When I first turned up at the golf club, I was hanging around in the pro shop in advance of my lesson, fingering the knitwear and trying not to scream, and two members introduced themselves. One was a woman whose husband had collapsed with a heart attack on the course the previous week, and she had dropped by this morning to return his motorised trolley, with many thanks for everyone's kindness. Whether the motorised trolley had accompanied her husband to surgery wasn't clear, but anyway it was back now, and the husband was in recovery. As she extended a welcoming hand to me, her first, rather startling words were, 'Are you thinking of joining us? Do you *have* a husband?' (She said this as if she strongly suspected the answer was no, and that I wouldn't get membership without one.) The other member keen to say hello was a man who claimed to be an airline pilot, but didn't ask me what I did. Without preamble, he said warmly that he was all in favour of women members sharing the tee equally. Scarcely knowing what he was talking about, I said, 'Oh good.' 'Yes,' he said, barely able to contain his amusement. 'I mean, fair's fair. Men can have the tee from nine in the morning till nine at night; and women can have the rest.' Shortly after this the lanky pro arrived, and we strolled out to an airy practice ground where I told him – in between gaily topping balls with a lofted club again – that I wasn't feeling terribly comfortable with the culture of this place already, and he said, to my relief, that he couldn't stand the members either, and was hoping to leave quite soon.

I really enjoyed the pro's company after that. His wife was also nice: in fact, I've just remembered how she advised me to go home and change, sharpish, when I first showed up at the course wearing a comfortable stretchy T-shirt and some jeans. 'I wouldn't want the members to be nasty to you,' she whispered. 'You must have some tailored shorts?

And a top with a collar?' I obediently jumped into the car and drove home, but in the full knowledge that 'tailored' and 'shorts' were words that didn't apply to a single thing in my wardrobe. I eventually turned up back at the course wearing a rapidly improvised combination of above-the-knee skirt, sleeveless blouse and pleading expression, and they let me off, but I knew in my heart that my not-in-a-million-years attitude to the tailored short was bound to cause trouble further down the road – which it certainly has. Having now covered 18 golf tournaments, I still go through the same despairing nothing-to-wear routine before each event: rooting through my cupboards in the insane hope of finding appropriate attire supplied by kindly pixies in the night.

One year I caved in and bought some proper ladies' navy gabardine golf trousers in the tented village at the Open, but I had to throw them away when I got home. There was something about the thickness of the material and the sturdy functional waistband – not to mention the satin lining that stopped at the knee – that made me feel denatured. When I had them on, I wanted to cry 'Unsex me here!' like Lady Macbeth. The idea of having them in my house really upset me. Another time – at the Ryder Cup at the K Club in 2006, where there was torrential rain on the Sunday morning – I made the reverse mistake and wore some rather lovely expensive linen trousers from Hobbs in a fetching shade of moss green. First they got very wet; then they got very muddy; and in the end it was like trying to wade through glue with a heavy weight tied round each ankle. I took them off in the hotel room afterwards and briefly thought about taking them to the cleaners.

But they smelled badly of fertiliser, and were beginning to rot, so in the end I put them in a plastic bag and left them in a bin in the bathroom.

But the point is, back at the golf club in Brighton: the pro genuinely loved golf, and that's what rescued the situation. Over the following weeks, he slowly let me into the secret of the golf swing, and it was fascinating. For example, one week he would say the golf swing was all about the left knee; the next week, he'd say it was all in the right shoulder; then it was about the plane of the hips. I began to deduce that a successful and graceful golf swing depended on a miraculous – some might say impossible – split-second co-ordination of all these independently swivelling bone-joints, muscle groups and body parts. Would I ever be able to do it? Well, the fact that many professional golfers were quite ungainly of figure yet could still perform this beautiful action was a source of inspiration and hope. And I got a bit fanatical as the weeks passed. On the pro's advice I bought Ben Hogan's book and read bits to friends who weren't interested. I practised my grip and my waggle whenever circumstances allowed, because the wonderful Hogan tells you (in capitals): 'PUT IN 30 MINUTES OF DAILY PRACTICE ON THE GRIP. LEARNING THESE NEXT FUNDAMENTALS WILL THEN BE TWICE AS EASY AND TWICE AS VALUABLE.' On the day I found myself waggling the grill pan handle in the kitchen, and letting the toast drop to the floor, I did wonder if I was letting my enthusiasm go too far. But I was in the grip and waggle of something I could not control. I really, really, really liked golf.

*   *   *

166

Since golf is the only sport I still write about (once or twice a year), I suppose it's fair to call it my favourite, even though I dislike the culture of the game as represented by the small-minded men in blazers. What one can't help asking is: does golf actually *make* people small-minded? Is it something about the game? The evidence does sometimes seem incontrovertible. Many people will remember the Channel 4 'Cutting Edge' documentary *The Club*, about the Northwood in Middlesex. This film was quite a snobbish enterprise, but it is rightly famous for including astonishing first-hand evidence of petty tyranny running rampant in a last bastion of lower-middle-class self-importance: the club's chairman threatening a dissenting member with expulsion (and then denying it); a bullying speech to the 'Ladies' Autumn Prize-Giving' from the club's president, in which he ticked off the assembled female membership for paying improper respect to his wife, by not remembering to give her flowers. 'My wife thinks it may be an intentional slur on me,' he said (he meant 'slight'). 'But I told her it was just a little mistake, and that it wouldn't happen again.'

The downtrodden ladies at Northwood were mere 'associate' members, of course, with limited access to the tee, and no voting rights. Their changing room had only recently been granted a shower. They were annually informed that the AGM had voted by a huge majority not to extend the vote to them. One of the older male members, in real confusion, said he couldn't imagine how a woman could be ready to play golf at nine o'clock in the morning, in any case. Weren't there breakfast things to be cleared up? After the documentary was shown, the board of directors was obliged to resign, and the women got full membership within the year, but, sad to say, the reasoning was still faulty. The board was criticised not for what the film exposed of the club's antiquated culture of high-handedness, Masonic solidarity, and institutional sexism. It was berated, but entirely for its lack of judgement in agreeing to let cameras inside the hallowed gates.

None of this did much good to the image of golf – but the game never learns, it seems to me. It is always telling people off for infringing rules; it is full of puffed-up little men. You can't use the front door on Fridays. Denim will be punished by flogging. You see this chalk line across the floor of the bar? Women may not pass beyond that point. I know a woman golfer who once reached the final stage of a competition, but when she turned up at the designated course to play her final round, the club secretary turned her away, on the grounds that it was Sunday. I was once at Augusta National, during the Masters, with *The Times*'s lovely golf correspondent, John Hopkins, and he invited me to a small party inside the famous colonial clubhouse. Halfway there, he stopped and apologised. He'd just remembered that the room selected for the festivities had a notice on the door saying it was men-only. The thing to do in this situation is to cause a scene by turning up anyway, and daring the Pinkerton security people to remove you by force – but I'm a rule-abiding kind of person, and I hate to ruin something nice, and I appreciated being at Augusta, so I went back to my desk instead and dolefully ate one of those special Augusta sandwiches with the famous cheese-and-pimento filling that looks (and tastes) like vomit. Clubs make rules, I reflected; and men make

clubs. One can't help feeling that God is logically impli-
cated further up the line. What are you going to do? One
of my favourite jokes is about an Englishman shipwrecked
alone on a desert island and not discovered for 25 years.
When found, he reveals he has not been idle: he's spent
his time building three structures. 'This is my house,' he
says, proudly pointing to the first structure. 'So what's that
one?' they ask, pointing to the second. And he says, proudly,
'That's the club I go to.' 'What's the third one?' they ask.
'Oh,' he says, as if the subject is painful to him. 'That's
the club I *don't* go to.'

Obedience to the rules is what golf is all about. On the
professional side of the game, there have been extraordinary cases down the years of the rules of golf being
bureaucratically applied against all logic, common sense,
or simple human compassion – but since that's the price
of being such a well-regulated sport, everyone accepts it.
But what about that chap (Welshman Philip Parkin) whose
small son had placed a miniature putter in his bag, thus
causing him to be disqualified from the Italian Open for
having too many clubs? Parkin found the toy in his bag
after he'd completed his round, confessed at once, and
asked the tournament organiser for a ruling. 'I asked
whether it would be classed as a golf club, and he said it
has to be at least 18.5 inches long to be classed as such,'
he recently explained. 'So of course we went off measuring and it was actually 19 inches long, meaning I was
disqualified.' The interesting part of the story is that Parkin
then asked what would have happened if the club had
been half an inch shorter, and he was told, well, then it
would have counted as an illegal club, so he would have

been disqualified for that as well. In other words, measuring it made someone in a blazer feel terribly important and authoritarian, but was absolutely pointless, in the circs.

Something similar happened to Ian Woosnam at the Open in 2001 at Royal Lytham. An extra driver in his bag (the fault of his caddie) incurred him a two-stroke penalty, which may have cost him the title. Meanwhile, what about the infamous case of Craig 'The Walrus' Stadler who, before kneeling on the ground to take an awkward shot at the Andy Williams Open in 1987, put down a towel to save his trousers and therefore broke the rule about 'building a stance'? Unaware that breaking this rule carried a two-shot penalty, Stadler was deemed to have signed an incorrect scorecard and was therefore disqualified. In 2003, at the Open, Jesper Parnevik and Mark Roe were disqualified for not exchanging score cards before teeing off. Recently, a chap in Canada got the chop because his caddie stood behind him while he putted. Neither of them knew this was against the rules. What makes me cross is that the religious players get away with claiming that Jesus is with them from tee to green. They seem to forget Henry Longhurst's admonition that if you call on God to improve the result of a shot while the ball is in motion, you are using an 'outside agency' and are therefore subject to appropriate penalties under the rules of the Royal and Ancient Golf Club of St Andrews.

Isn't it time they changed this score card business in professional tournaments, to acknowledge the presence of an official scorer? Professional players fall foul of this silly rule more or less continually. This is partly, I think, because they fill out score cards for each other, as if playing a social round at their local club, but since they scarcely speak to one another (no one ever said, 'What ya get there, Tiger? Was that an eight or a nine?'), it's a phoney situation. As I write this, Michelle Wie is still in shock after being disqualified from the State Farm Classic in Springfield, Illinois for forgetting to sign her score card until after she'd left the enclosure of the scorers' tent. She immediately went back to do it, but that wasn't good enough, and she was out. 'She was like a little kid after you tell them there's no Santa Claus,' reported the mean-spirited tournament official who had disqualified her. However, still ranking as the worst case of score card pettiness in history is probably that of poor Roberto DeVicenzo, the Argentinian who lost his chance to compete in a play-off for the Masters in 1968 because he signed a score card that incorrectly recorded a par on the 17th when in fact he had birdied. Instead of being disqualified, at least he came second, but the incident didn't reflect well on anyone involved in the ruling. DeVicenzo became popular with the American public, of course; especially because he is supposed to have exclaimed, in broken English, 'What a stupid I am!' But it did nothing for the reputation of the game, or of Augusta National. Moreover, the official Masters winner that year, Bob Goalby, was always somehow thought to have won it unfairly – or, at best, by default. Which, while we are on the subject of unfairness, was quite unfair on him.

There are a couple of basic philosophical contradictions that must strike anyone looking at golf. This issue of fairness is the big one. Golf is, by nature, a game of rules and etiquette; about the allowable and the unallowable – and for a perfectly respectable reason. The rules exist to prevent argument, and are therefore cleverly designed to cover every conceivable situation on the course, such as 'ball in movable obstruction – not found' and the subtly different 'ball in *im*movable obstruction – not found'. You might like to know that in the former case, here is the ruling:

> If it is known or virtually certain that a ball that has not been found is in a movable obstruction, the player may substitute another ball and take relief, without penalty, under this Rule. If he elects to do so, he must remove the obstruction and through the green or in a hazard drop a ball, or on the putting green place a ball, as near as possible to the spot directly under the place where the ball last crossed the outermost limits of the movable obstruction, but not nearer the hole.

Rules like this partly explain the phenomenon of 'slow play', by the way. It takes a good ten minutes to work out what's being got at here. However, as I said, the rules are all designed to make life simpler and fairer in the long run; to make sure no one gets an unfair advantage, which is surely a high ideal for any sport. And what about the handicap system? Golf is highly unusual in attempting to ensure that a player does not gain an advantage over his playing partner *even by being better at golf*. So my philosophical point is: why isn't golf a byword for egalitarianism? By rights, it should be. In the world of politics, the nearest equivalent to a brilliant player being hobbled so that he can play on level terms with a bad one would be those terrible old Maoist policies of getting ballerinas and opera singers to clean the lavs. Doesn't this make it all the more of a tragedy that this strenuously fair game has been ruled for ages (by and large) by intolerant and inflexible jumped-up misogynist bastards?

But I think I have the answer. I think that perhaps golf was, simply, designed for a race of people better than us. It is a very humbling game, as all thoughtful practitioners are happy to admit. Whereas in other sports, your performance is healthily affected by what your opponent does – by serving at you at 140 miles an hour; or punching you on the side of the head; or kicking the ball away from you at a crucial moment – in golf you are repeatedly forced to deal with the results of your own actions; you have no one to blame and nowhere to hide; every error is unforced; ultimately, you are called upon to stop and think. Golf is a scrupulous sport. It's all about strength of character; about inner resources; about honesty; even about good-ness, possibly. So it lays us bare. It's no wonder so many professional golfers turn to God when they weigh them-selves in such an exacting balance. It's no wonder, either, that in the face of such scary absolutes out on the course, man, little man scuttles off to the clubhouse afterwards, combs his moustache, adjusts the cuffs on his blazer and attempts to restore his wounded self-esteem by devising nit-picking rules about whether members can change their shoes in the car park, suspending outspoken members of the greens committee, and callously withholding basic plumbing amenities from the women.

'Human kind cannot bear very much reality,' wrote T.S. Eliot in *Four Quartets*, and I'm sure it will be discovered one day that, when he wrote this, he had just endured a disastrous afternoon at the Burnt Norton Golf Club. What I'm saying is: this game may actually demand more of people than they can give. John Updike's essay 'Moral Exercise' (collected in his book *Golf Dreams*) perfectly describes how golf makes a person face his true worth.

> What other four hours' activity can chasten a magnate with so rich a variety of disappointments, or unman a lothario with so many rebuffed desires? Golf is a square shooter. In the sound of the hit and the flight of the ball it tells us unflinchingly how we are doing, and we are rarely doing well.

I think it must be true, then, that the overwhelming philosophical magnitude of the game is, paradoxically, responsible for the kind of pigmy characters who give it such a terrible name.

In the wider world of sport, maybe something similar is going on – something that explains the sexism. Is it possible that men turn to sport to get away from women, because women remind them too forcibly of their failings? It's just a theory. But while I was writing this chapter, Sotheby's advertised for sale an original Bateman drawing of a teeing-off scene: a small, hunched and defeated-looking husband in plus-fours shrinking away to the tee from a large, curvy-calfed and strident female, who stands arms akimbo, with lipstick and rouge, wearing a beret and smoking a cigarette. The caption reads: 'Mind you beat him! If he beats you, I'll do the same!' Well, what a laugh, terrific joke, but

I believe this is where we came in. What one always has to remember is the well-known fact that the original aim of sporting competition was to sublimate carnality. Keep this in mind, and a lot of things fall into place. Sport was devised for the simple edifying purpose of keeping manly cocks safely dangling; it was designed to prove that, as a man, you could achieve quite satisfactory states of great excitement without doing anything dirty. So there is no mystery, is there? Does sport reject women because the activities themselves are fundamentally about sublimation? I don't think it's out of the question.

All this may explain, incidentally, the timeless mystery of why women's team sports never catch on with the public, despite being played to high levels, with earnest commitment, and with great organisation. The trouble is that when women play professional sport – even when they are hot-looking tennis babes – their play is plainly not about sublimating the sex urge; it's about celebrating physical liberation, which is a lot less interesting to watch. Hence the ho-hum response from the rest of us when they succeed or fail. This is a great shame. It shows how intrinsically unfair the world is. But it's true. Women can play games brilliantly to the crack of doom, I reckon, and no one, including me, will give a toss, because they make it too obvious they're enjoying it. Unlike men, they wouldn't rather be doing something else, you see. What they'd rather be doing is *this*.

THE SUNDAY

On Wednesday September 12, 2001, a small item about golf appeared in the British media. It was not front-page news, because holding on to a sense of proportion was something everyone was struggling to do at the time – this being the day after the attack on the World Trade Center in New York. However, as bathetic and distasteful as it may seem, a legitimately urgent golfing aspect to the events of 9/11 was already demanding attention, within 24 hours of the first plane hitting in Manhattan. The 34th Ryder Cup was scheduled to be contested by teams from Europe and America at the end of September 2001, at the Belfry, near Birmingham. In the light of events, should it go ahead or not? What on earth was the right thing to do in these exceptional circumstances? To cancel it? To postpone it? To go ahead and play it, but tone down the usual rabid jingoism? How about playing the first two days – of four-somes and fourballs – but then ditching the singles on the Sunday, which is usually when the trouble starts? *Oh for heaven's sake how can we even think about golf at a time like this?* Over the next few days, there was a proper flap, and it seemed right that golf – with its well-established passion for rectitude – should be the sport forced to handle such a thorny issue. Here was a golfing etiquette puzzler that even the Royal and Ancient's exhaustive rule book seemed not to have dreamed up an answer to.

Football just went ahead, of course. True, UEFA postponed a Manchester United match against Olympiakos in Athens on the Wednesday, but back in the UK, eight Worthington Cup ties were played regardless. Hugh McIlvanney (writing magisterially in the *Sunday Times* on September 16) was so shocked by this that he made comparisons with the 1972 Munich Olympics, and the monstrous decision of the International Olympic Committee's president Avery Brundage to press on with the games despite the appalling murder of eleven Israeli athletes. 'Brundage justified continuing as a refusal to yield to evil,' wrote McIlvanney, 'but to me the subsequent competition for medals was soulless, a circus in a graveyard.' Noting what other commentators had said – that here was surely a great opportunity to play the Ryder Cup in a sober and civilised manner – McIlvanney refused to be budged. 'Would it be sport, or a contrived exercise in social therapy? The results of games should never matter too much. But if they don't matter at all, nobody should bother to play.'

Elsewhere some quick (but not very deep) thinking was taking place at Monza in Italy, where the Grand Prix was scheduled for Sunday. Bernie Ecclestone of Formula One pronounced that the show must go on – but out of respect for the dead, Ferrari stripped all the logos off its cars and painted the nose cones black.

I'm not making this up, incidentally. Evidently, you see, it was the commercial aspect of motor-racing that would make its continuance offensive to people who needed time to absorb the significance of the attack on the World Trade Center, and to mourn the dead. 'Ferrari has taken the decision to show that it shares a sense of grief with the American people, with whom it has always felt close ties,' said a press release. 'Therefore, this weekend, with the full agreement of its sponsors and partners, and as a mark of respect, its cars will carry no logos relating to its commercial or technical partners. For Ferrari and its partners, Sunday's race will be a purely sporting event with no commercial implications, nor will it be a joyful event.'

To me, it was a bit easy, I admit. To me, it was cut and dried. Sport was not an essential part of life. It was supremely optional, a luxury of peacetime, and should know its place. Its own convenience should always take second place to real-world considerations – especially really big ones such as life and death. However, this wasn't how things usually turned out in practice, as I knew full well. It is in sport's interests to consider itself essential; one simple way it asserts its claim to immanence is by refusing to yield to any sort of interruption. This is a small example, I know, but I was once at a Saturday-afternoon Portsmouth–Sheffield United match at Fratton Park (a hell-hole; don't go), when a referee's assistant was struck to the ground by an incensed fan – and, to my utter astonishment, they didn't stop the game. I can still picture the victim: this poor, stricken bloke lying there on his face on the pitch, not moving, still holding his flag, one leg straight, the other bent at the knee. It was very shocking. Was he dead? While his assailant was quickly caught by security men, his body continued to lie there, motionless. Whistles were blown and a stretcher brought to remove him from public gaze. It was horrible. Everything went quite quiet. And then the game quickly re-started, whistle, flag, off we go, free kick, play on, with a new chap standing in.

I was truly confused by this. I think I had already zipped up my coat, stamped some blood into my frozen feet, and fished the car key out of my pocket, so convinced was I that this game would be automatically abandoned. Isn't there a rule that if you can't play nicely, you can't play at all? After something as serious as this, you surely don't just suspend this match; you suspend football altogether until after the public inquiry. But it seemed the reverse was true. Pitch-side homicidal attack was precisely the kind of thing you *don't* stop matches for. 'If they stopped the football it would send out the wrong message,' the seasoned chaps of the press box explained to me, wearily. 'Then every time a fan wanted to sabotage a fixture, he'd just bludgeon an official. They went ahead with the game at Heysel, you know. They reckoned it would be worse for everyone if they didn't play the match.' A few minutes later, we heard that the linesman had recovered consciousness and was being taken to hospital, so that was all right, then; but I was very disturbed by it, and I still am. In the Monday paper, I banged on about it, but I got no sympathy or support from anywhere. I still wonder where you draw the line, though, if not at an absolute. What if the linesman had been shot in the head? What if the assailant had used a crossbow, and taken out a few rival supporters as well? Would they have stopped the match then? Or would that have sent out the wrong message, too?

Of course, it showed how little respect I had for football – that I expected everyone to interpret an outbreak of violence as a signal to stop what they were doing immediately, go home in silence, and think jolly hard afterwards about what had happened. And I suppose I ought to confess here that when, at the theatre once on a hot evening a couple of years later, a chap in the audience for *The Postman Always Rings Twice* had to be removed (and might have been dead), I did not even consider gathering my things to leave; instead I waited in some excitement for the resumption of the play, and was hugely impressed that Val Kilmer and the rest of the cast were able to pick up the action exactly where they had left off. Their self-possession was magnificent, and it earned them an enormous round of applause at the end. However, this is not a fully comparable situation. The man in the stalls had – as it turned out – merely fainted. But even if it had been more serious (as many feared), he had not been knocked unconscious in full view of everyone by a shaven-headed hooligan under the direct malign influence of the action on the stage.

Anyway, the bigger point is, when sport comes face to face with reality, it freaks out. When asked to adopt a sense of proportion (even temporarily), it runs around in circles as if its bum is on fire. In the week following 9/11, when sport came face to face with one of the biggest doses of reality of my lifetime, there was a great deal of anxious soul-searching from the people who write about it. Richard Williams in the *Guardian* summed it up nicely when he wrote that 'those of us who earn our living from sport instinctively flinch from what feels like the sudden exposure of our essential frivolousness'. It seemed right for Radio 4's *Today* to drop its usual three minutes of larky sports news – but, on the other hand, if you want to argue that sport has nothing to do with real life, logically it might as well have just carried on as normal. An editorial in the *Observer* argued that if the Ryder Cup were cancelled, sport would thereafter 'always be considered expendable' – clearly an unthinkable proposition. Meanwhile, less elevated arguments for cancellation were emerging from the golfers themselves. Some of the chaps said some wise things about the humble place of golf in the greater scheme of things; but some of them also made rather less impressive not-on-your-nellie noises about not wanting to put their own precious lives at risk by stepping aboard transatlantic aircraft. Leading the way, Tiger Woods said on his website:

> I don't believe this is a proper time to play competitive golf. I feel strongly that this is a time to pause, reflect and remember the victims of Tuesday's horrific attack. I also fear that the security risks of travelling overseas at the present are too great.

Isn't there a rather big step from 'Golf is unimportant: let us sacrifice our games in full awareness of that fact,' to 'Golf is so important, oh my God, I might be a target just because I'm really good at it'? Yet several members of the American Ryder Cup team straddled both positions without apparent queasiness. The tall Alabaman Stewart Cink – a young man whose easy, loose-shouldered swing I am always pointing out to people as one of the most beautiful in the game (and it never works, because they conclude I just fancy him) – was the first golfer to be quoted as saying that the Ryder Cup might itself be targeted by terrorists. 'If someone wanted to strike at America, or freedom, or capitalism, the Ryder Cup would be a tempting event to hit . . . I have a wife and two boys and do not want to make them live without a husband and without a father just because I want to play in the Ryder Cup.'

In the end, good sense prevailed, and the event was postponed for a year – but with the extraordinary proviso that the make-up of the teams would not be revised in the interim. What this was meant to prove I never understood (the form of some players dipped dramatically in the next 12 months; other up-and-coming chaps missed their chance to play), but this resolution not to change the teams was presented to us as golf's small way of delivering one in the eye to Al-Qaeda, so nobody asked. At the opening ceremony at the Belfry a year later, on a cool green day in September 2002, both captains solemnly introduced their 2001 teams as if in tribute to 9/11. I suppose they could have painted their noses black as well, but fortunately there was no one around from Formula One to suggest it.

The Ryder Cup actually began its life with a disruption due to world events. It started, if you like, with a pause. The first organised meeting, scheduled for June 1926 at Wentworth in Surrey, is known as the 'lost' Ryder Cup because it fell foul of the General Strike and went off at half-cock. However, a year later, in 1927, the competition got going properly in Worcester, Massachusetts, and thereafter established a pattern of play that has lasted (so far) for more than eighty years, barring world wars and inconvenient terrorist atrocities. True, major things have changed in its constitution down the years – the size of the teams, the number of holes played, the number of points competed for, the number of days over which it takes place. Virtually every aspect of the competition has been adjusted over time, but it has now settled at:

Size of each team: 12, plus non-playing captain
Number of holes played per match: 18 (it used to be 36)
Number of points competed for: 28 (eight on each of the first two days; 12 on Sunday)
Number of days: Three

The few key features of the Ryder Cup that have survived intact from its inception are:

It is played every two years.
The two PGAs (Professional Golfers' Associations) host it alternately.
It is matchplay (where each hole is won, lost or halved), as opposed to stroke play, where it's the lowest overall shot total that wins.
It is an exciting mixture of paired games and single matches.
It starts with a dedication to the spirit of glorious sportsmanship, then quickly slips into complaint and/or recrimination, and finally ends up in muck, bullets, lifelong animosity, clubs broken across knees, and so on.

The biggest single change to the Ryder Cup's constitution occurred in the 1970s. It was not before time, either.

Until 1977, you see, the US played a team from Great Britain and Ireland whose official blazer might just as well have sported a special crest with 'Kick Me, Charlie' emblazoned on it in Latin. I am generalising, obviously. There were periods of up and down. But in broad terms, an examination of the history of the Ryder Cup's first half-century reveals the US team politely asking, every couple of years, 'Hey! Sucker! Your place or mine?' and then delivering a humiliating pasting of sickening proportions. The British and Irish traditionally limped away afterwards, vowed to try harder next time, and sulkily refused to accept that the contest was fundamentally unequal. After an 8–4 thrashing at Palm Springs in 1955, the president of the British PGA came over all Churchillian, saying that 'We are going back to practise in the streets and on the beaches.' In 1961, a chap writing in *Golf Illustrated* said it was always the same at the Ryder Cup: the GB and Ireland players started off overwhelmed by the occasion, 'and when they come to their senses their opponents are one or two holes to the good'. In 1967, at Houston, America's captain, the great Ben Hogan, secured the outcome of the event even before a stroke was played. At the pre-match dinner he introduced his team with the words, 'Ladies and gentlemen, the finest golfers in the world!' and the British and Irish were so demoralised that they gave up before even touching the soup.

Much as all this was good for the egos of American golfers, it did start to look a bit pointless after fifty years. Which is why, in time for the 1979 Ryder Cup at Greenbrier in West Virginia, years of common-sense campaigning by the competition-hungry Americans finally bore fruit and the Great Britain and Ireland team was extended to include Europe. This clever decision ultimately turned the Ryder Cup into what it is today: the third most popular sporting event in the world, after the football World Cup and the Olympics. Excellent mainland-Europe players such as Bernhard Langer (German), Jesper Parnevik (Swedish) and Sergio Garcia (Spanish) have played wonderfully in recent Ryder Cups. Back in 1979, however, the decision to extend the catchment area mainly meant that the charismatic young Spaniard Severiano Ballesteros could play against the Americans – although, sadly, at first the main benefit of Seve's inclusion was that the European team could add the heartfelt groan of 'Ay caramba' to the usual 'Oh fuck, not again' when they lost convincingly by 17 points to 11.

We tend to think that Ryder Cup Sore Loser Syndrome is a modern phenomenon, incidentally, but we are wrong. The history of this competition is rigid with examples of losers complaining about the weather, the course, the type of grass, the crowds, and even the unfair superior skill of the opposing team. In 1947, when the British and Irish team were beaten in Portland, Oregon, by 11 points to 1 (the one point was scored in the very last match, too), captain Henry Cotton asked for the clubs of the opposition players to be inspected for illegally deep grooves, so convinced was he that the Americans' success with back-spin could not be down to talent alone. Ten years later, at Lindrick (near Sheffield), the Americans suffered a rare defeat and complained about the biased Yorkshire crowds, and three of the team were so pissed off they refused to attend the prize-giving. 'They cheered when I missed a putt and sat on their hands when I hit a good shot,' whined Tommy ('Lightning') Bolt. In his frustration at losing by 4 and 3 to Eric Brown in the singles, Bolt broke a club across his knee. He told Brown that he hadn't enjoyed their match at all, to which the sportsmanly Brown is said to have replied, 'No, neither would I if I had been given the hiding I just gave you!'

In the decades prior to the Big Ryder Cup Post 9/11 Dither of September 2001, the supposed friendliness of the contest had been stretched to breaking point on several occasions. This was, I'm sure, one of the factors in the decision to postpone. What no one could face (although of course no one admitted it) was the idea of either:

a) pumped-up patriotic American golfers with ultra-conservative politics coming over here to kick ass in Sutton Coldfield, while their supporters grunted 'USA! USA!' in a warlike manner; or
b) depressed and shocked American fans all subdued and not chanting 'USA! USA!', making us feel really terrible if we beat them while they were down.

The thing is, since the mid-1980s, the Americans had been granted their wish: the contest had evened up, and they had found themselves the affronted losers on several occasions. In 1987, at Muirfield Village in Columbus, Ohio, they lost, narrowly, on home soil – moreover on a course that their captain, Jack Nicklaus, had himself designed. This sort of setback had tested their sportsmanship, and what a surprise, light-heartedness in defeat turned out not to be their best talent – just as Europe's has never been grace in victory, when it comes to that. 'We just love the Ryder Cup!' the Americans have continued to profess, but the teeth are now quite likely to be gritted when they say it. On each occasion I have attended the Ryder Cup (since 1997), the Europeans have lined up at the opening ceremony with beaming smiles, as if for a group birthday outing, while the Americans in their preppy blazers have looked tense, formal and grim – not to mention also pale of brow and oddly peanut-headed without their usual baseball caps.

It is unfair, though, to expect the golfers to get the balance right. The correct balance has, arguably, never been struck in the history of the fixture. Everyone who cheerfully wants the Ryder Cup to be a substitute for warfare still reserves the right to say, wagging a finger, 'Now, high spirits are all very well; but don't forget golf is a civilised game for civilised people.' I think this may explain why Tiger Woods – who diplomatically claims to adore the Ryder Cup – clearly suffers like a martyr on a gridiron every time he's forced to play it. I think his nature rebels. Golf, for him, is about winning by being the best. If he'd wanted to play team sports for a living, for heaven's sake, would he have chosen golf? It is often said that the current top American players are less good at bonding as a team than the more lowly-ranked Europeans, and this is sometimes blamed for their recent lack of success in the Ryder Cup. Are they maybe a bit spoiled? Are they too rich? Are they too *entouraged*? Well, it may simply be they are too good. It is completely understandable that a successful golfer should have difficulties taking one for the team, or enjoying a group hug. Golf is not a contact sport. It is, in fact, an *anti*-contact sport. As we have seen in the previous chapter, it is an ostensibly sociable game that in reality attracts people who are secretly (or not so secretly) misanthropic bastards.

Lovers of the Ryder Cup tradition are quick to remember moments of sportsmanship – as, for example, when golfers on the winning side have conceded missable putts, to take the pressure off of an opponent. In 1969, at Royal Birkdale, Jack Nicklaus famously picked up Tony Jacklin's marker, three feet from the hole on the 18th, and said, 'I don't think you would have missed that putt, but in the circumstances I would never give you the opportunity.' The result of Nicklaus's historic gesture was a 16–16 draw – although this wasn't quite as noble as it sounds, since the rules state that the defending team retains the Cup in the event of a dead heat. But how terrific of him, and what a great way to put it – 'I would never give you the opportunity'. This lovely story makes me think of the shiver-up-the-spine moment at the end of the movie *Batman Begins*, when Lieutenant Gordon says to Batman, 'I never said thank you,' and Batman replies, 'And you'll never have to' – before spreading his cape and diving off a parapet to swoop into the night.

However, such superhero moments are rare in the history of this competition, and in recent times there has been a lot of head-shaking about the Ryder Cup getting too bellicose, especially after the meetings in America in 1991 and 1999. Taking place against a background of global conflict, the 1991 Ryder Cup was played at Kiawah Island in South Carolina, where the us team got so infected with Desert Storm patriotic fervour that the press dubbed the event 'The War on the Shore'. In 1991, the US hadn't won the Cup for eight years, and were pretty sore about it – but still, how they managed to confuse golf against Europe with bombing Iraq was never adequately explained. There was an unprecedented unpleasantness about Kiawah Island, which the Americans finally won by 14½ to 13½, the whole result turning on a single missed putt by Bernhard Langer, the horror of which has arguably marked the poor chap for life. Corey Pavin and other US players wore Desert Storm caps. Galleries whooped, bellowed and screamed. The Europeans were subjected to insults, offensive prank calls, spectators chucking decoy balls onto the course, and even a daft campaign (started by a local radio station) to deprive them of sleep by yelling outside their hotel in the small hours. After the victory, US player Paul Azinger said: 'American pride is back. We went over there and thumped the Iraqis. Now we've taken the Cup back. I'm proud to be an American.'

I wasn't there in 1991, but I have a vivid memory of the Sunday afternoon eight years later, at Brookline, Massachusetts, in 1999. It was a famous day, for one reason and another. The Americans had finished the Saturday four points down, which meant that, to win the Cup, they needed at least 8½ points from the 12 available in the singles matches – which, frankly, looked like a tall order. No winning team had ever started the Sunday with more than a two-point deficit before. We Europeans were culpably light-hearted about how well things had gone for us in the preceding two days; we had celebrated tactlessly (there was even, I'm ashamed to say, cheering in the press restaurant); we were fools not to register the intensity of the anger and wounded pride now pulsing through our opponents. La la la, we trilled. Hey ho, lighten up you guys, it's just a game, but aren't we good at it, la la la la la, New England in the Fall, what could be nicer, la la la la la? Imagine a blithe little lamb with a ribbon round its neck skipping about in front of a wounded and starving lioness, and you get the idea. I always remember our collective euphoria in watching the 19-year-old Sergio Garcia paired with Jesper Parnevik on those first two days: in the four matches they had played together, first they had beaten Tom Lehman and Tiger Woods, then they had beaten Phil Mickelson and Jim Furyk, then they had beaten Payne Stewart and Justin Leonard, and then they had halved against David Duval and Davis Love III. Bloody hell. Could this really be happening? They larked about together, Sergio and Jesper. They hugged and high-fived. They jumped into each other's arms. Can you imagine how obnoxious this behaviour must have been to their opponents? At what temperature, I wonder, does human blood literally start to boil?

All week the Europeans had infuriated their hosts by appearing to take the contest lightly, their captain Mark James setting the tone by being hilariously flippant in his public statements – in contrast to the deep, full-fathom-five solemnity of the US captain, Ben Crenshaw, who said things were 'very, very meaningful', and that Sergio Garcia had a 'very, very wide arsenal' (scary moment there, actually). James's press conferences were completely disarming. He said the thing he feared most about the Americans was their dress sense. It was like watching a person repeatedly cheeking a humourless US immigration officer, and getting away with it. 'What was your best decision today as captain?' James would be asked, and he'd say, 'I had the hamburger for lunch instead of the turkey sandwich, and I really enjoyed it.' Asked why he parked his captain's buggy at a particular place on the course, he said he usually chose a spot where he could catch a bit of sun. 'Tell us about Miguel Angel Jimenez,' a reporter pleaded. 'Well, I don't know a huge amount about him,' said James. 'He's got a Ferrari.'

Boy, were we asking for it. And boy, did we get it. On the Saturday night, according to legend, Ben Crenshaw invited George W. Bush, then governor of Texas, to fire up his men by reading to them a stirring appeal-for-help letter written at the Alamo. The next morning the US team arrived on the course pumped up to a frenzy of battle resolve, and incidentally wearing the ugliest shirts you've ever seen. It was shock and awe time again, basically – and before the happy little European lamb could say 'Baa?', it was torn to pieces, reduced to nothing more than an interesting spatter pattern, a stump of woolly hoof, and a poignant strip of ripped and bloody ribbon caught up on a bit of shrub. In the first six singles matches, the US players absolutely slaughtered us, and the crowd got the taste for blood. One by one, the Europeans were simply blown away. In the end, only four of our boys were able to make a game of it on that Sunday – Padraig Harrington, José-Maria Olazabal, Colin Montgomerie and Paul Lawrie – but no one has ever accused the Europeans of choking. On the contrary, those who scored points against the Americans are regarded as heroes. The crowd was so appallingly abusive to Colin Montgomerie that his dad left the course in disgust. Mark James's wife was spat at. All day the crowds just shouted at the Europeans to go home.

Personally, I was exposed to only about an hour of this. Given the deadline difficulties of filing copy from America to London (the first deadline is around 1.30 p.m., and the last is around six), it was necessary to spend most of the Sunday working in the air-conditioned press tent, watching the singles matches unfold on TV screens, and updating pieces for each edition. However, at last spotting a gap between deadlines, I walked out to the nearest point of the course in time to see Colin Montgomerie and Payne Stewart come by, and it was one of the most shocking discontinuities I've ever experienced. Passing from the TV version of the event to the reality was like walking out of the Reading Room of the British Museum and into the trenches of the First World War. It was unnaturally dark out there, for a start. The atmosphere was almost unbreathably thick; people were yelling abuse; there was an air of violence. As someone who had spent three years mingling with football crowds, I was no stranger to this sort of thing. But I had never felt it on a golf course before, and I hope I never will again.

This was all prior to the events on the 17th hole – events which every person considering what to do about the Ryder Cup in 2001 must have had in mind, even if they didn't say so. Having already secured eight of the required eight and a half points, a number of excited American players were gathered at the 17th green to cheer Justin Leonard in his match against José-Maria Olazabal. Olazabal had been four up earlier in the match, but Leonard had putted beautifully, making birdies, and had eroded Olazabal's lead until they were all square after 16. If Leonard won the 17th, he would ensure a half-point for his team, and therefore victory. If he halved it, he still stood the chance of winning (or losing) the match on the 18th. Arriving at the green, Olazabal had a twenty-foot putt for birdie; Leonard was putting from around forty-five feet, also for birdie. With one of those shots that ring around the world, Leonard made that brilliant putt, with the result that his team-mates, whooping and shrieking, charged onto the green in triumph. They knew Leonard hadn't won the hole yet, but they went berserk anyway, and the pictures of that mad moment became instantly iconic: the American players and caddies surging, leaping onto the green in the foreground; an impassive Olazabal in the distance, head bowed, presumably battling to contain his feelings (as I suspect he always is). This was the moment when all that guff about golf being a gentlemanly sport simply went up in smoke.

Now, the Americans had had a fantastic day. Despite the considerable hindrance of the hideous shirts, they had played magnificently. They had staged the biggest fight-back in the history of the competition. But the fact that they ran out onto the green at the 17th before Olazabal had had a chance to putt was, in golf terms, a heinous sin, and unforgivable. Had Olazabal halved the hole, and gone on to win the 18th (and as it happens, Olazabal *did* win the 18th), he would have prevented – or at least delayed – the US win. Given that the eventual score was 14½ to 13½ (and Europe needed only 14 points to retain the Cup), Olazabal's putt was just as crucial as Leonard's had been.

But he not only had to wait for the celebrations to die down; the crowd then yelled abuse at him. Nowadays, as part of the generous campaign to forget Brookline and not point the finger at anyone (because it just makes the US players defensive, and doesn't achieve anything), Olazabal is often quoted as saying, in a saintly way, that had the boot been on the other foot, who knows whether the Europeans would have behaved similarly. At the time, however, that was not what he said. At the press conference afterwards, he congratulated the Americans but said that 'What happened today should not have happened. We are playing a match and we should show respect to each other and what happened was not the right thing to do.'

When people refer darkly to the events at Brookline in 1999, this is what they are talking about. When the PGAs tore their raiments in agony in September 2001, deciding whether or not to postpone, they knew that the event under consideration was more than just a straightforward golfing competition, it was potentially a bloodbath. Those events on the 17th at Brookline had shown us what happens when you mix golf with war, start meaning it, and leave yourself with no way to get back. On both sides the memory was fresh, and people were still very sore about it. It no longer cut much ice to console oneself with, 'Yes, but Jack Nicklaus did say that fantastic thing to Tony Jacklin back in 1969.' It is a harsh thing to say, but postponing the competition by a year and then playing it in the shadow of a terrorist atrocity was, as it turned out, precisely what was required. It lent a bit of perspective. I've never heard anyone say this, but perhaps the horrific events of 9/11 were responsible, in an ill-wind kind of way, for saving the Ryder Cup.

My main memory of the 2002 Ryder Cup at the Belfry is of being in the wrong place at the wrong time – so no change there, then, I hear you say. But it's the chief reality of on-the-spot golf-writing that there is no optimum place from which to view an unfolding golf tournament, except in front of a telly, listening to Peter Alliss sending private warm wishes over the public airwaves to the party with fairy cakes going on today for the 90th birthday of the ex-pro Sandy MacHoots at the Old-Bastard-on-the-Wold Golf Club. (I do wish he'd stop doing that.) If you opt to follow a match for 18 holes – which involves walking several miles, crouching motionless in the long grass when required to, and jotting down umpteen yardages and club selections – you must do it in full knowledge that in terms of getting a useable story you probably might just as well have stayed at home and groomed the cat. The story of the day will arise wherever it chooses to, and is impossible to second-guess. On the Sunday at the Belfry in 2002, I was assigned to the match between Lee Westwood and Scott Verplank, which looked all right on paper, but turned out to be an odd, dreamlike affair, with no story in it for anyone concerned. Basically, Westwood didn't look like winning, by contrast to most of his team-mates, who were blazing a trail towards an eventual victory of 15½ points to 12½. He won a hole here; lost a hole there. Elsewhere on the course – as tantalising distant roars frequently attested – all was going fabulously well for Europe, and I was very glad just to hear about it on Radio 5 as I plodded round regardless. The virtually unknown Philip Price was beating Phil Mickelson. Jesper Parnevik was heading for a half with Tiger Woods. Padraig Harrington was slaughtering Mark Calcavecchia.

As always in these circumstances, I used no journalistic initiative. I stuck with Lee. Where a better journalist assigned to this match would have dashed off to get a better story (and all the rest of them did), I didn't have the heart. And to be honest, it has now become almost a point of pride for me to pick a naff match on the Sunday of the Ryder Cup. At Valderrama in 1997 I went out with Ian Woosnam, who lost to Fred Couples by one of the most horrific margins ever – 8 and 7. In 2002, I got Westwood. And in 2006, at the K Club in Dublin, in a drenching downpour, I was allotted Sergio Garcia, who immediately started losing so catastrophically to Stewart Cink (five down after seven holes) that John Hopkins – knowing from experience how stolid I can be in such circumstances – came out to intercept me after the front nine, pulling me out of the squelching mud, and officially taking me off this awful non-story. I wouldn't have minded, but the bloody rain stopped the moment I went indoors. Anyway, at Louisville, Kentucky (2008), the pattern was finally broken. Noticing my jinx effect, perhaps, my bosses begged me to keep away from the players altogether on the Sunday, so I stayed in the tent with all my outdoor paraphernalia piled untidily around my desk, and wrote about the very real mental agony of having to revise my prejudices concerning Ian Poulter (still a bit of a git, but incontrovertibly the most impressive player on the European team).

I missed going out, of course. One of the reasons I love covering golf is that you get to walk round with the players. I mean, you don't chat with them or anything. You don't say, 'I'd aim for that TV tower if I were you,' or 'I was surprised you chose the wedge.' Your presence is something they blank out, which is fair enough. I did once help David Duval look for his ball in some gorse, but I'm pretty sure I was invisible throughout, and I kept my distance anyway on account of that awful gobbing. Generally you stay near to the ropes, and you have to kneel or crouch when the shots are taken, so the spectators can see over your head. It is no stroll, however. Ambling is not an option. While the golfers stride down rolling velvety fairways, we hacks have to scramble over tussocks of long grass and occasionally slip and fall over (to cheers from the crowd). The marshals who control the crossings will often wait for the players to pass and then, just as we approach (yelling 'Wait for us!'), they open the ropes, so we have to fight our way through crowds of spectators, streaming from one side of the fairway to the other. We are often a fairly merry band, however. We have a laugh. 'Ten foot putt?' we say, peering towards the green. 'Twelve,' says someone. 'Fifteen,' says another. I am usually listening to the radio commentary, so I tend to pass on what the commentator has said ('He says eight'), so we can all agree a number. My own method of calculating distance on the green is to imagine laying a number of six-foot golfers end to end, but I wouldn't dare mention this to the guys, obviously, because of the scope for innuendo.

Notepad and pen are all that the guys carry, by the way, and I can't imagine how they do it. I am permanently in awe at their sheer chutzpah in the face of four or five hours in the unpredictable outdoors. They just strap on an arm-band with 'PRESS' on it, click a Biro, and out they go. By contrast, every time I go out on the golf course, I not only change into a completely different outfit (golf shoes with soft cleats, waterproof jacket, jumbo waterproof trousers), but I pack into a knapsack enough wardrobe options and essential survival items for a weekend on Dartmoor. While the chaps merely pay attention to the golf and jot down the occasional note (some of them pretend they can even follow the flight of the ball, but I don't believe them), I am forever re-arranging my possessions: passing from hand to hand any combination of gloves, hat, glasses, binocu-lars, sun cream, radio, switched-off mobile phone, purse, wallet, allergy tablets, yardage guide, spare batteries, jumper, novel, spare glasses, back-up radio, tin of mints, tissues, sunglasses, sanitary towels, contact lenses (in case I lose all the glasses), bottle of water, glucose tablets, banana, first-aid kit, set of splints, fold-away stretcher, portable resus-citation unit and emergency distress flares. No wonder I never know what's going on. No wonder I can never find my bloody notepad and my bloody pen. What is inter-esting is how the chaps are tactful enough never to comment on all this stuff I'm freighting about, but at the same time they won't have anything to do with it, either. If a chap sneezes and I say, 'Ooh, I've got a big box of tissues in here somewhere,' I've noticed the offer is always declined quite sharply. If a chap is in visible need of a sustaining banana, I have equally learned not to say anything about having a spare apple and an individual fruit pie if they're interested. It appears to be a male-pride thing, and I am bound to respect it, even without understanding it. Some men just don't like to be offered things, do they? And they would rather die than ask. Mind you, I think my fellow golf writers are mainly worried I'll one day magically produce a fully-erect hat-stand out of that bag of mine, like Mary Poppins. I'm actually quite worried about that myself.

Back at the 2002 Ryder Cup at the Belfry on the Sunday, of course, there was no one to offer a fruit pie to besides Lee Westwood himself, because the smarter blokes had so wisely buggered off elsewhere. On the first two days, Westwood's current supposed lack of form (he was ranked 148 in the world, having sunk dramatically since the team was fixed in 2001) had seemed a mere irrelevance. He and Sergio Garcia had played in all four sessions, and won three points – despite some rather costly juvenile heroics on the 10th. But now, on singles day, the miracle had been revoked, and the fact that Westwood managed to hang on to Verplank until the 17th was a huge achievement. He made a terrific birdie putt at the fourth (my notes say it was 30 feet, but I suspect I was mentally laying five golfers end to end again here, so this may not be a reliable figure). On the eighth, he did it again. But you just knew that, whatever he did, this stuff wasn't going to make it onto the telly. Out on the leafy, autumnal course with only his wife in support, and only one journalist (me) still taking an interest, Westwood v Verplank was the remotest edge of the action. I kept wondering, 'Should I go off and follow someone else? Where did all the guys go? Oh no, was it all my fault for offering that cheese board at the eighth? Oh come on, it was only a bit of brie and a few Bath Olivers!'

But on the other hand, I couldn't just leave Westwood now, could I? It would look so rude. I remember how Lee's wife vented her feelings when captain Sam Torrance and team-mate Padraig Harrington eventually showed up in support on the 15th. 'Finally, we get some help,' she said. 'Hear, hear,' I echoed, quietly.

There was an air of 'finally' about the whole Ryder Cup that year. Everyone was glad to get the damn thing played at last – and to move on to a new era in which no War on the Shore and no Brookline Outrage could occur again in our lifetimes. Postponing by a year put the events of 9/11 at a distance, but its true value was in shifting Brookline further into the past. Sadly, as it happens, history repeated itself at the first opportunity. Europe won again in 2004 and 2006. In 2006, in fact, someone at a press conference at the K Club in Dublin dared to suggest to the losing American captain Tom Lehman that, with the contest getting so one-sided these days, maybe it was time to change the rules again: maybe the US team should be opened up to include players from other parts of the world, just in the interests of making the contest more even? Lehman said that the question was 'a little insulting in some ways', by which he meant it was very offensive. He said there were cycles in these things, and that the American golf world was full of great players.

But while his team lost with exemplary good grace – taking turns to hug the recently widowed Darren Clarke, for example, and talking a lot about respect – the effect was ever so slightly creepy, and those of us with a sense of history knew where this three-losses-on-the-trot thing would ultimately lead, and so it did. In September 2008, Europe was duly trounced at the Valhalla course in Louisville, Kentucky – with lots of unlovely crowd behaviour – and honour was restored.

Miscellaneous Sports, Travel, and All the Misleading Bollocks I Had to Put Up With

To many people in the sports-writing profession, Richard Ford's excellent novel *The Sportswriter* comes as a disappointment. The main trouble is that its hero, Frank Bascombe, works from home. True, he writes magazine profiles of big-name American football stars, but (oh my God) did I mention this? He works *from home*. True, he also embodies a recognisable anomie, and has a few child-like traits that make him unpopular with more emotionally mature people, but, look, for goodness' sake, he works from home, so how the hell does that count as sports writing? Sorry to be so literal-minded where a Great American Novel is involved, but, good grief, it isn't clear even whether Frank Bascombe owns a laptop (unlikely, since the book was published in 1986), let alone has acquired a cumbersome 20-piece set of telephone connectors for essential dial-up use in all the more bizarrely socketed countries of western Europe. Has he ever delivered 900 words ten minutes before the whistle in a stadium packed with jubilant Italians all using up the available Vodafone signal? Has he ever tried to park near Stamford Bridge after 10 a.m. on a match day? Has he turned up, week after week, at far-flung football grounds all over England only to be told by miserable blokes in donkey jackets, 'You can't come through here'? Has he ever attempted to drive with a dangerously empty fuel tank from Liège to Antwerp at midnight when all the petrol stations are mysteriously closed and the effing road signs have been draped with effing tarpaulins by those effing, effing Belgians? I think the answer to all these urgent questions must be no, because if Frank Bascombe *had* done any of these things in his career as a sports writer, let me tell you, there's no way a novelist as good as Richard Ford could possibly have left them out of the narrative.

The main reason I've waited several years to write this book is that it took me all that time to calm down. For at least five years after I stopped sports writing, all I remembered about it was the stuff that made me scream – the stuff that one of our photographers memorably described as 'The Agg' – such as calling the Edgbaston Thistle from the road ('Can you give me directions from the A45, please?') and having the person at the other end say, 'No, sorry, I can't. But I know the way here from my house in Redditch if that's any use.' Even now, when people say, 'Why was it golf you decided to keep doing?' I never say anything about the beauty of the game, or the structure of the tournaments, or even the exhilaration of being outdoors near the sea for a pleasant week in July. With ill-suppressed passion, I burst out that, with a golf tournament, at least a girl gets a guaranteed indoor desk to work at, a guaranteed bed in a house she knows the route to, plus a guaranteed place in the car park. Not only that, but the same conditions pertain for a whole week.

They could honestly send me to cover illicit bloody kitten-juggling if all these things were offered in the deal.

It was getting lost that was the worst thing. And in case this sounds quaint and antique in the days of sat-nav, I should point out that I was quite well equipped with maps and books with up-to-date information; it just happens to be in the special nature of large sporting events that normal road systems don't apply: regular routes are closed, one-way systems are instituted, signposts are covered up as if to confuse the Germans, and the police will bash the side of your car with their truncheons if you try to stop and ask them a question. It also happens to be in the nature of sports arenas (especially football grounds) that they don't see the point of signposts in any case, partly because they are quite large structures, but mainly because the supporters know the way. As kick-off approaches, you see the fans mindlessly thronging in the right direction, following mysterious ancient trails like moribund elephants heading for their final resting place. Not one of them ever stops with a puzzled expression that says, 'I wonder if it's down this street or the next one?'

For the first-time visitor who arrives a few hours earlier than everyone else, therefore, things can be quite tough. I have deep and bleeding mental scars from the night I was carefully following detailed directions to Anfield ('Pass Showcase Cinema on left after 1.8 miles; after further 1.9 miles turn left, signposted Widnes') and ran into a road block. Veering by necessity from the prescribed route, I drove in desperate circles for the following half-hour, hyper-ventilating and performing illegal U-turns in residential streets, and finally pulled up outside a chip shop and ran inside yelling, 'I can't find Anfield! How can they put up a road block when there's a match on? There's an FA Cup match starting in four hours! Don't they know people have to be able to find the ground?' At which the chip-shop proprietor patiently took me to the door and pointed up at an angle of 45 degrees to the tell-tale floodlight towers standing just beyond the Victorian terrace opposite.

There are other reasons for preferring golf, but to be honest they still mostly have to do with not getting the car broken into by hooligans, and not having hotel receptionists deny all knowledge of your booking. The highlight of my tenure as a sports writer will always be seeing Dennis Bergkamp score that magnificent last-minute winning goal for Holland against Argentina in Marseille in 1998 (it's the best thing I ever saw, and the Velodrome was the coolest stadium I was ever in), but for a long time the memory of Bergkamp's superhuman ball control was more than off-set by all the bloody 'agg' that surrounded it. Had *The Times* booked me into a nice hotel in Marseille, convenient for the stadium, for this match? Well, take a guess. Despite expecting me to come up with lovely local colour about loony Dutch fans with carrots tied to their heads (it's to do with their orangeness) and the pungent fishy whiff of the dockside restaurants, the office had dispatched me to Marseille by stuffy train from Lyons a couple of days before the match, then told me to catch another stuffy train to Avignon (100 kilometres inland) and await instructions. At Avignon, glad to be in the fresh air at last, I was told to go to the Ibis Hotel next to the station – which was when I made the big mistake of thinking I'd at last be able to unpack, have a shower, and write my daily column. Because I turned out not to have a booking at this nasty little Ibis Hotel, you see – or so the high-handed check-in people claimed. They suggested I might in fact have been booked by mistake into the Ibis Hotel in the quite different location of Avignon Sud (an industrial suburb), and would need to get another train and then a cab, although naturally they couldn't promise anything about there being a bed still available at the Avignon Sud Ibis Hotel when I eventually got there, because someone else might have got there first and taken it.

I phoned the office from under a tree outside Avignon station and told them this had stopped being funny quite a long time ago. I was hot and tired and already miles from where I really ought to be; meanwhile a deadline was looming, in case they hadn't noticed, and I hadn't seen any Dutch fans at all, either with or without the comical veg. They assured me they were hot on the trail of a suitable (i.e. cheap) hotel room 'in Provence', so things could still be all right. It was at this point that I broke down and wept. I'd been in France for three weeks already. I'd had to fight the whole time. I'd had to be fantastically organised, getting from one city to another, one stadium to the next; improvising methods for transmitting copy in apparently hopeless circumstances; managing on a tiny, minimal wardrobe without access to hotel laundry facilities (because the hotels were always too basic to have them, and I was never anywhere long enough for things to dry if I washed them myself); and having to cope, above all, with all the utter misleading bollocks I kept being fed in place of information. And now the office was telling me they might have located a room for me . . . in Provence? The last time I looked, Provence was an administrative region of south-east France roughly the size of Switzerland. 'Do you mean in Aix-en-Provence, which is a town rather than a region?' I wailed. No, just Provence, they said; we'll call you back. I stayed under my tree for the next hour, snivelling on my upturned suitcase, until a dear nice *Times* colleague thankfully arrived from Paris ('Kevin McCarra! Thank God!'), and we came up with a plan that involved staying in a stylish converted monastery in Avignon that Kevin had luckily heard about. During my Beckett-y wait under the tree outside the station, incidentally, a taxi driver had sidled over and said discreetly I could always go home with him if I wanted, because his wife was away. So, on top of being abandoned, I got propositioned as well, which made me feel all the better.

I shan't go on with all this complaining. I know how it gets people's backs up. Being a sports writer is considered such an almighty privilege by all people who love sport that they simply won't condone any grumbling. Sports editors won't condone it either, but for a different reason. With them it's down to an interesting physiological quirk: they are born with hearts of stone. When applying for the job, they are subjected to special tests: they are strapped to polygraph machines and then shown distressing images of sports writers tangled in barbed wire and screaming for help. If their eyes don't flicker, and their pulse continues to flatline, they're in. 'You can't expect sympathy from me; you're under a tree in the South of France, and I'm in Wapping' was the standard response to any whinge from a writer in the field, however justified. Naturally, this attitude added considerably to one's already quite powerful sense of existential loneliness. But that was probably the idea. 'Oh dear, pillows not fluffy enough?' they would interrupt, if you started to point out that there were no trains back from Macclesfield after half past eight.

What used to annoy me much more than the 'I have no sympathy' reflex, however, was the thoughtless assumption that I must be enjoying a fabulous social life involving other sports writers. 'Off to the bar now, I suppose?' they'd chuckle, after I'd filed from Ewood Park or somewhere, and was already back in the parked car with the heater on and the doors locked, trying to read the road atlas by the light of a lonely street lamp, with the radio tuned to Radio 5 for the phone-in. Off to the bar? What bar? I never saw a bar. And with whom, in any case, would I be off to the bar? When I was staying in a cheerless apart-hotel in Antwerp during Euro 2000 (where every morning for a whole month the receptionist asked me brightly whether I was checking out), I drove down to meet one of my bosses in Brussels and he asked me in a friendly fashion whether there was a 'gang' of us staying in Antwerp. I remember just looking at him with my mouth open. What sort of gang did he think I belonged to? Did he know something I didn't? Oh good grief, why had no one introduced me to all those other middle-aged women football writers who railed at the misleading bollocks all day, got soundly rebuffed when they appealed to the office for help, and did needlepoint watching the TV alone in their hotel rooms (watching the footie) on all their nights off?

* * *

Dancing on the edge of sports writing involved dancing on the edge of a variety of different sports, which only added to the stress. I was always setting off to Goodwood, or Silverstone, or Murrayfield, or the Hurlingham Club, or Headingley, or the National Indoor Arena, or Olympia, or Wentworth, or Frimley Green – and always doing it for the very first time in my life. 'Lynne Truss at Trent Bridge', the byline would announce under a cheery photograph on the Monday morning – and good heavens, didn't it sound straightforward when it was put like that? As if I sort-of lived there. As if I had my own locker. Other sports writers did, of course, have regular stamping grounds, and I couldn't help absolutely resenting and hating them for it. It was clear that the press box at Trent Bridge (or wherever) was indeed their second home. The only people who roamed as widely as I did were the chief sports writers – people like Richard Williams at the *Guardian* and Paul Hayward at the *Mail* – but theirs was nothing like my situation. These were men of vast journalistic experience achieved over decades, who just seemed to materialise effortlessly in all the major sporting venues, equipped with not only a sound magisterial overview of the forthcoming event but also (damn them) a thorough working knowledge of the relevant topography. By the end of my four years, the only place I regarded as a stamping ground was the now-demolished Wembley Stadium. It was a gritty, dank, dilapidated and unattractive place in many regards, the old Wembley, but knowing which door to use really brightened it up for me. Confidently swinging my weighty computer bag, I would whistle on the escalators and head straight for the press room, where I knew the ropes about tickets and team sheets and could say hello to the press officers by name. I even established a preference for which type of half-time sandwich. But Wembley was the exception. Everywhere else, I first had to work out how to get the car as near as possible, and then I had to fight, plead, argue and scream to get in.

'You can't come through here,' they said. Even when I'd found the right bloke at the right gate, he would scan his list, tell me I didn't exist, and send me to the box office, or club reception, or the gift shop – and they in turn would send me to the chip van or the players' entrance (or whatever), and they in turn would finally send me back to the man at the gate. This was why I generally turned up at least two hours early for any event – to allow for all the time-wasting misleading bollocks, which could somehow never be averted, just endured. What I discovered about human nature during this period was that there are many people who cannot say 'I don't know' when that's the truth of the matter. For reasons of pride, perhaps, it is beyond them to do it. They think it is better to make something up, because it makes you go away. 'Is there a press car park?' you might ask, and instead of confessing their cluelessness, they'd stroke their jaws as if in genuine thought and then say, 'Right. You need to go back to the A437, OK? Then take a left for half a mile, then go round the back of the old brewery, and then follow the signs. There'll be a shuttle.' Half an hour later, when you returned with the tragic news that there was no truth in any of that, they first of all wouldn't recognise you, and then they'd say, 'Really? Well, whatever. You can't come through here.'

Still, there was a positive aspect to all this. By the time

the actual sporting action commenced, it was – relatively – heaven. When you've just spent an hour explaining to a jobsworth that you don't have a parking voucher because the only way to obtain a parking voucher is by going inside, which involves *parking first*, it is bliss to look at a team sheet, a blank scoreboard and a bit of grass with lines on it and think, 'Here at last is something organised. I know where I am with this.' I went to some rum and improbable events in my time, but however unfamiliar I might be with the rules of darts, or croquet – or indeed those of quite big sports such as cricket or rugby union – the rigidly circumscribed comings and goings of an unfolding game stood in wonderful contrast to the random petty annoyances and difficulties presented by real life outside. I remember Simon Barnes telling me (the first time I met him) how sport always got you this way, and that he'd once been immediately sucked – quite against his will, apparently – into the drama of a lumberjacking competition involving axes, logs, a lot of frantic chopping and an enormous shower of wood-chips.

I soon realised he was right. They sent me to Olympia for the show-jumping once, and on the undercard (as it were) was a dog agility competition that turned out to be sheer drama. There was a Great Dane called Blake who was clearly capable of all sorts of top dog agility, but would tantalisingly weigh up the pros and cons of each obstacle before deciding to take it on. For the impartial spectator, whose only interest was in sporting tension, this was dynamite. Would Blake go up the seesaw and down the other side? Well, it was touch and go. With precious seconds ticking by, Blake would stop first and give it some serious doggy thought. And then, with a visibly resolute, 'Yep, OK, I'll do that!', off he would bound, to huge encouraging applause from the crowd. What about this little tunnel, Blake? Yes? No? Come on, boy, what do you think? 'Yep, OK, I'll do that!' What I loved about Blake's approach to his sport was the way he repeatedly excercised (and indeed embodied) the sometimes forgotten principle of free will. Stan Collymore used to do the same thing in the footie, didn't he? But without the equivalent charm.

However, the best gig I got, I reckon, in the whole four years, was the BDO World Darts Championship at Frimley Green on a cold weekend in January 2000 – and not only because the round trip from my home in Brighton to Frimley Green (in Surrey) was so agreeably short. No, it was just that it had everything you could possibly require from a sporting event, if you are prepared to leave out fresh air and athleticism. From the moment I arrived for the Saturday semi-finals (Ronnie Baxter v Co Stompe from the Netherlands; Ted Hankey v Chris Mason), I knew I was going to love watching this stuff. It took place in a large, packed, carpeted and artificially-lit function room usually used for knees-ups and weddings. It was billed as sport but the blokes had corny nicknames and silky capes and 'walk-on music', like professional wrestlers, and the place was full of families in holiday mood. The stage was spangly, and there were big screens on either side. The all-day bar was emphatically open, and there was a range of high-cholesterol hot food for sale in a spot-lit buffet. Since Holland produces many top-ranking darts players (such as Stompe), there were many larky Dutch people present – although, sadly, none with root vegetable adornments.

And since darts is one of the few sports the BBC can still afford to cover, the dearly beloved Garry Richardson was in attendance – a circumstance that has never failed to raise my spirits.

It was larky, this semi-finals day, but it was also very serious. These players had already played three rounds to reach this point. Darts turned out to have the same sort of organisational palaver as boxing, with rival outfits staging their own world championships, and attempting to lure players into separate leagues – so there was the honour of the BDO (British Darts Organisation) at stake here, on top of everything else. By the time play commenced, I'd learned a bit about the players (Co Stompe used to drive a tram!) and was avid for oche action. And I had already worked out some of darts' potential advantages over other spectator sports – which mainly concerned how straightforward it would be to officiate. No room for the players to contest any line calls here, for example. No need to consult a snickometer. No hunting for lost darts in the rough. No dodgy penalties awarded by blind-sided refs. Darts is, in fact, a doddle of a game, save for the lightning mental calculations entailed when suddenly everyone in the room knows that if you need 158, you quickly subtract 3 x 17, then 3 x 19, and then 50. Another interesting fact about darts is that, whereas in cricket 'throwing' is sometimes illegal, in darts it is positively encouraged. In fact, without throwing, there is absolutely no game to speak of.

To my shame I'd never heard of the semi-finalists before, even though young-gun Chris Mason had apparently been making a name for himself all week, charmlessly casting aspersions about the other players. Instinctively, I supported the Dutchman, partly because he wasn't the usual shape for a darts player (his nickname was 'The Matchstick'), but mainly because I found it very touching that he used to drive that tram. But the first semi-final, between Stompe and Ronnie Baxter, was in all respects the lesser contest of the day, and Stompe didn't put up a great fight. Matchstick-like, he snapped under the strain. It was the best of nine sets (each set consisting of five legs), and Baxter took his winning five sets rather easily and gracefully (the eventual score was 5–2). I didn't particularly warm to Baxter, nicknamed 'The Rocket', but I did admire his choice of walk-on music. Queen's 'Don't Stop Me Now' was very well suited to his style of play. But although there was skill in this match, there was little drama. There was tension, but not much. At the end of the first semi-final, I still had no idea what glories a good game of darts had to offer.

The second semi-final pitched Ted Hankey ('The Count') against this young chap Chris Mason ('The Prince of Dartness'). Having a nickname when you're a darts player seems to be non-negotiable, by the way, but the unsmiling Hankey took the joke further than most. Pale and balding, he played up his resemblance to Dracula, chucking vampire paraphernalia to the fans, grimacing, and occasionally transmogrifying into an immense black dog (oh all right, he didn't go that far). Hankey was the number five seed in this championship; Mason was unseeded, but the bookies' favourite. From a superficial look at the two players, I jumped to the happy conclusion that here was a classic true-grit contest between age and youth – the tight-lipped old gun-slinger teaching some manners to the young, twitchy rodeo punk; John Wayne v Montgomery Clift. Someone would end up humiliatingly headfirst in a rain barrel at the end of this, I thought, and it probably wouldn't be Hankey. It was at this point that I checked the player information and found that Whipper-Snapper Mason was 30, while Old Geezer Hankey was 31, so bang went that idea.

The game was again best of nine, and Mason led from the start, on account of superior finishing, but from the beginning the standard of play on both sides was obviously exceptional. This match was to set the record (I think it still holds it) for the number of perfect 180s scored in a nine-setter – Hankey and Mason threw a total of 38 between them. But Hankey was having trouble with that old rule about ending with a double, and by the interval, Mason was up 3–1 and looking pretty smug. When Hankey retrieved a set to make it 3–2, Mason quickly upped his game again and re-established the two-set margin. With the score standing at 4–2 (i.e. just one set from defeat), Hankey looked washed out, stricken, deflated – a bit like the way Dracula does when someone carelessly parts the curtains. He sweated lot. He looked deathly pale. He put his hand inside his silk shirt and adjusted a medallion. Was he turning to dust in front of our very eyes? He *really* didn't look 31, by the way. I simply couldn't get over that.

But just when Mason was looking unbeatable, Hankey fought back – and all one's hopes about true grit were rewarded. In the seventh set, he started to put pressure on the younger man, and Mason responded by making mistakes and talking to himself! Mason didn't have what it took! *Thud, thud, thud* came those relentless 180s from Hankey. *Thud, thud, thud.* People were leaping to their feet to yell their appreciation. Hankey won the seventh set and then the eighth, pulling level at 4–4. By this time the Kid was seriously rattled. He threw wildly and talked to himself even more. And suddenly he was trailing! He'd been two sets up, and now he was fighting to stay in the match. Honestly, a Borg v McEnroe five-setter was only ever so slightly better than this, in the wider sporting scheme of things. Come on, Ted. Show him how it's done, son. This is all about character. You know you can do it. In the final set, Ted won the first leg, and the second. In fact, suddenly, hang on, Ted required only 45 to win the match!

We held our breath. He shot a five, and then – oh no – missed the double 20 with both remaining darts. Oh my God, don't you play darts *for a living*, Ted? This gave Mason a chance, but he likewise blew it. The pressure was beginning to tell on everybody. People in the audience were dancing with agony. Ted tried for the double 20 again. He got a single! He tried for the double 10. He got a single there as well! With the last dart, he tried for the double five. Some of us couldn't bear to watch. Dividing five is notoriously difficult in a world consisting only of simple integers. If he missed the double again, he'd have to wait his turn and then go for a one and a double two. And then, if he got only a *single two* . . . The world stood still. Get the double five, Ted, for God's sake. Get the double five. (He did.)

'Tragedy' by the Bee Gees was played for the benefit of Mason, who didn't need reminding: he was openly in tears. Dealing with defeat was not something Mason had any ambitions to be good at – and he wasn't. On the telly afterwards, he told Garry Richardson, 'I was the best player here this week, but my name wasn't on the pot.' So no old Corinthian nonsense about the best man winning on the day, then. But it had been a brilliant match, and in people's memories I believe it has quite overshadowed the final, which was played the next day. A complete let-down, the final was, a whitewash, with Hankey beating Baxter 6–0 in the fastest BDO final on record (46 minutes). Personally, I never went to darts again, but I felt I didn't need to, after an experience as perfect as that. According to the internet, all these blokes are still playing, but not at the same level, and not all for the same organisation.

It's quite interesting, though. Chris Mason re-nicknamed himself, for example. Nixing the rather clever 'Prince of Dartness', he became 'Mace the Ace'. He has been in trouble with the law a couple of times – once earning himself 180 hours of community service; and you can't help thinking that this particular figure was picked for a quasi-humorous reason, when the bench knew it was dealing justice to a professional darts player. Meanwhile, Ronnie Baxter jumped ship from the BDO to the PDC (Professional Darts Corporation) and his world ranking (at time of writing) is 15, which isn't bad. But there is tragedy in Baxter's story, too: in the 2008 Las Vegas Desert Classic, he threw his first ever nine-darter in a qualifying round, and it wasn't televised. Co Stompe stuck with the BDO until 2008, and then joined the PDC, as a result of which he dropped down the rankings. After 2000, the furthest he got in the World Championships was the last 16. Finally, Ted Hankey won the title again in January

2009, bringing him – suitably – back from the dead. In the intervening years he had gained a reputation for complaining about crowd behaviour and for quarrelling about whether the air conditioning should be switched off; in 2008, at the BDO World Championships, he received a warning for punching the dartboard, and told Ray Stubbs on the BBC that he was considering quitting the game. You can put a lot of this stuff down to chronic vitamin D deficiency, but I suspect he doesn't want to know.

Some sports were slower and more reluctant to reveal their treasures, sadly. They didn't all have the simple *thud, thud, thud, hurrah* of championship darts. There is a story beloved of sports writers (and it's told about different people, so its origins are probably now lost) of one sports writer saying to another before an equestrian three-day event, 'I think I'm going to enjoy this,' and the other one saying, 'Ah, you can enjoy it; I have to understand it.' Part of my remit was to strike an interesting triple variant to this usual professional axis of enjoying and understanding sport: I had to a) enjoy the fact that I didn't understand it; b) understand exactly how far I didn't understand it; and c) understand and enjoy the fact that I couldn't enjoy it as much as people who understood it. This was naturally quite tiring, and sometimes it couldn't be managed. Sometimes I merely got grumpy and said, 'I'm not enjoying this and I don't understand either.' Attending just the one Grand Prix at Silverstone, for example, I wanted to gnaw my own leg off, I hated it so much. For once, I had no fellow-feeling with the spectators; I thought they were mugs. A well-meaning man in a draughty cafeteria tried to strike up a conversation with me by saying, 'Great day out,' and regretted it instantly. 'How is this in any way at all a great day out?' I snapped at him. 'You can't see anything, mate,' I said. What's the point of a spectator sport where you can't see anything? Even if you've paid hundreds of quid for a decent grandstand seat to sit in (open to the elements), you still have to watch on a big screen and listen to a commentary, just to have a vague idea of who's winning. Lesser mortals who had paid a mere 75 quid for admission (Yes! £75!) got nothing at all. They had merely bought the privilege, it seemed, of wandering around this puddly and bedraggled former air-field, trying to negotiate a route avoiding all the unexplained roped-off areas, in search of a free bit of miserable chain-link fence to watch a bit of track through.

I thought the Grand Prix was preposterous. Whereas in all other sports, there's a reason for the writers to go outside and watch it for real (instead of on the TV), at a Grand Prix you'd have to be mad. Even when the cars zoomed right past our press box above the pits, it was noticeable that none of the blokes tore themselves from their screens to run over and give the drivers an encouraging wave. In the end, I left the press room and found a high windowsill in an out-of-the-way ladies' lavatory from which I could peer out at a segment of faraway track and glimpse the cars for real while listening to a radio commentary – but it didn't add anything valuable to the experience beyond a stiff neck from the draught. Everything in motor-racing was about sponsorship and conspicuous wealth, and I loathed it for pretending to be about anything else. Everything had 'Seudaria Ferrari Marlboro Asprey Shell

Goodyear Pioneer TelecomItalia NGK arexons SKF USAG brembo TRB sabelt BBS' written on it, including the drivers. The best thing about the day was that Michael Schumacher's big end went. I have no recollection of who won. I do remember the traffic control system afterwards which directed you for miles at glacial speeds down country lanes to a B-road and then didn't tell you which one it was. Motor-racing was not for me, I told the office on Monday. 'We noticed,' they said, and never sent me to anything engine-related again.

Horse-racing was a different matter. I cheerfully loathed horse-racing too, but only because being a surprise female guest of the racing press garnered the sort of reaction you'd get if you turned up to do a striptease in a mosque. 'She's not writing for *us*,' one of the chaps broad-mindedly explained to another chap (and how I loved that third-person treatment). 'She's writing for the Hampstead luvvies.' Honest amateurism was clearly not a quality much embraced by men of the turf, and naturally I could respect that. But it was a shame, because racing had lots of appeal otherwise. Those beautiful animals, for a start. The bewildering speed with which one race followed another. The opportunity to win £37.50 without deserving it. The chance to wear a broad-brimmed hat in the line of work. The endless circuit of down to the paddock, out to the bookies, back to the stands, and up with the binoculars. In particular I loved the brain-teasing aspect of studying form under pressure – using the race card and all the newspapers – which reminded me of those old logic puzzles in which Peter has three friends, Rebecca has red hair but doesn't eat nuts, and Julian is friends with Peter but failed to catch the 10.56 from Paddington. You could spend your whole life (and people do) trying to evaluate the different sorts of information available about horses running in the same race. Tippex Joy was a disappointment last time out; Red Bucket likes the going soft; Business Class is a one-time frustrating maiden; Mouse Mat Muesli never wins in months with an 'r' in them (but this is June); Council Flat is owned by Sheikh Mohammed; and Simon's Moron is a 'stayer'.

I won't go into how unpleasant it was in the press box, but you can understand why the racing press would have a certain Masonic air. They are pundits, these blokes; their job concerns divination – and it's well known that people in the oracle profession prefer to form secret societies and to keep their juju dark. A chap who writes about horse-racing will do the usual journalistic job of writing features about owners and trainers, and he will also report the races afterwards, but his main job, obviously, is to get on a rocking horse every night at home, with his eyes closed in a meditative trance, and then rock backwards and forwards until he reaches a state of frenzy and yells out the name of the winner of tomorrow's 2.45 at Newmarket. In no other branch of sports writing are the chaps judged on how well they predict results. In racing, it's everything. Naïve to a fault, I remember asking my boss whether racing correspondents were allowed to place bets themselves. I wondered whether this was properly consistent with the job of advising others. But betting turns out not to be a sacking offence, not by a long chalk. What my boss told me, in fact (and this came as quite a big shock to Little Miss Pollyanna), was that a professional racing journalist who didn't add at least £100,000 to his salary from bets each year wasn't a chap worth employing.

Under the heading of 'didn't enjoy, didn't understand, and didn't enjoy not understanding', I think the worst experience was a trip to Paris to see basketball. I suppose I needn't go into the logistics of getting to and from the Palais Omnisports at Bercy during a transport strike. You know all about that irksome stuff by now. I needn't tell you that the check-in staff at the hotel were emphatic I was booked for one night only, when I needed to stay for two, because I'm honestly not banging on about that any more. In theory the basketball event looked very interesting, and I spent my time on the outward Eurostar journey swotting up on the differences between NBA and FIBA rules – about the amount of time on the 'shot clock', for example – and trying very hard to care. I tried to memorise terms like 'burying a jumper' and 'pump fake'. I tried to imagine skywalking. A thousand journalists were due to attend this event, apparently. The 13,000 seats of the Palais Omnisports had sold out. Paris was very excited. In a championship sponsored by McDonald's, basketball teams from Europe and the wider world (but not the USA) were to play each other in an 'open' knockout competition, and in the final stages the winners would be pitted against none other than Michael Jordan and the Chicago Bulls – who would, of course, make short work of beating the living pants off them.

By good fortune, at the event I found myself sitting next to a very well informed American man with a fantastic job. He was the European scout for the Cleveland Cavaliers, which meant he lived in Florence (Florence!) and his only responsibility was to keep an eye on all the beanpole-shaped young Yugoslavians currently playing basketball all over Europe, and occasionally approach one of them to ask whether he'd ever fancied wintering in Ohio. The preponderance of Yugoslavians was very noticeable on the team sheets at the Palais Omnisports that day. Teams were ostensibly from Barcelona, Paris, Argentina, Italy and Greece, yet virtually every player was pale, with a very long face, and had a surname ending in '-ic'. I asked the scout about this shot-clock thing. He said it was important. He also drew diagrams of burying a jumper and so on. We discussed that excellent documentary film *Hoop Dreams*. The challenge for the Americans today would be in dealing with zone defence, he explained. Under NBA rules, a player marks an opponent; he is not permitted to defend in a general kind of way. But in this competition, zone defence would be allowed. This would give an advantage to the Europeans.

So I was properly up for a day's worth of basketball. Each match being 48 minutes, I reckoned I could concentrate that long on this alien game. I furrowed my brow and prepared to be swept along by the action. Which was where I made my big mistake, because the infuriating thing about basketball is that it no sooner starts than it stops again; then it re-starts and stops, re-starts and stops, re-starts and stops. If you have an attention span of any length whatsoever, it is a kind of mental torture. Even during the play you can't pretend that the game has its own organic

223

momentum, because irritating count-down music is played the whole time, shoes make ear-splitting *squeak* noises on the polished floor, you feel rushed and bamboozled – and then someone calls for a time-out (arbitrarily, as far as I could see) and the game is mystifyingly suspended for precisely 90 seconds while acrobats come on, and some pop music blares, and mascots clown around, and small boys with mops clear the sweat off the playing surface. My brain really couldn't cope with all this, and nor could my patience. With all these interruptions, each match represented the longest 48 minutes I had ever endured. It occurred to me that those of us who can watch a whole 45 minutes of football *in one go* ought really to congratulate ourselves for what it says about our superhuman powers of concentration.

It was great to see Michael Jordan, of course. One of the French papers had announced that having Michael Jordan in Paris was better than having the Pope: it was 'God in person'. Those who had hoped to see Jordan's two pretty famous Chicago Bull team-mates Scottie Pippen and Dennis Rodman were disappointed, because Pippen was injured and Rodman was ill. (The Cavaliers man was gutted about Pippen, and said I ought to be gutted too.) But looking on the bright side, their absence may have prevented further blasphemies about the Holy Trinity, and I suspect Jordan did not resent being left alone in the limelight in any case. For he was indeed like a god, compared with everyone else. It was impossible for the other players literally to resemble pigmies because they were all eight feet tall, but in all other respects besides height, pigmies is what they relatively were, when seen beside the colossus of Michael Jordan. Evidently he wasn't even trying very hard, but he ran and soared and made graceful plays (and *squeaked*), always with the ball somehow miraculously adhering to his horizontally outstretched palm.

And there was statistical evidence for his supremacy, if you don't believe me. In the course of the final against Olympiakos Piraeus, which the Bulls won by 104 points to 78, Jordan was responsible for 27 points, scoring 11 field goals for 22 of them. But I resent even writing this down, to be honest, because the thing I hated most about basketball was that it was all about numbers. The clock ticked down, the points ticked up, statistics kept pressing themselves on your attention. And all the while that maddening damn music played, driving you out of your mind. I found myself adding the number of Jordan's defensive rebounds to the number of his offensive rebounds, just because it seemed the right thing to do. And I sat there pining for a good old straightforward game of footie. I remembered how an American friend had said an odd thing when I'd taken him to his first football match and apologised that there didn't seem to be a scoreboard. 'Will you be OK?' I'd said. And he had replied, somewhat scathingly, 'I think I can keep track of the number of *goals*.' Well, having watched the basketball, all was now explained.

The final game I didn't understand and didn't enjoy much either was rugby. This may come as a surprise, when all women are supposed to be fantastically turned on by the sheer heft of the rugby-playing physique, but I can only protest that a meaty male thigh shaped like an upended lightbulb has never done a thing for me. Naturally, I always felt bad about not warming to such an important national sport, played by amenable popular heroes who sometimes go on to become stars of reality television, but there was an insuperable obstacle to enjoyment in the case of rugby, which was to do with the plain fact that, as far as I could see, it was a game that no one watching it fully understood, because that would entail having the mystic ability to read the mind of the ref.

Every few seconds the game would stop for one side or other to be penalised. No one could tell you why. 'Oooooh, offside, probably,' they sometimes said, but it was clear they were bluffing. Isn't this a basic flaw in a spectator sport? Shouldn't something be done? I loved the atmosphere at rugby matches, and could appreciate the toughness of the players, but it drove me nuts that the game turned so often (and so significantly) on rulings that were accepted by all and sundry as unfathomable. You just have to trust the ref, you see. I saw one game between England and Italy in a downpour in Huddersfield where there were 47 penalties. Forty-seven. In 80 minutes. What was that all about? But no one else minded. 'I played rugby myself for years and I still don't understand it!' the chaps said, whenever I asked what the hell had happened now. In football, when a player commits a foul and a free kick is given, one knows who to blame and can even evaluate the damn-fool reasoning that made him do it. In rugby, there's a load of pushing and then a whistle is blown. What did the ref see? What happened? Will we ever be allowed to know? The fact that the players always obey the ref in rugby is significant, I think. Because my suspicion is, they don't have a clue about what's going on either, which leaves them no grounds for objection. Only the ref knows what has occurred. The entire effing game is played for the benefit of its officiator.

Nowadays at least the referee wears a microphone and is obliged to explain himself for the benefit of people watching at home. One hears him telling players which rule they've infringed; he dresses down 20-stone giants as if they were 11-year-olds, saying he doesn't want to see any more of that kind of nonsense, does he make himself clear? Thus, I suppose, the true star of the show is duly acknowledged – but it surely makes things even worse for people in the crowd. In my day the ref had to perform internationally-recognised hand gestures to signal his reasons, so if you could be bothered to study his body language, you stood a (small) chance of interpreting fragments of mime. But they weren't self-evident, I must say. Peering through binoculars, one would discover the ref gesturing with open palms, fingers pointing downwards. What did that mean? Well, what it looked like was 'Oops, I dropped my tray.' There was another gesture I spotted that involved stroking one hand up and down the inside of the opposite arm, as if to say, 'And I still can't get rid of this rash.' A third seemed to involve the miming of setting doves free ('Fly, my little one!'). None of this was helpful in following the game.

In 1999, of course, there was the rugby World Cup. I expected it to win me over, but it didn't. I got quite bored, and I wasn't the only one. It was generally thought to have been too drawn-out, to lack drama, and to lack much decent offensive play. Plus England got knocked out in Paris by that South African with the golden boot, and the final between Australia and France at Cardiff was largely boycotted by the disappointed Welsh (the crowd was top-heavy with South Africans and Kiwis who had booked their seats in a state of hubris). The memorable result of this mix-up was that Shirley Bassey (star of the pre-match entertainment) had to walk to her little stage in virtual silence, when she had come out of the players' tunnel with her arms out, expecting wild, spectacular applause. The Millennium Stadium hadn't been quite ready in time, and the pitch got scabby. In short, there were many reasons to complain. Personally, I don't remember the details of a single match I saw – and I went to five, including the South Africa–Australia semi-final at Twickenham and the final. I just remember yelling 'Pass it wide!' miserably, week after week, at chaps who knew more about it than I did. 'Why don't they pass it wide?'

As an outsider, I felt that the rules of rugby would definitely benefit from simplification (how about having fewer players?). It also occurred to me that an excellent England reply to the New Zealand or South Sea Island *haka* would be a rendition of the Birdie Song. Nowadays the boys stare it down while the crowd sings 'Swing Low, Sweet Chariot' to drown it out. But I still think a camp disco routine originating in the 1980s (with arm flapping) would be a great deal more effective in taking the wind out of their sails.

Cricket

Among sports writers, it is generally agreed that the worst sport to cover is cricket. This has nothing to do with the game itself, just the life-destroying way in which it's organised, with a national team on tour to the Indian subcontinent for weeks on end, or to the Antipodes, or the West Indies. Such extended periods of travel in exotic lands sound lovely in theory, but it's an unusual marriage that can survive so many lengthy separations, and divorce is common. One of the big flash-points in the married lives of all sports writers must, I reckon, be the issue of holidays. Once international travel becomes a mere necessary evil, it's hard to think of it as a source of pleasure. Moreover, once you have been *everywhere in the world*, the main attractions of marriage and family are bound to be exclusively hearth-related. The end result is that the wife and kids stand no chance whatever of being taken abroad by you.

'I fancy the Caribbean,' says the wife, wistfully.

'Really?' huffs the sports writer. 'Do you know what I fancy? I fancy sitting in the garden with this cup of tea.'

'It's a long time since I had an exotic rum-based drink,' sighs the wife.

'It's a long time since I had a cuddle with the dog,' comes the unanswerable reply.

The wife's chin wobbles. She gathers her children to her skirts and surreptitiously waves a freshly-peeled onion under their noses, so that tears stream down their little cheeks.

'It would be really nice to stay in a hotel for once,' she sobs (she and the children have slept in their own beds every night for the past five years).

'Well, send me a postcard when you get there.'

'We all think you're being very selfish!' says the wife.

'*I'm* being selfish?' he yells.

And so on, and so on, predictably, until the chap finds himself back in the press box in the Windward Islands, staring at his decree nisi and a tattered photo of his kids, sipping his tenth exotic rum-based drink of the day, dreading his hotel, and calculating on the back of an envelope how much of his salary will be left over to rent a small room in Bucks after all the alimony and school fees have been extracted from it at source.

Obviously I was not in this kind of fix myself. While I was sports writing I had a nice boyfriend who was very supportive of the enterprise. The longest I was away was five weeks in France in 1998. Since the boyfriend lived in Yorkshire and I lived in Brighton, he particularly approved of all the northwards driving I was obliged to keep doing. 'I've got Elland Road next week,' I'd say, and he'd be jolly pleased and start tidying. He often told my friends and

relations the droll story of how I had asked him specifically, when we first met, whether he was interested in sport,
and had said 'Thank God' when he said he wasn't. I realised
that this was his way of pointing out, ever so tactfully, that
he had initially signed up for a literary and quite feminine
sort of girlfriend who had turned, overnight, into this
fixated sports fan who argued with strangers in pubs about
the future for English goalkeeping. I did feel bad about
this unlooked-for transformation, of course. I did worry –
more for his sake than mine, really – that I was turning
into a bloke.

However, the funny thing is, even knowing all this
recipe-for-a-dismal-life stuff, if I had my time again, I
reckon it's cricket I would go for, because it doesn't take
much to see that cricket is by far the most rewarding game
in the long run. It's not just that, being generally stringy
and long of limb, the cricketer conforms to my personal
taste in athletic frames (Australia's lanky Glenn McGrath
embodying the ideal). It's that every match has potential
for an enormous and fascinating range of outcomes. The
way the game unfolds is simply more interesting than
anything else offered by sport. It is designed to reward
thought. Maybe it's the drugs I've been taking for this
cold, but it seems to me there is a solid-geometry aspect
to cricket: every development alters the three-dimensional
shape of the game, turns it inside out, flips it round. Ricky
Ponting is bowled for 23 (say), and the cubic limits of the
possible have to adjust themselves so quickly and radically
that you can almost feel the draught. On top of that, from
an atavistic point of view, cricket is the spectacle of one
lonely bloke at the crease, staunchly facing down a whole

pack of eleven other blokes, who surround him and his currently powerless partner like hungry hyenas and have no other purpose than to wear him out and tear him down. But hark at me. A woman who can't tell her deep square leg from her third man, or her extra cover from her backward point. Stop mainlining the Night Nurse, that's probably the answer. Stop taking that Night Nurse at once.

While I was on duty for Sport, there was a Test series visit from the Australians in 1997, plus the 1999 cricket World Cup. The World Cup was marked by some stupendous, epic one-day games, and also (sadly) by some quite remarkable post-match pitch invasions. These took the edge off some of the victories, I thought. The players were never able to clap each other on the back and enjoy the moment, because at the second the words 'That's it' were spoken, they had to pull the stumps and sprint to the pavilion, dodging and slipping through a great crowd of spectators charging the other way. I happened to go to the theatre one night in the middle of the tournament, and at the resonant curtain line ('Go, bid the soldiers shoot'), I felt a momentary impulse to duck under my seat, on the assumption that the audience would dash on stage and steal all the props while the actors fled for safety to the dressing rooms.

But the excitement of the crowds at the cricket World Cup was certainly understandable. Aside from the weird non-event of the final between Australia and Pakistan at Lord's (a dodgy business which has never been fully accounted for, in my view), it had all kinds of carnival atmosphere, all kinds of last-over drama, a bit of unseasonal sunshine (it was held in May and June), and some passionate cricketers excelling themselves all over the country and in all areas of the game. The cricketer who made the biggest impression on me, I remember, was the young, scowling, skinny and fascinating Pakistani fast bowler Shoaib Akhtar. This was before Shoaib was officially classed the fastest bowler in the world, but even an ignoramus could see (as she tried not to swoon) that he wasn't exactly a slowcoach; also that his technique earned his team great results, and that he had magnificent nostrils.

I was sent to several matches, the first a supposed 'warm-up' match at Hove between South Africa and Sussex which was rained off completely, and was not a good start. True, I met a lot of very nice South African cricket writers who talked lark dis, and I learned how to use a tricky, newfangled hot drinks machine in the press area – a life skill that has subsequently stood me in good stead. But in terms of raising excitement for the upcoming tournament, there was nothing. Covers were rolled up and then unrolled again. Men in blazers stood under umbrellas with their arms outstretched. Children played baby cricket on the outfield. Spectators stayed shivering in their seats because their bottoms kept the seats dry (there are few things more demoralising in life than getting up for a bit of a walk-round and coming back to a wet seat). There was a smell of beer and chips. I spent the day mostly under cover, fishing for information about the South African team (among them Allan Donald, Shaun Pollock, Hansie Cronje, Herschelle Gibbs) and getting a bit transfixed by the name Lance Klusener for the shamefully irrelevant reason that it reminded me of 'Lars Porsena of Clusium' from the once popular reciting poem by Macaulay about Horatius holding the bridge, with its famous thumping rallying cry, 'Who will stand at my right hand,/And keep the bridge with me?'

My mother had recited parts of 'Horatius' to me when I was a child – usually when I was ill in bed and too weak to stop her – and it had made an impression. Neither of us knew who 'Lars Porsena of Clusium' might have been, incidentally, and all I know now is that he was a first-century Etruscan whose fabled attempt to invade Rome was turned back by the equally fabled heroism of Horatius. But it's a name that can truly stick in the mind when it comes in the first line of such excellent verse.

> Lars Porsena of Clusium
> By the Nine Gods he swore
> That the great house of Tarquin
> Should suffer wrong no more.
> By the Nine Gods he swore it,
> And named a trysting day,
> And bade his messengers ride forth,
> East and west and south and north,
> To summon his array.

As things were later to turn out for the staunch Lance Klusener, the poem about Horatius holding the bridge all on his own (while it was destroyed around him) got more and more relevant as time went on. But this is to get ahead of ourselves.

My second match was England v South Africa on a pleasantly warm Saturday at The Oval. You may remember this occasion. It was a bit like Armageddon. Sports fans never quite prepare themselves for outcomes as horrifying as this one was. We go along cheerfully thinking we know the extent of what can occur ('We won the toss, tiddly-pom; what can go wrong, tiddly-pom'), and end up screaming, 'Make it stop! For God's sake, make it stop!' The thing was, England opted to bowl first, then had a hard time making any headway against the opening batsmen (Kirsten and Gibbs had reached 111 runs before the first wicket fell), but then did a fair job keeping the South Africa total down to 225 for seven. Mullally bowled Kallis for a duck; Pollock (admittedly batting at eight) was out to Darren Gough first ball. I noticed that my new best friend Klusener was not out for 48. Apparently he was a terrific all-rounder, this stolid, sandy, bun-faced chap. He also spoke Zulu. He got more interesting all the time.

But I soon wished I hadn't known about that Zulu connection, because what happened next was pretty much the story of Rorke's Drift. England's openers Nasser Hussain and Alec Stewart went out (which in cricket should strictly be 'went *in*') and came staggering back almost immediately, in a state of dumb shock, with the cricketing equivalent of six-foot spears sticking out of their chests. We watched in horror. They had got only two runs between them. Stewart had got none at all – and he was the captain! And from then on, well, it was a scene of carnage, basically. A classic, humiliating batting catastrophe. With terrific efficiency, the South African bowlers got the whole side out for 103 in 41 overs, the highest individual scores coming from Graeme Hick and Neil Fairbrother, who each clocked up a measly 21. It was Fairbrother I felt most sorry for on the day, despite his relative success with the bat. His honourable longevity at the wicket meant he had to watch at close range while, sickeningly, Hick fell, and then Flintoff, then Croft, then Gough. To adapt the famous line, he counted them all in, and he counted them all out again. Such a waste of young life, he must have thought. (Or alternatively, I suppose, what a bunch of tossers.)

My next match was quite an oddity, again involving South Africa. For reasons lost to history, the Kenya–South Africa first-round match was played in Amsterdam, which was more than a bit surreal. 'Which way to the cricket?' is the sort of question that, in Holland, makes people assume you've been at the dodgy fags again. But it was true. In Amstelveen (a leafy suburb, with rustling trees) there was a serviceable cricket ground where a match could be played in an exceptionally laid-back atmosphere, if you know what I mean. 'TEST STATUS FOR HOLLAND NOW' said a hopeful sign, and it got quite a few appreciative laughs. Had there not been a local transport strike that day (oh yes), a few more spectators might have shown up. But there were 3,500 people there, which was fine. There was a curious but familiar scent on the breeze. I spent most of the day sitting next to the Duckworth-Lewis official – a graduate of Brainbox University with a slide rule and calculator whose job was to apply a complex mathematical formula in the event of rain stopping play. He was extremely entertaining, this Duckworth-Lewis man. We had a great time. But so did everyone in Amstelveen that day, I think, aside from the hapless Kenyan team. In the end, when the South Africans had won by seven wickets, we all said, 'Is it finished?' and then we said, 'Hang on, remind me where I am again,' and then we said, 'Seven wickets? Wow. That's like, I mean, wow, seven. *Seven*? That's like, wow.'

Obviously, the main feature of the day was its weirdness – partly because it was *de facto* weird, but also because it was May 26, 1999, a date that lives in the memory of many English football fans because it was on May 26, 1999 that Manchester United played Bayern Munich in Barcelona in the Champions League final. Naturally, passing the day in a peaceful woody enclave outside Amsterdam, I had a very clear sense of being in the wrong place for the wrong fixture. On the plus side, however, I knew that if I could only overcome the serious transport difficulties of getting back to my hotel in time (the late Ian Wooldridge and I exhausted all our combined ingenuity to achieve this, and it was still touch and go), I could watch the match in the evening in my room on Dutch TV. A nearby bar in the heart of Amsterdam would have been a better setting, but as usual my hotel was sterile and out-of-town and didn't have a nearby anything, so watching in the room would have to do. And the great thing was, I could have a beer or two and get into my jim-jams. Best of all, I wouldn't have to make notes, because no one was expecting me to write about it.

So I was just dancing round the room afterwards shouting 'Unbelievable, two goals in added time, amazing, what a very strange day, what a very, very, very strange day,' when my phone rang and the office said, 'Did you watch it?' And I said yes of course I'd watched it, what did they take me for, and by the way the pillows weren't halfway fluffy enough, if they really wanted to know. And they said, how about writing it up for the front of the paper? And I said, puzzled, 'You do remember I'm in Amsterdam, not Barcelona?' And they said patiently that they did know this, yes. 'I watched it in Dutch,' I explained. 'Yes, but football is an international language,' they reminded me. So I switched on the laptop and turned in 800 criminally under-informed words in about half an hour, with an especially sinking heart because I knew my piece was destined for the front of the paper, rather than the back.

Writing for News when you are a sports columnist, I should explain, is like laying your babies in front of a combine harvester and then having to look at their mangled bits and pieces prominently displayed in a national news-paper the next morning. In fact, it's worse than that, because the mangled bits are presented under your byline, in a manner to suggest you are the person responsible for them. If you tell a fellow sports writer that you are filing 'for the front', they pat you on the back and say they're sorry. But I couldn't really say no – or not after making the initial mistake of answering the mobile, anyway. In the piece I made it very clear that I was not in Barcelona, because I can't abide deception of that sort. But the news subs automatically stripped out all such irrelevant sticking-to-the-truth nonsense, so that the next day – at a literary event in Sussex – people asked me all about the match, convinced that I'd been our woman on the scene of sporting history, when in fact I'd been our woman in a deck-chair in the Netherlands, having a snooze in a glade.

Two or three days after Amsterdam, the scene was Edgbaston. Bowing to the inevitable, I nowadays found the hotel by going first to that woman's house in Redditch and letting her lead me in. India were playing England this time, and I'll save you the misery of suspense by admitting at once that, in a match spread over two days due to rain, India beat England by 63 runs. Again we failed to bowl out the opposing side in 50 overs. Again they got us all out, although Hussain survived 89 minutes and scored a paltry 33 (from 63 balls), but Stewart was out for two (from nine balls). This time, however, the stakes were a bit higher: with Zimbabwe beating South Africa elsewhere, against all the odds, England had needed to beat India to get through to the next stage of the competition (called the Super Sixes). Their failure to do this meant they left the competition. The remaining teams in the World Cup were Pakistan, Australia, South Africa, New Zealand, Zimbabwe and India.

After the match, David Lloyd, the England coach, accused his disgraced players of not standing up to be counted, but in the context of cricket it was a stunningly bad choice of metaphor. Cricketers are counted the whole bloody time, surely, and that's the very beauty of it. I had started to realise that the zen moment of cricket was the scoreboard set at *Total 0, For 0, Overs 0*. It was necessary to gaze at the board in that state, breathe deeply, and meditate. After that, once there were any numbers at all to look at (any numbers *at all*), one set about mentally dividing and subtracting and adding up – but whereas I disliked this aspect of basketball, I saw it as the great boon of cricket, perhaps because cricket gave you more time to do the calculations, and to ponder their significance for the game. The numbers told the story so far; they kept it completely alive in your mind; but they also teased you, led you on, tempted you to anticipate what was still to come. And the positive thing was, the mental activity was somehow its own reward, even when it confirmed that India were going to win this and you really might just as well get back to your tiny Dairylea-shaped room at the Edgbaston Thistle and set about sawing your head off.

For example, say your team has got 47 for two after 14 overs (in a 50-over match), and needs 233 to win. Forty-seven from 14 overs isn't much, is it? In fact it is a rather poor 3.35 runs per over. The team now needs 186 from 36, which works out at 5.16 runs per over. 'Is this poss?' you write on your notepad. 'Given measly 3.35 up to now?' Later, when the team is facing the reality of 118 for five from 31 overs, you do the calculation again. The run rate has improved slightly (to 3.8) but they now need just over six runs per over, which would be a jolly fine thing, but only in a flying-pig kind of way, given their record so far. At Edgbaston on those two fateful days the situation got steadily worse, until the figure required was nine or ten per over, and it was officially hopeless. The last men standing were Gough, Mullally and Fraser (all bowlers). Ultimately, there was no escaping the maths.

While England was folding to India, we watched the scoreboard for the Zimbabwe–South Africa game with considerable alarm – especially when it started off with: 0 for 1 off 0.1, which looked at first glance like binary code, but in fact meant that a South African batsman had been dismissed with the very first ball of the match.

We kept looking, and we couldn't believe our eyes. After 7.3 overs, they were 25 for three. After 8.2 overs, they were 25 for four. In the 12th over, they were 34 for five, then 40 for six! Those bastard South Africans were shafting us again – but this time by pretending they didn't know how to bat! Klusener would have no part of this rotten strategy, I was relieved to see. He was not out for 52. But on the other hand, in Zimbabwe's innings he had taken only one wicket from nine overs, which was piffle by his usual high standards.

On Thursday June 17, 1999, the second semi-final of the cricket World Cup took place between South Africa and Australia at Edgbaston, and I was there. A shiver runs up my back as I type those words, because it was the great match of the tournament and one of the best things I ever saw. Australia had finished fractionally higher than South Africa in the Super Six stage of the competition (it was a tiny matter of run rate), which meant that in the extremely unlikely event of a dead heat, they would go through to the final. They had also met South Africa already, just a few days before, at Headingley, and beaten them in a very close game. Steve Waugh, the Australian captain, had notched up 120 runs on that day – helped by a famous dropped catch. Herschelle Gibbs has apparently never lived down the fact that he fumbled and dropped the catch that made that century possible. 'Mate, you just dropped the World Cup,' Waugh is supposed to have said to Gibbs, by way of manly comfort. Interestingly, however, he has always insisted that he didn't.

It was a variable day, sunshine-wise. At the start, when Australia went in to bat, there was no sun. On a

241

shadowless and heavy sort of pitch, they lost Mark Waugh almost immediately (for a duck from four balls), but then Gilchrist and Ponting got 50 fairly comfortable runs between them, making them 54 for one from 13 overs. At this point, of course, it was too early to extrapolate from these figures the likely outcome of the match, although naturally it was tempting. Then Allan Donald – wearing a fetching war-paint combination of Breathe-Right plaster on his nose and ghastly white zinc sun protection on his thick lower lip – bowled his first over, and shook things up considerably. Off the first ball of the 14th over, Ponting was caught by Kirsten; off the last, Lehmann was caught behind. So, suddenly, Australia were 58 for three from 14 overs, which looked a bit wobbly; but on the other hand, Steve Waugh was coming on, which looked great. I mean, it's all very well for batsmen to survive and protect their wickets, but when overs are limited they have to score runs as well, surely – if you'll pardon me for being controversial. As I may have mentioned, cricket is a terribly thought-provoking game.

So Australia just needed to dig in for a bit and get some runs – which is largely what happened. True, Gilchrist bought it in the 17th over (caught by Donald, off Kallis), but since this brought the excellent Michael Bevan to the crease, it turned out to be quite a good thing. The usually devastating Gilchrist had been in for ages, but had scored only 20 runs, so was the cricketing equivalent of a bed blocker, in my view (see highly original runs-v-wicket argument above). With the sun out now, Steve Waugh and Bevan steadily pushed up the total to 158 – but by this time 39 overs had been used up, so it wasn't spectacular. In the 40th over, Waugh was out for 56 (caught behind off Pollock), and Australia seemed to be in trouble again. Suddenly that score looked a bit weak. 158 for five off 39.3 overs? With just ten overs to go?

New batsman Tom Moody fell to Pollock in the same over as Steve Waugh. He went in; he stuck his leg in front of his wicket to stop the ball (novice mistake, surely); he was out again. Australia were now 158 for six, with ten overs to go, and were starting to look a bit pants – but that's how cricket goes, you see. Even those of us who have no direct experience of cinematography know all about the 'zoom in, dolly out' technique made famous by Steven Spielberg in *Jaws*, when he closed in on the face of Roy Scheider when someone shouted, 'Shark!' on the beach at Amity. The effect is that the subject remains in focus, and doesn't even get any bigger in the frame – but the background falls away, and it's like an attack of vertigo. A perceptual, grip-the-arm-of-the-seat 'zoom in, dolly out' thing happens umpteen times in the course of a dramatic cricket match. It happened when Tom Moody was dismissed for 0 in three balls. I mean to say, hang on, so that means 158 for *six*?

Bevan was still batting, of course. Shane Warne was the next man in. Between them, Bevan and Warne got 31 off 30 deliveries, but Warne was eventually caught in the 48th over by South Africa's captain Hansie Cronje, who performed a flying somersault to secure the ball – although he probably knew that, had he dropped it, he wouldn't have dropped the World Cup, because there were only two overs left. Warne had made 18 runs from 24 balls, which wasn't bad. His dismissal meant that Australia were 207 for seven, with only 12 balls left. Seven? Mm, suddenly there seemed to be more than enough Australians in reserve; in fact, one wondered whether they'd been a bit too careful with them. What were they saving them for? Christmas? But then Reiffel was bowled by Donald off the first ball of the 49th over, and Fleming followed just two balls later. Neither of them had scored a run. Good grief, it was so hard to know what to think. A little while ago the Australians were 207 for seven. Now they were 207 for *nine*. There were virtually no Australians left to come in. Just the willowy Glenn McGrath, in fact, who craftily took the first opportunity (without having struck the ball) of getting to the non-striker's end, thus putting Bevan in the firing line. Bevan upped the score to 213 and was then caught behind by Boucher (who did all the other catching behind for South Africa, by the way – I just didn't want to keep repeating that information).

So that was that for Australia's batsmen. All out for 213 in 49.2 overs. At this very interesting halfway point, it was *still* much too early to extrapolate from those figures anything remotely resembling the outcome of this match. You will notice I never mention fielding positions, incidentally; or types of delivery. 'It was a full toss driven to extra cover.' I just think it would sound bogus if I did.

With a target of 214 runs from 50 overs, the South Africans went in to bat. Kirsten and Gibbs – who you may remember notched up 111 together against England at The Oval before a wicket was lost – got settled in again. Wise heads were saying that such a low total was not one the Australians would try to defend. Instead, they would be going for wickets. However, they waited until the 13th over to bring on the brilliant leg-spinning wicket-taker

Shane Warne, which seemed a bit perverse, but probably had a perfectly good technical explanation involving advanced theories of propulsion, lateral revolution, flight and bounce. Or perhaps he had a headache. Anyway, with the score standing at 48 for 0, Warne came in to bowl, and got Gibbs out with his second ball. Shortly after this, in the 15th over, he bowled out Kirsten, and two balls later he got Cronje as well (caught by Mark Waugh for 0). Extrapolating from these figures, this looked like curtains for South Africa – or at least with Warney coming at them. They certainly looked quite shaken by what had happened. For a long period, Rhodes and Kallis stayed in together, raising the score to 145, but the play was nervy and there seemed to be countless dashes towards exploding stumps. In terms of the run rate, moreover, they were trailing their opponents. Rhodes was eventually caught in the 41st over, and I think most of us around this time opened our laptops with a little sigh of resignation and started to write our pieces about what a disappointingly one-sided semi-final this was. At which point Shaun Pollock went in and started to hit sixes and fours off Shane Warne.

I can't remember whether the sun was in or out by now. I think it was out. I think the temperature had risen considerably. But suddenly, with less than seven overs to go, the South African batsmen decided to make a fight of it. It was as if a bell had been rung for the final lap, or a signal had been flipped. Warne responded to Pollock's disrespectful slugging by getting Kallis out for 53; but Kallis was replaced by Klusener (batting at eight) – who took one run from Warne's last ball, and then a very confident four from the first ball from Fleming. *What was it about this man?* He had been man of the match on other occasions; he was destined to be man of the tournament. He lost his ideal batting partner when Pollock was yorked by Fleming in the 46th over, but he showed no sign of discomfort. He was Macaulay's Horatius, basically. Blokes might stand briefly on his right and left, but this keeping-the-bridge business would ultimately all be down to him.

The last three overs were pretty tense, to say the least. The South Africans needed 25 runs from 18 balls. Unfortunately Boucher was on strike, facing Fleming. Top priority was therefore to get himself out of the firing line and swap ends as quickly as possible. This didn't happen, agonisingly, until the fourth ball of the over. However, once it had been managed, the fifth ball was struck by Klusener for a four. The sixth was intercepted by Moody at the boundary, for a two. South Africa now needed 18 runs from 12 balls, and some of us in the press box could feel hot blood starting to leak out of our ears. There was something very special unfolding out there, but what? What? How was this going to turn out? With Klusener whacking fours about, 18 from 12 balls was achievable, but he was at the wrong end again now, with McGrath bowling the first two deliveries of the 49th over to the hapless Boucher, who succumbed to a yorker on the second!

South Africa were now 196 for eight, with only 10 balls left in the match. The number 9 batsman Elworthy went in to face McGrath. He got one run, putting Klusener back on strike. Good man. I think I even wrote down, 'Good man, Elworthy.' Then Klusener opted to take two runs (this being a sensible even number, which would mean he kept the strike) and Elworthy was taken by surprise by the second and was run out by McGrath! I promptly crossed out 'Good man' and wrote 'Git' instead. How could he not realise that they had to go for two runs? There were an anxious couple of minutes while the third umpire ruled on the run-out, because from some angles it looked as though McGrath had caught the ball all right, but had maybe knocked the bails off with his hand. But the third umpire finally ruled that Elworthy was out – which was just as well, as the player had already returned to the pavilion and taken his pads off. With South Africa needing 16 from eight, Allan Donald (the last man) replaced him at the wicket. Did Donald make a mental note, 'Don't get run out like the last bloke, eh?' We shall never know. McGrath bowled to Klusener and he belted it high and long, right over the head of Reiffel at the boundary rope, who parried it but didn't catch it. It was a six! Bloody hell. Bloody, bloody hell. South Africa now needed 10 from seven. From the last delivery of McGrath's over, Klusener got a nifty single, to put himself in position to bat to victory.

It is the last over of the match, then. Six balls left in this semi-final. Nine runs required. The contents of our brains are starting to dribble out of our noses. I am pressing wads of tissue to all the orifices of my head. Fleming bowls to Klusener, and he smashes it as if he were playing base-ball. It's a four. *A four!* All one can do is whimper, watch it fly, absorb the cheering, and keep trusting the Kleenex. The second ball is bowled and Klusener drives it hard and long to the boundary for *another four*. Oh my God, oh my God. The scores are now tied, and the South Africans require one run to win. They have four deliveries to do it from. But they have no more wickets, you see. There's the rub. No. More. Wickets. And it is *still* not possible to extrapolate from these figures the outcome of the game. Requiring one run from four balls, Klusener mis-hits the third delivery of the over and decides not to run. It is at this point that we notice, with alarm, that Donald, at the other end, has been anticipating a run, and has therefore 'backed up' (i.e. jumped the gun) by a considerable distance. Oh no. On realising his mistake, he scrambles back to safety with bat outstretched, and is saved only when the rolled ball misses the base of the stumps. Laughing hysterically with relief, one reflects on what a dick-head Donald must feel at this moment. Imagine getting run out in these circumstances, Allan, with the scores dead level. How would you ever forgive yourself?

And now we are down to the last three balls of the match. Fleming bowls to Klusener, who whacks it – and runs. This is it! This is it! Klusener is running for the match! But for some reason, Donald is going backwards again. Why on earth isn't he running? What is he playing at? This is a fucking nightmare. Run, mate! Fucking run! As Klusener reaches his end of the pitch, Donald visibly realises, Oh hang on, where did he come from? Better make a start. He is like that Great Dane I saw at the dog agility championship making up his mind to attempt the slalom through the bendy poles. 'Yep, all right, I'll do that.' But he's much too late. Having already dropped his bat, he abandons it and moves off, but by the time he's covered a quarter of the distance, the Australians have already run him out and are celebrating their astonishing hair's-breadth escape from defeat with their backs turned firmly towards this lonely, stranded, batless figure dressed in green. No one can believe what they've just witnessed. Débâcle is the only word for it. It might have been a famous victory; instead it is a débâcle of horrifying proportions. Klusener has left the field already. At the end of his run, he just kept on walking. It is the most desperately ghastly ending to a World Cup match ever.

It is cricket, though. That's what they all say. It is, quintessentially, cricket.

As you can tell from reading between the lines of the above, I know nothing whatever about cricket. And this is one of my bigger regrets. During the thrilling 2005 Ashes series in England, I actually pined to be back in the press box – an emotion that really took me by surprise. I felt seriously envious. My friend Gideon Haigh – talented and prolific cricket writer from Melbourne – was here to cover the series for the *Guardian*, so was on the spot for every delivery, and I couldn't quite cope with the idea that I wasn't there too. He would tell me who he'd been sitting next to, and I'd snivel, lamely, 'I know him.' In the end, I consoled myself at home in front of the telly by sending nuisance texts to Gideon at moments of high tension. He would be concentrating on unfolding events, tirelessly tapping out his blog with one hand, making notes of scores with the other, and he'd get a text from me that said, 'What about Pietersen then?' In the introduction to his bestselling *Ashes 2005*, Gideon thanks me for letting him use my flat in London and says generously that I 'lived every ball' of the series. He knew this to be true, because his phone went 'beep-beep, beep-beep' every bloody ten minutes when he was trying to do some work.

I could imagine Gideon being exemplary in the press box. He would be in his element as I never was. In most cricket press boxes, I had no idea how to behave. They are very much smaller and quieter places than footie ones, which makes them more sociable, but at the same time made me more self-conscious. There is less representation from the tabloids, which also has an effect. At the risk of over-simplifying (and getting it entirely wrong), cricket writers are generally quite tall, very amusing, a bit Aspergers, and well informed on highbrow topics such as art and music. They are also utterly pampered, compared with the writers covering rougher sports – being allowed to sit under cover, behind plate glass, and being supplied with regular trays of food. I was at a match sponsored by Benson & Hedges once, and someone came in and gaily tossed free packets of fags to all corners of the press box. This wasn't even a surprise: one bloke said, 'They were a bit late with the Bensons today,' as he stuffed a few packs into his briefcase. But, congenial as all this ought to have been, I didn't relax at the cricket and have chats about Mahler with these tall and amusing men, for the simple reason that I couldn't: sadly, I needed to concentrate much harder than everyone else just to follow the game. In fact I panicked if anyone tall and amusing started telling me a joke or something, because it might mean I'd miss some subtle development on the pitch, such as a wicket falling, or a legendary diving catch at deep backward square leg, or England being all out (again) for 76.

What a tragedy. What a waste. Most of the matches I attended were big enough to have commentary on the radio, so that put the tin lid firmly even on listening to other people's conversation. From start of play, I sat studiously with my earphones in, and with a trusty, dog-eared diagram of fielding positions open in front of me. And I listened very carefully, matching the description to the reality, checking that it all made sense. This isn't what radio commentaries of cricket matches are for, of course: they are meant to supply the pictures for people who can't be present for some reason – the ideal listener would be a lonely lighthouse-keeper in the Azores, his ear pressed gratefully to the patrician tones emanating from the tinny speaker while grey waves crash against the rocks below ('Shoaib Akhtar runs up, he bowls, and good heavens, I don't know about you, Johnners, but I've never seen nostrils like it!'). Listening to this stuff when the game is actually spread out right in front of you is a bit strange, especially when you're aware that the broadcasters are upstairs in the same building, probably less than ten feet away, observing precisely the same view. But I loved it. When the commentator said Tendulkar had cut the ball to Twose at deep square leg, I could look at where the ball was going, then consult the diagram, then hold the diagram up the other way, then check it was indeed Twose who was occupying deep square leg, and then think, 'Right. Got that. Phew.' I performed this lame sequence of actions for every ball of the match – and I mean that. I did it for every ball. I felt it was important just to keep track, you see. I knew that keeping track of cricket was the very limit of what I was capable of doing.

* * *

When I gave up sports writing, it was partly because I was ready to face facts: I was never going to get any better at this. With cricket, I would always have to consult that diagram of fielding positions, and lean on *Test Match Special*. Looking at the disposition of the fielders (three chaps close together at one o'clock, two o'clock and three o'clock; one chap on his own over there at a quarter past seven), I wouldn't have the first idea how a captain might have chosen it – to suit either the style of a bowler or even the orientation of the batsman. On a simpler level, I watched umpteen men explain spin bowling, but it still looked like witchcraft. I have just opened my (signed) copy of *Shane Warne: My Own Story* (1997) and discovered that every page has underlinings and little comments, showing my frustration at still not understanding how spin bowling was done. Next to the words, 'I bowled a maiden first up and gathered some confidence. They were landing where I wanted them to land,' I have written in pencil, 'I want him to describe *bowling*.' Next to his words, 'I tried a flipper to Richie and it just came out of the hand perfectly,' I have written, 'Oh good. *HOW?*' But it's not all criticism, you will be relieved to hear. When Warney explains that young blokes on the team should 'earn their way up the auto-graph bat' – i.e. not sign at the top when they haven't played as much as the others – I have written a thoughtful 'interesting'.

But the main reason I could never feel comfortable about cricket is that there is clearly no substitute for a lifetime of enthusiasm. It can't be faked or mugged up, no matter how many times you pick up C.L.R. James or Neville Cardus, or struggle to find humour in Siegfried

Sassoon's famous description of the Flower Show Match. This stuff has to go deep, you see. And for me, it doesn't. When they open me up after death, they will find no Test scores carved on my heart – and they won't find any stored in my brain either. I have no personal memories of Don Bradman or Fred Trueman, or even (really) Ian Botham, except as a fairly controversial TV personality doing ads for Shredded Wheat. On my first trip to Headingley in 1997, chaps filled me in on the famous events of 1981 and it was honestly the first time I'd heard of them. No wonder I was more comfortable with football. With football, a sense of history is so unimportant as to be virtually meaningless. No one seriously sits around comparing the achievements of (say) Alan Shearer and Jackie Milburn; or Fernando Torres and Kenny Dalglish. They can usually tell you how long it's been since they won the league, or the Cup, but that's different. That's about showing off how much they've suffered. 'Eighteen years, mate! Can you imagine? Eighteen bloody years!'

I keep thinking of a friend I had twenty years ago, who used to complain about her cricket-loving husband. Apparently the only books she ever saw him reading were yellow-jacketed, quite thick, and had the word 'Wisden' on them – and it annoyed her very much. She was in despair at his monomania and general dullness. 'He even reads old *Wisden*s in bed!' she said. 'He reads old *Wisden*s in the bath! He has old *Wisden*s in the car!' In those old days I was firmly on her side. I think I used to advise her to kill him. Nowadays, however, I feel nothing but sympathy and warmth for this poor, hounded chap. It wasn't his fault.

One of the attractions of cricket, surely, is that it requires a lot of thinking about afterwards. In fact it's a sport that largely takes place after it's finished, in the splendid and reassuring comfort of the inside of one's head.

Football Again and the
Necessity of Weeping

In September 2000, I decided to stop sports writing for *The Times*. I phoned them up, I said I was sorry, and I jacked it in. There seemed to be no alternative. I felt I was on the edge of a nervous breakdown, and that if I had to argue with just one more man with just one more clipboard, I might start screaming and hitting – and then I'd end up in court, or in a mental hospital, or on a park bench with a bottle in a brown paper bag, and no job was worth that, not even one that other people would kill you for. But what on earth could have precipitated this sense of – well, precipice? I know what you're thinking. It was England's poor performance in Euro 2000. It was bloody Gary Neville. But no. Depressing though the Euro 2000 England campaign assuredly was, my reasons for quitting my job and burrowing under a duvet for the next two years were not connected with sport. The short explanation, which cannot be avoided, is that my sister died. I apologise for not mentioning this before. The right moment never seemed to come up. Kay, my only sister (indeed, my only sibling), was diagnosed with inoperable lung cancer at the start of the rugby World Cup in 1999 (I was on a bus coming home from a launch with the All Blacks when she told me on the phone), and she died less than a year later on the morning of Sunday September 24, 2000, on Day Nine of the Sydney Olympics. I can be so specific about what was concurrent in the world of sport because, the evening before, I had assured my boss that I would definitely be OK on that Sunday morning to file my usual 900 words about the BBC coverage of the weightlifting (or whatever) before setting off for the hospice.

'What a shame you missed the Olympics,' one of the other sports writers said to me, rather tactlessly, a couple of months later, at the Christmas party. I had been accredited for Sydney, you see. I had been due to go. My sister had even ghoulishly promised not to die till I got back. But I had wrestled with the dilemma and finally decided it is a good thing to be at the deathbed of one's closest relative if you can manage it, even when there is the alternative of being on the opposite side of the planet watching fireworks. And so I cast the whole idea from my mind. Four years later, in 2004, I was invited to Melbourne for book promotion purposes, which meant that my publisher needed to apply for an Australian visa. 'Well, that was a waste of time,' they reported back. 'You've already got one. Why didn't you say?' I was at a loss to explain it. How did I have a visa? I had never been to Australia. I had never planned to go. For a week or two I entertained paranoid fantasies that someone had stolen my identity – and then I remembered the Olympics. Missing the fabulousness of Sydney 2000 had clearly not been a festering regret, then. Four years later, I had forgotten that it had ever been on the cards that I should go.

In any case, I didn't miss the Olympics in Sydney. I watched them with a great deal of grim emotional intensity at home. Other people may think they have a special raw, racking, sobbing connection to the sight of a coxless four from Great Britain taking the gold by the tiniest of margins, but let me tell them they don't have the first idea of the feelings it can evoke. Kay and I watched the games in the night together, when she couldn't face going to bed. In the early hours I would drive to my mother's to sleep; then I would wake up to the BBC coverage in the mornings. And so the Sydney Olympics framed the long days in the worst week of my life. I found solace in them, and I also hated them. I wanted them to stop and I also wanted them to go on for ever, because I didn't think Kay would survive them. Every morning I would start work to the accompaniment of Heather Small's anthemic song 'Proud' – 'I step out of the ordinary; I can feel my soul ascending.' And I would cry and cry for my poor helpless sister with her oxygen cylinder and her gasping terror of death. And then I'd pull myself together, and set about suppressing all these distracting howling feelings – pegging them down and flattening them and burying them – in order to deliver lively stuff on deadline about (say) that plucky non-swimmer from Equatorial Guinea who took almost two minutes to complete 100 metres in effortful doggy-paddle and soon became immortalised as Eric the Eel.

When Kay died on the Sunday morning, I think my boss was the first person I called, to tell him I was sorry to let him down. A few days later, I asked if I could leave. I had no idea how I would make a living. In terms of remuneration, sports writing was the best job I'd ever had: ditching my contract to stay at home and write radio scripts was madness. But there was no way I could go on, if only because the screaming and hitting scenario was not far-fetched at all. It had been a very stressful year, what with one thing and another, and I was already dangerously close to losing control. One of the bonuses of bereavement, I have learned, is that it makes you honest. It strips you of the lies you usually tell yourself, so you have no choice but to face facts. What I saw with great clarity at this critical time was that the press box at Stamford Bridge would be the wrong environment for me to grieve in, because it was the wrong place for me to be in, full stop. I was only there on sufferance. No one would miss me. Even after four years, friendly faces were few. And while I was in this mood for cards-on-the-table, the other points I made (to myself) at the time were:

You have a lot of other work to get on with;
This comfortless masculine lifestyle never suited you and it was sheer masochism to endure it for so long;
The sporting calendar is on a perpetual loop and will steal your life if you're not careful;
All this crying and sobbing will do no good at all to the cause of women sports writers if you do it in front of the blokes;
You have coarsened as a person because of this job;
You don't really believe sport is a subject worth devoting your life to; and, finally:
A joke's a joke.

My boss was extremely kind about all this. He had seen it coming. What I said earlier about sports editors having hearts of stone – perhaps I was hasty. But what argument could he possibly put up against grief? Here was an undeniable obstacle to business as usual. What use is a funny writer who has, overnight, stopped finding things amusing? What use is a football writer who thinks football is meaningless, that sport is meaningless, and that life itself doesn't have a lot of point in the long run, either? No, the truth was, I was no longer prepared to be a good sport – about football, or about anything that went with it. I didn't have the strength. For four years I had turned anything unpleasant into a joke at my own expense. I had suppressed my hatred for hooligans singing obscene songs. I had tried not to make a hysterical scene when, at important matches, my colleagues got tickets, while I was put on a waiting list. I had stopped my ears when blokes talked freely in my company about the sexual rapacity of the women they'd picked up the night before. I had even made entertaining copy out of the miserable fact that the only entertainment for the lone professional traveller involves lapdancing and blowjobs. I had tried not to blame anyone else for the fact that I often shook with fear as I set off in the dark for my car in some alien industrial wasteland. But enough was, finally, enough.

For obvious reasons, though, it was the life-and-death argument that was the most powerful. How can you waste your time on sport in a world that people die in? I kept remembering something that had happened during the football World Cup in France, when I'd dashed back to England to see my mum in hospital, after she'd been involved in a bizarre accident. The paper had been terrific: organising tickets so I could get back on Eurostar and then fly back to France the following day, so that I didn't miss a match, and didn't miss a piece either (I was in the paper every day of the tournament). But I'll never forget how I felt when I got the news that my mum had been hurt. I had just got settled in my seat at a damp and dreary Parc des Princes in Paris, for an evening game between the USA and Germany, and I was already feeling pretty fragile – mainly because the journey to the stadium had been like something from a Coen Brothers movie. Against my better judgement (my *Times* colleague had thought it was a fine idea), I had agreed to accept a lift from an unknown fellow British journalist who promptly set off the wrong way round the Périphérique and then made matters worse by shouting things like, 'We're going to be late! Where are we? I've never been to the Parc des Princes, have you? It's got to be this way, doesn't it? Do you know where it is? Oh my God, we're going to be late!'

It was one of the worst journeys of my life. It was pouring with rain. Kick-off time was indeed approaching. We were travelling in the opposite direction from our preferred destination, at considerable speed, and I was apparently in thrall to a psychopath. I kept wondering whether I would ever have sufficient nerve to open the door of a moving vehicle and hurl myself out. My colleague and I dared not look at each other – especially as I had made a strong case for taking the media bus, which was a mere ten-minute ride in the safe hands of a French person who knew the way. Passing motorcyclists thumped the side of the car because our driver was straddling lanes; at one point, he swung off the Périphérique onto a slip-road and slewed the car to a halt, parking across two lanes in the smoking rain so he could jump out and ask directions from the bewildered, emergency-stopped Parisian motorists he had just attempted to kill. And on top of all this, while he was driving he took calls from London on his mobile about his job for the evening – which he fielded with a great show of professional competence ('Five hundred by half time? All right, Kippo, leave it with me!'), after which he'd go to pieces. 'They want 500 by half time. How do you do that? What are they talking about? How can you do 500 words when it hasn't finished yet?' And all we could do was yell, 'Turn round! Turn round for pity's sake! We'll tell you everything you need to know if you'll just turn round!'

So I was rattled by this journey, and also by the usual teeth-grinding, shrugging-French-person waiting-list business. And then I got the call about my mum being in hospital, and suddenly everything else – especially the football – seemed bonkers. Luckily I was sitting next to the colleague who had shared the journey, and I felt he owed me something, so I told him what had happened. Having calmed down once I'd got my press ticket, you see, I had suddenly got a great deal more agitated again, and I felt I ought to explain why I kept standing up and sitting down again, and muttering and whimpering, when my attention ought to have been focused on the perfectly good World Cup match unfolding on real wet shiny grass just a few yards from where I was sitting. Jürgen Klinsmann was on excellent fairy-footed form, as it happens; the USA were gamely battling to compete; interestingly, there was a player on the US team who'd been naturalised as an American citizen just a week before the tournament, apparently, and spoke no English. But it was impossible to concentrate on the supremacy of the German goal-making machine when I knew my mum was all on her own, in pain, in hospital, hundreds of miles away. 'I shouldn't be here,' I moaned. 'My mum's in hospital and I'm at *football*? How did this happen to me? I shouldn't be here. I ought to go. I feel torn in half by this. How can I be at *football*?'

So we had a little heart-to-heart, this chap and I. And what he said, kindly, was that he absolutely understood how I was feeling. He had been there and done it. Moreover, something similar had probably happened to everyone else in this press box at some time or another. But what he said didn't cheer me up at all. Some of the blokes here had been abroad when their children were born, he said. Some had been abroad when their parents had died. Some had been reporting the second round of the Frisbee championships in Timbuctoo when their wives had gone off with the bloke next door. I said this was one of the saddest things I'd ever heard. But he said no, it was just the price of being a sports writer. He himself had missed his father's death, and then he had missed the funeral as well, because it all coincided with a busy time in the athletics calendar in the Far East. But such was life, you see. What was the point of beating yourself up, he said, about something that couldn't be helped?

But it's a well-known fact that human beings are quite shallow really, and that a sense of true proportion can never be maintained for longer than 90 seconds; thus, when you are depressed because a) your sister is terminally ill and b) against all that is holy, Gary Neville has been selected for England *again*, the two facts can loom equally large, and all you can do is observe this truth and accept it. The truth is that England, the football team (who are looking rather perky at the time of writing), had really started to get me down, to the point where I all but hated them. Everyone had warned me that watching England beat Holland 4–1 at Wembley from an airship on a balmy midsummer evening was not to be taken as a representative experience of supporting the national side. And, crikey, how right they were. Over the next four years I turned out for umpteen blizzardy qualifiers and friendlies as well as matches in the big tournaments, and I was for most of the time as miserable as sin. Having once walked in a Shearer Wonderland, I had now ceased to believe in that particular postal district; or only if it was a new name for one of the circles of everlasting torment. From being a neophyte Pollyanna, I was football disillusionment in human form. I had started off almost in love with David 'Safe Hands' Seaman. Towards the end of my period of duty watching England, someone cruelly referred to him as 'a piece of meat with eyes', and I not only laughed, I wished I'd thought of it first. As for Glenn Hoddle – well, to be honest, even now I can't hear his name mentioned without wanting to stab myself in the face with a pencil.

To be fair, I did see England play well a couple of times. People forget how fabulous they were at St Etienne against Argentina in the 1998 World Cup, for example. But by far the best performance I ever saw from them was a World

Cup qualifier in Rome against Italy in October 1997 – when England, miraculously, played like Italy and came away with a magnificent goalless draw. It was a night later famous for its tremendous pre-match tension, superlative midfield passing, reprehensible police violence, and Paul Ince running round with a bandage on his head so that (in Paul Gascoigne's famous description) he looked like a pint of Guinness. The two teams were battling for automatic qualification as winners of the group. England, at the top of the points table, required a draw, while Italy required a win. In advance of the match, no one was optimistic for England's chances. They remembered what had happened last time. In the previous qualifying match between the two countries, at Wembley, Hoddle had disastrously experimented with weedy Ian Walker in goal (ugh) and the lumbering Matt Le Tissier alongside Alan Shearer in attack, and Italy had won 1–0.

Neither Walker nor Le Tissier ever recovered from the ignominy of that night. In fact it was amazing afterwards that Le Tissier didn't do himself a mischief, so appallingly emphatic was the Wembley crowd's message to him that he was a useless, lazy lump of humanity who would do everyone a favour if he buggered off and died. It was like something out of *Nineteen Eighty-Four*: 75,000 people all turning the full force of their collective hatred onto one bloke, trying to shrivel him up on the pitch. Le Tissier was a large, low-bottomed and frankly sloth-like Southampton striker with a bad fringe who had been mooted for an England place for years, and whose record at the Dell was exemplary; but he hadn't played for his country in Euro 96, so some of us were rather pleased to see him given his chance to impress the fans, and were dismayed when, dismally, he didn't. There may have been a rocket up his bottom, but if there was, it failed to light. The result was that he made 75,000 personal enemies on the spot and for ever after took the blame for the defeat. Looking back on it a couple of years later, however – when one knew more about the weaselly psychology of Glenn Hoddle – one couldn't help thinking how convenient it was for the England manager that all responsibility for the loss of a crucial match could be laid at the door of this one poor abused dobbin-like player who simply disappointed on the day.

Anyway, back in Rome, Hoddle did surpass himself. As did the team. Wickedly, I would like to point out that the injured Alan Shearer was not playing on that glorious night. But for the time being, I will say no more about that. The team that lined up against Italy at the Stadio Olimpico was: David Seaman, Sol Campbell, Tony Adams, Gareth Southgate, David Beckham, Paul Gascoigne, David Batty, Paul Ince (captain), Graeme Le Saux, Teddy Sheringham and Ian Wright. You will notice that the midfield is quite strong in this line-up – but if you were the worrying sort, you might also notice its collective potential for temper, brainlessness under pressure, and alcoholic amnesia. In the week before the match, incidentally, Hoddle had fed rumours that young David Beckham was at death's door with the 'flu, and that Southgate might also be unfit to play, neither of which scare stories turned out to be based on more than a smidgen of truth. If there was one thing Glenn Hoddle enjoyed more than anything, it was making things up to confuse the opposition, even if it meant losing essential credibility with the fans and really getting on the tits of the football press.

I will outline my own experiences that night, just because they remain so vivid. For a start, I was not in the press box. *The Times* had set me up with some corporate hospitality, so I was a guest of Carlsberg, whose offer was to fly a party of fans to Rome, take us to the match, and treat us to a lavish dinner afterwards. This sounds extremely lovely-jubbly, I suppose – but wait. By now you are wise to the cautionary tale that invariably attaches itself to even the most wonderful treat where this ungrateful female wretch is concerned. So here's the beef. The problem was that the Carlsberg travel arrangements did not dovetail terribly well with my journalistic duties. Our flight to Rome was very early on the Saturday morning, and the match started quite late on the Saturday night (kick-off was 8.45 local time), and I was at no point in charge of my own destiny. Because of the return flying times, I would need to file copy by 11.30 on Sunday morning, from the hotel, without seeing any British papers, and (crucially) without the required technology. This being my first football assignment abroad, I had been issued with a brand new office laptop – but with some alarm I quickly established on arrival that the mobile phone that came as part of the kit did not work in Rome, and that the phone sockets in the room weren't compatible with the leads I'd been given. (It was after this trip that I invested in a bag of tele-adaptors, for use in every country in the world.) No other journalist was staying at my hotel, so I couldn't get help or advice. The IT support team in Wapping didn't work on Saturdays. Thus it was that I spent the Saturday afternoon in Rome (intended for sight-seeing) looking in vain for a shop that sold data connectors, as opposed to exotic-flavoured ice creams or little plaster models of the Coliseum.

Now at this point the special conditions that applied to this match need to be factored in. This was a big night for Italy as well as for England, and the stadium was a riot in embryo from the start. The police presence was the most menacing I ever experienced. When we disembarked from our coach, we were greeted by heavily armed *carabinieri* in robocop garb who wordlessly marched us miles away from the stadium in the dark, and rifle-butted people who asked questions about where we were going. During the match itself, they baton-charged England fans in their seats. And after the match (which ended at 10.30) they made us remain in the stadium for an extra hour and a half – partly to allow angry Italians to disperse; and partly, perhaps, to give the English time to set up makeshift field hospitals for the dressing of wounds – before marshalling us out in what was, to my mind, the scariest and most idiotically irresponsible part of the whole evening: funnelling thousands of people down narrow staircases, and risking having hundreds crushed to death.

Once outside, having run the gauntlet of yet more *carabinieri*, the Carlsberg group regained its high spirits. Personally, I thought it had been a fantastic evening of football, but enough is as good as a feast, I was a bit tired now from all the singing, and if I could get to bed before 1 a.m. I'd be a very happy girl. Maybe I had forgotten about the dinner included in the deal. Or maybe I assumed that the lengthy delay in the stadium would mean it had been cancelled. Either way, I was in for a shock, because one lone voice saying 'Back to the hotel then?' made no impact at all on this hospitality crowd who were all crying out for their promised five-course Italian blowout. Sure enough, having re-boarded the coach, we were driven for something like 45 minutes to an out-of-town restaurant where an enormous evening of food, drink, colour, heat, smoke, laughter and noise was awaiting us – and where brightly-clothed guitar players came weaving between the tables, playing jaunty Neapolitan tunes like 'Funiculi Funicula' and getting the punters to join in the chorus.

'Will this take long?' I kept asking. Well, it took till nearly five in the morning, and by the time the first food arrived, I calculated I had been awake for over 24 hours. I was too tired to eat, and I would have been mad to drink anything, given the deadline in the morning. I assumed a glazed smile, sipped a glass of water, rested my cheek on a mound of fruit, and waited quite patiently for it all to end, although when the guitar players were joined by women in red gypsy frocks, if I'd had a gun, I would have shot them. All I wanted was to escape, crawl on my hands and knees back to the centre of Rome, and solve my data connection problems. The shaven-headed fellow guest sitting next to me turned out to be a very wealthy publisher of pornography, and a supporter of Millwall. So that was nice. Feeling a bit like the Queen, I tried to take a polite interest by asking questions such as, 'And do you find that takes up a lot of your time?'

When we got back to the hotel, I slept for two hours, then woke up and wrote my piece – all the time in the worrying knowledge that I probably didn't have the means of sending it. At around 10.30 a.m., I put some shoes on and carried my open laptop downstairs, with the lead attached, and – having got the attention of the man at reception – mimed the act of plugging it in. His response was to mime a big shrug of indifference, and then to do another, throat-cutting mime to indicate that breakfast was *finito*, so he hoped I wasn't expecting any. But I still had reason to be glad I had gone down, because it was while I was standing in despair in reception that I happened to spot a British football journalist outside on the street. Here was a stroke of luck. I went outside and said help, help, what can I do? And it turned out that many members of the proper accredited British media were staying in a quite modern hotel right next door to mine, and that this hotel had a fax machine that would take the lead I had, although I might need to reprogramme the tricky copy-filing software to include some international codes. Well, that all sounded quite acceptable. In fact, it sounded great. My coach was leaving in twenty minutes, and I hadn't showered or eaten yet, but at last I felt I was winning: kneeling on the floor of a back office in a neighbouring hotel, groping for a universal phone socket behind a photocopier, saying 'Thank you thank you thank you' in Italian, and praying that the stuff would go through.

In these days of universal wi-fi, bluetooth and tri-band mobiles, these transmission problems seem quite primitive and tragic, I suppose. But in 1997 we thought we were up to date just saying the word 'modem'; we were ahead of the curve having portable computers that weighed a mere three stone and had a battery life of more than 15 minutes. At night I would dream not of ponies or heaps of gold, but of the far-off invention of the lightweight laptop and of a newspaper that would one day accept copy sent by email. As things stood, the software for filing copy from the *Times* laptops was a laborious one which seemed to send your pieces one word at a time, weighing them for quality in the process, and always reserving the right to reject the whole thing if it found something it didn't like. 'It's going!' one would gasp, as the correct initial connection message came up – but then the worrying started. An image like a protractor (a semi-circle on a flat base) would indicate the tortuous progress of a file transmission with a dial going slowly through 180 degrees. 'I think it's going,' you whispered, as the dial started to move. What you soon learned was that getting over the hump of the 90 degree mark was no guarantee of success. It just ratcheted up the tension. 'Halfway!' you would moan, with head in hands. Many was the time that the dial would get to 137 degrees (or maybe 140) and then pause, stagger, and conk out.

On this occasion, on the third attempt, I was lucky. It went! '*Grazie grazie grazie,*' I said to the hotel person who had helped me. At this point, a normal sports writer would have gathered his stuff, whistled a tune, and put the whole thing behind him, but I knew I wouldn't. I would brood on this. Improvising under pressure gave me no satisfaction. Quite the contrary: it made me seethe. But thankfully there was no time to dwell on anything right now. With ten minutes to go, I ran back to my own hotel, got washed, changed and packed. Mission accomplished, I boarded the bus to the airport, dragging my laptop case, and started thanking those generous Carlsberg people for my lovely-lovely-jubbly weekend.

* * *

But would I have missed this match? Not for anything. Not for worlds. The atmosphere in that stadium was phenomenal, for a start. It is traditional for triumphant footballers to thank the supporters for their part in proceedings, but there was no doubt that the non-stop lusty *Great Escape* stuff from the crowd that night grew out of a quite valid kind of magical thinking: with the team playing so well from the outset, the chanting must never stop, never. As long as the fans were singing, the boys would maintain this amazing football, this enchanted football, which was like watching eleven blokes with a history of poor co-ordination balance a priceless egg on their combined fingertips and miraculously deliver it intact across a minefield. England's clear ambition was to keep the ball: to play Italy at their own game. Their performance required skill, and control, and collective intelligence; above all, it required them to *take care*. And bloody hell, they did! When the English fans sang the taunting variant of 'Bread of Heaven' that goes 'You're suppo-osed to-o be at home', it was brilliantly apt. Not only did the Italians appear not to have home advantage, but the English players had apparently just walked in and stolen their tactics. England looked very much at home in the Stadio Olimpico. There were no long balls. There was no putting it in the mixer. There was no Route One. The side of the elegant English foot was employed as never before. And what made matters especially wonderful was that it drove the Italians crazy. As Gazza put it so well afterwards, 'It was great to see them running after the ball for a change. They were desperate, and it was a really nice feeling to see that.'

Great matches sometimes reveal themselves rather late

in proceedings. Not this one. From the start, you could see qualities in the English game-plan that were so much like answered prayers that it was hard to believe one's eyes. Here was Gazza consistently outwitting Albertini and Baggio. Here was Paul Ince throwing himself into tackles, but not in a manner to get sent off. Here was the 22-year-old David Beckham keeping cool under provocation. Here was David Batty with a clear linchpin role, acting as a human shield. In defence, Tony Adams was at the height of his remarkable powers (and of course, he should still have been England captain, but we'll come back to my feelings about Alan Shearer later). The point is that from the start of the match, everywhere one looked on the pitch, one saw not-very-English footballing traits such as guile, subtlety, control, elegance and forward thinking. While the Italians ran around exhausting themselves, our chaps used their energy efficiently, and seemed to be ruled by the idea of not letting each other down. The Italian fans threw bottles and coins onto the pitch, but they ignored them. A banner said, 'GOOD EVENING BASTARDS'. They ignored that, too. Mentally speaking, throughout the whole 90 minutes, the match was a logically impossible stasis in which one team was always smoothly and consistently going forward and the other was always frantically scrambling back.

Afterwards, Italian defender Paolo Maldini (son of the coach Cesare Maldini) announced that his team had been 'psychologically destroyed' by the match – which was highly gratifying, obviously. Striker Gianfranco Zola said, rather oddly, that he would have given his finger to win the game (which one?), but that Italy had been outnumbered in midfield, so his talents had been wasted, as he'd been obliged to keep pedalling back. 'I found myself running after Batty like a madman. In such conditions, I burnt up precious energy. Let us tell the truth, I was neither fish nor fowl. I say honestly, to play such a role it would have been better to have had another player than Zola.' The Italian papers in subsequent days had headlines like '*Povera Italia*' (poor Italy) and 'Courage Drowned in a Sea of Incompetence'. An editorial in the *Gazzetta dello sport* said England had contented themselves with controlling the game against 'an opponent that managed to explore nothing but its own impotence'. What music to one's ears.

On that night, I can honestly say I loved the England team. When Sheringham hugged Beckham for post-match pictures, I was in tears of joy and pride. As the Italian fans quickly left the stadium in disgust – empty-pocketed, presumably, after flinging anything portable at the rival fans, or onto the pitch – it was a fabulous moment of togetherness for us. We didn't even notice we'd been locked in. England had qualified for the World Cup, and had done it beautifully. David Beckham's cold had got better. Glenn Hoddle was a genius. Ince had been a hero. Adams would live for ever. It was a fine night in Rome. The *carabinieri*, despite all their best efforts, hadn't actually killed anyone. And, just as a sentimental bonus, Gazza had returned to the stadium of his old club Lazio and shown them what he could do when he was trying.

Too much has already been written by genuine life-long football fans about the exquisite misery of the long-suffering supporter. The tiny ups and the lengthy downs, the heart-break, the locking oneself in a shed for five years. So as a way of dealing with my bitter disillusionment with England, I'll just get Alan Shearer off my chest, because it was such a curious thing, the way I quite quickly grew to loathe that man, and to rant at anyone who dared to stand up for him. Now that Shearer's England captaincy is in the past, I find I can put the whole thing behind me. On my desk as I write this is a little model of Shearer in Newcastle strip which I look at regularly for inspiration. People with cruelly good memories will gladly remind me that, during Euro 96, I not only offered myself as mother to Alan Shearer's children, I even had a happy dream about him working in a furniture shop. But in the dark days of 2000, if he was named man of the match, I would say, 'Oh for Pete's sake, what's wrong with you people, don't you have *eyes*?' and heartily spit on the floor.

I blamed him, you see. He was captain of a consistently under-performing England team. At a time when it was fashionable to refer to certain individual players (such as Eric Cantona) as 'talismanic', Shearer's personality seemed to influence the England team, and in only negative ways. In Shearer's image, England was mean, dirty, tight-lipped, bullet-headed and pointy-elbowed. It expected to get away with stuff, and huffed when it didn't. It had all the grace and daintiness of a bulldozer. It was opportunistic instead of inventive. It waddled instead of ran, and always had its arm up in appeal for a penalty. It didn't deign to look side-ways or backwards. Its goal-scoring record in no way justified its arrogantly high opinion of itself. Worst of all, in a world of sexy football, beautiful football, and lanky, nifty football, it was resolutely unattractive. Basically, it had thick white yeoman legs with hairs on the backs of its knees.

What really got to me about Alan Shearer, however (oh yes, there's more), was that different rules seemed to apply to him. This was the thing that drove me crazy. He fouled all the time, yet he wasn't booked or sent off. He played half-heartedly, yet he wasn't substituted. He seemed to exert a power that wasn't commensurate with his true value as a footballer. What was going on? Did he know where bodies were buried? Why was everyone scared of him? Famously, when Ruud Gullit dared to leave him out of the Newcastle team, the decision was interpreted as an extreme folly for which Gullit would (and did) rightfully pay with his job. Some might argue that the loyalty shown to Shearer by a succession of England managers is sufficient evidence of his worth. And to be fair, many people told me I was barking up the wrong tree, and that having Shearer leading the England team from the front gave it bulldog qualities of strength and purpose. 'Alan Shearer knows where the goal is,' they would say, meaningfully. But at the height of my Shearer obsession, I considered such arguments mere propaganda. It seemed really obvious to me that the non-negotiability of having Shearer in attack was limiting England's options in disastrous ways. Why did tactics – and team selection – have to be tailored to suit this bloke? Why was he exempt from criticism? Why was he untouchable? Why did no blame attach to him after St Etienne, when it was his foul on the Argentinian goalkeeper that lost the match for England (when Sol Campbell's goal was disallowed, and Argentina ran off and scored while England were still celebrating)? I remember a Football Writers' Dinner where I was lucky enough to sit next to Ted Beckham (David's dad), and instead of asking him to marry me (what a wasted opportunity), I just moaned on and on to him about Bloody Alan Shearer.

The last match I attended for *The Times* was in October 2000, a few days after my sister's funeral. And the good news is: Alan Shearer wasn't in it. However, the bad news is: it was still unwatchably awful, so he might just as well have been. His mean little spirit still hovered above it. It was a 2002 World Cup qualifier against Germany at Wembley (the first of our campaign), and even on first sight it seemed to contain every ingredient for a paradigmatically miserable afternoon of English football. Somebody had decided to make this a celebratory occasion by entitling the match 'The Final Whistle', but this was never going to be a party, no matter how many Cross of St George flags were sold to unsuspecting children down on Wembley Way, and no matter how many times the aggravatingly upbeat stadium announcer played 'Three Lions' over the PA and yelled, 'The world will be watching! It's a family occasion! It's a World Cup qualifier! Don't run off at the end of the match, we've got a show that's fantastic!' This was, you see, to be the last match played at the old Wembley before demolition, and equivocal feelings abounded. It was, on the one hand, rather melancholy to reflect that the ghostly echoes from 1966 of 'They think it's all over' would be silenced for ever by the wrecking ball; on the other hand, the place was dank, stinky and uncomfortable and deserved to be struck by lightning. When the Red Arrows failed to show up (pleading weather conditions), one could only applaud their good taste. Nothing to celebrate here, mate. Nothing to celebrate here. You mark my words, the England fans will soon be singing, 'Stand up if you won the war,' because it will be the only pathetic little straw they can grasp at.

Why anyone thought an England–Germany game with important points attached to it would make a suitable last fixture for the old place, I couldn't imagine. True, they couldn't have predicted it would be cold and raining, but they must surely have known we would lose. England's performance in Euro 2000 had been pretty terrible, and it was clear by now that, as manager, Kevin Keegan had only ever had one idea: build the team around Alan Shearer and see what happens. By this point, sadly, Keegan's supposed motivational skills were no longer a source of wonder. His talent for tactical idiocy, however, was universally acknowledged; in fact it was reckoned to be unsurpassed at this level of the game. On this occasion, for a World Cup qualifier against the Germans, Keegan put out a midfield of three – Beckham, Scholes and Barmby – and set Southgate the task of patrolling behind them. In the press box, some of the blokes looked at this line-up and put their heads in their hands. It was the work of a madman. It was insane.

Personally, I cried. I never stopped crying, in fact. This being a few days after my sister's funeral, I started crying because of personal circumstances, obviously – but there seemed to be no practical reason to cheer up once I'd started, so I didn't. On arrival, I realised that I'd been allocated a seat next to Brian Glanville, a veteran football writer of high renown, tangled ascetic appearance and haughty intellectual condescension, who had never made a secret of his dislike for me (sometimes he even did it in Italian). A couple of years before, at a Charlton game, he'd been given my ticket by mistake, and when a steward asked him for it he'd said, rather shockingly, 'If I'd known it was for her, I'd have torn it up.' Now, for four years fortune had spared me the necessity of sitting next to Brian Glanville, but naturally I had kept myself keenly prepared for the eventuality. By way of practice, for example, I had recently dealt quite successfully with one of his like-minded woman-hostile colleagues, by saying as I sat down, 'Look, I'll only say this once. But if there's anything you don't understand, *just ask*.' It would have given me considerable satisfaction to say something similar to Brian Glanville. One day the opportunity would arise, I was sure of it. I was ready for him. I had nothing to lose.

But today, when I saw him sitting there in the next seat – damn it, I just welled up and cried. And since he steadfastly ignored me (possibly in Italian), I felt I had full permission to give vent to all my feelings. In this noisy stadium, no one would notice, after all. So I cried throughout the pre-match stuff, which included a playing of 'Jerusalem' (which had been sung at my sister's funeral). I cried during the fireworks, which we couldn't see because it was daylight, and in any case, they were on the roof. I cried with everyone else when I saw the team sheet. I cried when I spotted the Wembley groundsman, with whom I'd once spent a really pleasant day learning about sports turf management; I cried when the England fans booed the

German national anthem; I cried right through the match and the half-time sandwich, cup of tea and orange-flavoured Club biscuit. And after the defeat, when Kevin Keegan announced his resignation as England coach, I cried at that as well, not because it was such a shock but because it was the opposite: it was so miserably inevitable. When you are in a state combining personal grief with despair for England, nothing is a surprise, you see; bad things just confirm your worst fears. So *of course* Keegan would choose this moment to quit the England job. Hadn't he abandoned clubs and jobs all his life? Hadn't I been saying he would do this at the worst moment, when we had another vital qualifying match in just a few days' time? Wasn't that just *typical* of him to slink off but dress it up as the honourable thing?

In a way, though, I reckon it was fitting that I should spend the whole of my last ever football match openly piping the eye and wringing out tissues. Sport doesn't permit a really good cry, and I had begun to think that this was one of the main things wrong with it. Although it's a widely acknowledged fact that watching sport is an emotionally gruelling business, isn't there an unsatisfactory gap where the catharsis ought to be? You get all worked up – and then, because no one dies, you gradually calm down again and nurse a curious sense of emptiness. People sometimes say that sport educates the emotions, but the range of feelings it promotes is pathetically small, when you think about it. Anxiety, frustration, unbearable misery and almighty relief – that's about it. Whenever the subject of 'Is sport the new religion?' came up in my day, I'd say no, or at least it's no substitute, because sport is designed to make people anxious whereas religion is supposed to do the opposite. Watching sport is about placing your temporary emotional well-being in the hands of a bunch of fallible athletes; religion makes you put faith in an infallible God for the sake of your own ultimate spiritual security. The fact that people make 'gods' out of footballers is merely a symptom of paltry understanding and bad taste. When Kevin Keegan had made his flit from Newcastle in January 1997, the quasi-religious grieving was quite shocking. Fans with fresh 'RIP' tattoos on their stomachs hung around outside St James' Park, hoping to see him rise again. One fan pledged to explain about Keegan to his toddlers 'when they were old enough'. 'He Never Forgot Ordinary People', ran the headline in a local Newcastle paper. At the time, Keegan was advertising Sugar Puffs on the telly, and in this climate of religiosity I remember thinking it would have been quite a simple matter to change the Sugar Puffs slogan to 'Eat these and think of me'.

But the very reason sport is so ascendant in our day, I reckon, is that its drama requires such shallow emotional engagement. It isn't very complicated. It is self-centred. It's unhappy/happy. It's lose/win. Empathy doesn't really come into it, let alone anything so profound and human as pity. Sport legitimises quite shameful feelings such as naked triumphalism and – especially when German people are involved in a rare defeat, tee hee – *schadenfreude*. Sometimes we might feel sorry for losers, but it's up to us; it's optional. I remember quite a yelling match I had on the night of England–Argentina in 1998, when my boss called from London and told me to focus on Beckham's red card, and the issue of pity came up at an extremely bad moment. This sending-off incident was one of the lowest points of my sports writing career, I must confess – not for what it represented in the history of English football, but because it happened right in front of me and I missed it. I was bent over my keyboard at the time, and looked up only when I heard the roar from the crowd and the yelled expletives from all round me in the press box. What I saw on the pitch was Beckham inexplicably untucking his shirt and striding off. *What?* The crowd was going mad. *What on earth –?* People in the press box were hopping up and down. And I just sat there, swallowing and blinking; waiting for an explanatory replay on a nearby monitor, and all the time thinking, 'If I ask what just happened, I'm dead.'

Anyway, back in London they wanted me to 'go for' Beckham. They had obviously mistaken me for some rottweiler alter ego, who went for people. I don't know. I can't explain it. I just knew it was pointless asking me to call for David Beckham to be burned in effigy, and that, luckily, I worked for a newspaper that would not insert the words 'I hereby call for him to be burned in effigy' unless I actually wrote them. And I wouldn't. 'If we lose this, they'll crucify him!' my boss yelled. (He was hoarse by the end of the night from yelling to his troops in the cacophony of St Etienne.) And I yelled back, hopelessly, 'But I feel sorry for him!' And he'd shout, 'He did something really stupid!' And I'd shout, 'Pardon?' And he'd shout, 'He deserves what's coming to him!' And I'd shout, 'That's why I feel sorry for him!' I had to re-file my piece twice because it wasn't strong enough, but I still refused to have a go. I said Beckham was incredibly talented, and it was tragic that there was nothing he could do to repair his mistake. In the end, the last edition went and my voiceless boss was obliged to forgive me my milksop girlie failings; characteristically, he never referred to the incident again.

What he always loyally loved to tell people afterwards instead was that I was the only one of his writers in France who had predicted the home side to win the World Cup, which is a bizarre sports writing distinction I can't not mention here, since it's the only one I have. The paper had asked all its footie writers for its 'top four', you see, and printed them before the tournament. My prediction was: France, Brazil, Holland, England – which was extremely uncanny as things turned out, being correct in three out of four cases, with the top two in the right positions. More learned chaps such as Brian Glanville had gone for Brazil, Argentina, Italy and Germany (not that this gives me any pleasure to recall, you understand). However, my success was mostly fluke. Also, as I was always quick to point out, I had misunderstood the question in any case. I thought that by 'top four' they meant the teams that would make it to the semi-finals. It was only when colleagues reported to me, chuckling with mirth, 'I see you tipped France to win, Lynne,' that I found out what I'd done.

The End of the Affair

So now I'm back to knowing nothing about football again, which is quite liberating. I wouldn't say I had returned to normal, because that would raise too many complex questions. But I have established some distance, which was a conscious objective, and I no longer wake up screaming that Brian Glanville is working in a furniture shop and that he's torn up my ticket for the public burning of David Beckham, but I'm in an airship so I can't get there on time, and anyway I can't park here and I don't have the right kind of mobile. For a couple of years after my resignation, I did rail against sports writing's shortcomings as a way of life – but I had faith that the reflex bitterness would pass away in time. One day, I solemnly hoped, I would be able to look at this little statuette of Alan Shearer without wanting to bash its smug little head in with the Sellotape dispenser. In the meantime, it was very therapeutic to burn some of my hideous (but warm) footie outfits, and ceremonially bury the set of universal tele-adaptors in a special place in the garden.

Retrospective anger is quite a normal feature of break-up. For a while the ex-football writer is bound to rant against football's failings: how selfish it was, how it always left the toilet seat up, how it dumped wet towels on the bed, stubbornly refused to ask directions when lost in Croydon. 'You're better off out of that,' friends would declare, supportively, afterwards. 'Football never understood you. I don't know what you saw in it in the first place.' Occasionally, in those tender first days of separation, news about football would filter back to me, and I'd try to be brave and send it good wishes. If football was getting on perfectly well on its own, I had no right to complain. After all, the idea that we go our separate ways had been entirely mine. My only consolation was in a perverse kind of pride. Had anyone ever left football so successfully before? I couldn't believe they had, what with football being so damned attractive, so damned fascinating. The whole point of loving football is that you commit yourself for life. You clamber aboard the carousel (usually aged about six), cling on tight, and go round and round for ever. And here I was, jumping off after four revolutions, with no regard for injury or dizziness – and doing this, moreover, just when the fabulous Thierry Henry was starting to reign supreme at Arsenal.

It wasn't a simple reaction against sports writing. Obviously I had run out of patience with the lifestyle, but I was uncomfortable about something else; something very important. I was beginning to accept as normal a culture I knew to be horrible. Being aware of this was profoundly unsettling, especially for someone with only a shaky sense of their own identity in the first place. Put simply, it seemed to me that while I was still capable of being shocked by the stupidity and unhelpfulness of the donkey-jacket brigade, I was still me. When I stopped being shocked, I was lost. There is a powerful description in a book by James Hamilton-Paterson of what it's like to be swimming alone in the ocean and mislay your boat. He explains that, because your eyes are a mere six inches above sea level, you can see only about ten feet in all directions, depending on the swell. Being up to your neck in deep water, there is nothing you can push against to make your head go higher. This may strike most people as obvious (especially anyone who does a lot of snorkelling), and I suppose it is, but I still find it a panic-inducing thought, and it reminds me of how I felt by the end of my sports writing career – frustratingly cut off from the natural landscape of my former life, in which I had sometimes cooked meals, and tended herbs in pots, and spent Saturday afternoons cosily indoors watching *Sherlock Holmes*, and remembered people's birthdays. I couldn't even *see* any of that namby-pamby stuff any more; I was up to my neck in donkey-jacket misery, without any means of levering myself up. I was sure the male sports writers managed to keep work and life more healthily separate than I did, but probably (and I try not to be peevish about this) they had wives at home to help.

Did I also feel that I had started knowing too much? Well, that would be stretching things a bit, but I certainly felt I had seen quite enough sporting history made already, and that if I carried on, I might have to start questioning what sporting history was supposed to be exactly. It's the main reason I felt I had to write this book – because if there's one thing I'm endlessly fascinated and amused by, it's the human struggle to establish a true perspective, or maintain it in the face of other people's. If there isn't a

New Yorker cartoon on this, then there ought to be: the astronaut's wife saying, 'Yeah, yeah, you went up in space and the Earth looked like a beach ball. That doesn't mean you can't wash the car.' Personally, I've found that dropping sport was as much an interesting experiment in perspective as taking it up in the first place. Looking back at specific long-ago matches, fights, games, cups, bouts and championships (for the purpose of this book), I have relived their claims to historic significance, at the same time as knowing that many of them lived on in people's hearts and minds for about 24 hours at the most. Taking that great FA Cup semi-final between Middlesbrough and Chesterfield, for example, wouldn't it be reasonable to suppose that teeny-weeny Chesterfield FC would still treasure the excitement of that very special match? That it would be screened once or twice a week in the town hall for the edification of the populace? But does the club even sell an official video? No. At the time of writing, Chesterfield has just been knocked out of the Cup and is offering a half-season pass for under twenty quid, which suggests there are immediate concerns that take precedence over nostalgia. The website offers a menu of Home, News, Match, Team, Tickets, Club, Fans, and Commercial. You will notice how 'Glorious Cup Runs of Yesteryear' is absent from this list.

And yet, that match at Old Trafford seemed jolly historic at the time. Is this all a con trick, then? Is it sheer propaganda, this idea that a great feat will live on? When those over-excited Sky Sports commentators say 'one for the annals', do they think 'annals' is a synonym for 'bins'? That bloke in Newcastle who said he'd be telling his kids about

Kevin Keegan when they were old enough – well, I'm beginning to suspect he forgot all about it the minute he got home (and anyway, since then, Keegan's been back to Newcastle and then gone again, so the kids probably wouldn't want to hear about him anyway). Sport is all present tense, and its present tense is packed with event, so there's no time for much of a backward glance. Open the newspaper any day at 'Today's fixtures' and you will see races to be rowed, ridden, driven and run; games to be played; fights to be settled; championships to be claimed. If there is not a major international football tournament being played today, by definition there are qualification rounds in progress, with a points table and goal difference. The main thing that worried me about sport from the outset was its sense of its own importance, especially when its everyday feats (conducted for profit, don't forget) were reinforced with glorifying abstract nouns such as 'greatness' and 'meaning'. Every piece of sport I've written about in this book seemed truly significant on the day it took place (even the darts match) – but was it? The only reason I can imaginatively reach back to these events after a gap of years is that, for me, the gap of years contained, mainly, trips to the theatre, some remedial herb-gardening and a lot of talking about commas and semicolons.

Sport goes on and on and on, you see. You have to run on the spot to keep up. Events just keep on coming: moreover, they keep coming in exactly the same order, year after year, which is sensible, but also a bit depressing if the sporting calendar's rigid cycle dictates your actual life.

What I grew to realise was that, in order to relish the eternal, cyclical nature of sport (as opposed to resenting it), you need a combination of mental capacities that are all quite alien to me: one of which (oh, the shame of it) is the simple ability to retain cold information such as who won last time, who won the time before, and by how much.

Possibly this does not come as a surprise, but it is worth reiterating: the ability to remember who won last time, and who won the time before, is pretty much essential to a sports writer. You can therefore imagine my dismay when I realised I did not have it. Whenever I applied to the appropriate sporting-statistics area of my brain for some quick answers about scores or results, all I found there was the set used in *Teletubbies*: a broad, rolling landscape with a rainbow and twittering birdsong, with hopping brown bunny rabbits in the foreground to provide a sense of scale. When someone asks, 'So who won the 2008 Open at Birkdale?' a sports writer should be able to reply, 'Tsk, Padraig Harrington, of course. He finished with a 69.' It is no good if, like me, you initially find the question abrupt and slightly irrelevant and therefore puzzling. Who *won*? After all, the Open took place over four days, and the winning bit happened for only about an hour at the end. Birkdale, for me, was where Greg Norman made his amazing comeback. There was no Tiger Woods, because of his knee. The rain was torrential. Ian Poulter did extremely well on the last day, and Sandy Lyle gave up on the Friday because his glasses kept steaming up. But who won it? Who *did* win it? I remember we were all very pleased, which ought to be a clue. Think Sunday afternoon, Lynne. Think 18th green with long shadows.

You stood at the back of the green to watch the last putts. Tip of the tongue, truly. It wasn't Padraig again, was it? And as the fog clears, do you know something? I'm beginning to think it was! I can see him now on the 18th! Yes. Padraig Harrington it certainly was. And jolly well deserved too.

I knew I had this statistic-retention problem quite early in my sports writing career. Winning and losing made much less of an impression on me than they did on others – which was another persuasive reason for keeping my mouth shut in the presence of proper sports writers. Once, at a Leicester–Liverpool match in the 1998–99 season, I insanely remarked to an amicable chap from the *Sunday Mirror* that I'd attended the same fixture the year before. I remembered because the match had provided my first in-the-flesh sighting of the young Michael Owen. But this was a conversation I should never have started. 'What was the score?' the *Sunday Mirror* man asked – and I honestly don't think he was trying to trick me; he thought I'd be able to tell him. So that was the end of our little chat; and probably the end of me, as far as he was concerned. Chewing the lip, I had to admit I had no idea who'd won Leicester–Liverpool in January 1998, let alone the scoreline. (I've just checked: it was a goalless draw.) My principal memory from that previous match was a visual one: of seeing Owen clattered and left for dead on the touchline by someone considerably stockier than him. I remembered a pathetic little red heap of clothing that didn't move. I remembered, at a stretch, that the atrocity had been perpetrated by a big man dressed in blue. But as for any other details – well, I'm sorry, officer, I think I've told you everything I know.

This issue of memory was always a big one for me. It seemed to me that my main disqualification as a sports writer was that my memory for statistics is staggeringly short-term, while my emotional memory is the sturdy means by which I navigate life. Unfortunately, a love of sport requires these positions to be switched. You must remember scorelines stretching back to the dawn of time, and at the same time possess the emotional recall of a gnat. Fans are blessed with an ability to live in the continuous present, as if under a beautiful spell of forgetfulness, in which every day is a clean slate and hope triumphs over empiricism, and in which it is sheer wicked heresy to say that Tim Henman probably won't win Wimbledon (on the grounds that it's obvious), or that England's footballers will more than likely go to pieces when the chips are down. Just as I felt embarrassed on account of my inability to store Open champions on a convenient page of my mental ledger for more than a couple of weeks, so I was continually confused by the way I was supposed to forget quite big things such as how much it hurts when England doesn't win at football. In life it is surely a good policy to guard against disappointment by adjusting expectations. For example, if Christmas is always a disaster, you stop looking forward to it. This is a simple matter of self-preservation.

But fans don't have this self-preservation instinct. They always come back with hope in their hearts, as if nothing bad has ever happened. At club level, they even get fanatically attached to individual players, when the age-old convention of musical-chairs football transfers ought to tell them not to. Instead of forestalling the inevitable, however, they wait for the blows and then roll with them.

It's touchingly simple. One week you are a Spurs fan so devoted to Dimitar Berbatov that you get the Bulgarian national flag tattooed across your face; and the next week, when he's signed to Manchester United, you go out and buy a balaclava. You don't dwell on it, that's the main thing. You might shout 'Judas!' at him on his first re-visit, but then you let it go. I suppose you are too happily occupied recollecting every Leicester–Liverpool score since the dawn of football. Or maybe you are too busy studying an old straggly frond in your goldfish bowl for the hundredth time today and saying, 'Blimey, that's attractive. Is it new?'

It's perfectly all right to have no emotional memory – after all, psychopaths generally manage without, and you don't hear them complaining. But unreal expectations of sport aren't just about not remembering; they arise out of magical thinking, which is what you get if you add wilful obtuseness to unchecked sentimentality and then allow yourself to get wildly over-excited into the bargain. As an example of magical thinking in sport, we only have to think of that match at Wembley between Germany and England in October 2000. People at the highest level of the game could see all the dismal England football performances under the reign of Kevin Keegan, yet they could still organise an England–Germany match as the Wembley swan song. 'We could win that!' they will have said. 'It would be great to beat Germany in our last Wembley match!' Even the sports writers (and the sports editors, for other reasons) are not immune to this sheer mad logic – and it used to make me quite scared for their mental well-being. They would imagine the wished-for result – England wins back the Ashes, *in Australia*! Tim Henman finally wins Wimbledon! – and then they would start not only excitedly believing it, but even planning how to cover the victory parade. The moment England scrapes into any tournament, it's the same old story. 'There's nothing to stop us winning this, you know,' they start saying. 'We've got six or seven world class players in there.'

The one policy issue I used to argue about with my boss was this irresponsible hyping of British (specifically English) chances in major competitions. The fact that false hope sells newspapers is no excuse. But I think the corollary disagreement we had was even more infuriating. This was the one that invariably took place after England was knocked out at the group stage – or Lee Westwood missed the cut – or Henman reached his predictable (but still very respectable) limit in the quarter-final – when the office would say, dogmatically and harshly, 'That's it. No one will be interested now. You might as well come home.' That used to make me very cross. For a start, I was sure our football-loving readers weren't all raving jingoists. For another thing, if all the excitement around this tournament had truly been attached only to national expectations, *who was to blame*? And third, although I was careful not to say this too clearly in print (for fear of hurting the already tender feelings of the England fans), I positively adored all competitions the moment the red herring of England's chances was safely off the agenda. It was such a great relief to *get on with the football*. What bliss to watch Holland–Italy, and not worry about hundreds of semi-naked English thugs rampaging in some quaint foreign town and finally being contained by water cannon. As for the annoying people-will-lose-interest-in-Wimbledon-now argument,

I used to point out that, before Tim Henman came along, there had been decades without a realistic British hope, and the fans had happily rooted for Australians, Americans, Germans. All my anti-jingoist arguments fell on deaf ears, though. Presumably the sales figures proved me wrong.

To be fair, however, I don't think sports coverage would be much cop if it woke up one day with a completely realistic attitude about all this. 'Yes, it's Super Terrific Sky Sports Super Terrific Sunday and blah blah are at home to blah blah, but the likelihood of it producing anything memorable is pretty small, so look, we thought we'd give it a miss, because life is precious, have you noticed, and football is quite often a bit disappointing, and besides it goes on and on and on.' No, better to carry on peddling expectations, and being either totally gob-smacked when things go badly, or justifiably elated when everything turns out well. The supporters expect this Year Zero mentality; for some reason, they don't even see it as dishonest. Yes, they live to remember who scored what, when and how; who won last time, and who won the time before; and to forget entirely what it felt like. In the end, this kind of wilful amnesia is a gift, and I'm quite envious of people who have it. 'Why don't I ever *learn*?' is not a question they ask themselves. Which, in itself, satisfactorily explains why they never will.

If it's any consolation, I have made a great discovery. The less you know about football, the more you can enjoy it. After a break of eight years or so, I have tentatively returned to footie, and found it fascinating. For a start, footballers have actually changed shape in the intervening period. It's very noticeable. It's as if they have all been stretched and moulded until they are of identical proportions, using the slender David James as the template. Footballers have got taller and leaner and lighter on their feet, with smaller knees and spatchcock shoulders. This means they all look very fit and nifty, but are much, much harder to tell apart. Whereas a team lining up in the late 1990s might have contained some terriers, an Afghan, a pit-bull, a chihuahua and a few mutts, now every premiership team is 100 per cent greyhounds. Referring to footballers as athletes used to be stretching things, but not any more. It is astonishing how quickly matters have altered to the detriment of square-shaped blokes like David Batty. An England team with Matt Le Tissier in it now seems like something from another world. Paul Gascoigne, with his thin legs and pigeon chest, would today be laughed off the field.

Other things have changed, too. Rules-wise, they have clamped down on goal celebrations and have dickered with the offside rule so that even the commentators are throwing their hands up. Meanwhile, personnel-wise, it's hard to know where to start. No Ron Atkinson, which is good. No David O'Leary, either, who used to preface all his remarks with 'I don't want to sound arrogant', 'I'm not trying to be arrogant' or 'Stop me if this sounds at all arrogant'. What immediately struck me was the way scary hard-man players such as Mark Hughes and Roy Keane have gone into management, and look just as murderous in the dugouts as they ever did on the pitch. As it happens, I was once at Stamford Bridge when Mark Hughes (then on the visiting Southampton side) was awarded a rose bowl in recognition of his years with Chelsea, and I know what you're thinking because I thought it too. A rose bowl? Yes, not the most thoughtful of gifts for old Sparky. You could imagine the scene at Peter Jones the night before: Chelsea chairman dithering about what to get, and the assistant saying, 'Well, if you say he likes flower arranging . . .' Hughes was removed from the pitch in a state of concussion during the ensuing match, and I have to say I did worry about that gift of his. Would any of his team-mates remember to put in on the bus? Would it be left in a corner of the dressing room? Would it be back on the shelf in Peter Jones by Monday lunchtime?

But anyway, back with having General Ignorance about football, it is honestly great fun, and I can recommend it. It's as if I have been in a lengthy coma – or perhaps (nicer image) living in a cave. Thus, I am genuinely agog for information about what ever happened to David Platt (say), but since I have to ask the question, 'What ever happened to David Platt?', it's obvious that I haven't cared sufficiently in the intervening period to know the answer for myself. I'm sure it's quite irritating, this *faux naïf* act that isn't even quite *faux*, but I can't control it. I only have to spot a chatty football fan and I start in with the questions. I'm like one of those mischievous old people who come up with things like, 'Have *you* ever seen a square-shaped plate?' when you're in the middle of negotiating a complex system of round-abouts and the car is on fire. 'What happened to Nottingham Forest?' I demand. (And, interestingly enough, it turns out that this question is virtually synonymous with 'What ever happened to David Platt?') 'Where did Hull spring from? What on earth is Anelka doing at Chelsea?

Who is Fernando Torres, and is he any good? Did Ruud Gullit run to fat? Does anyone else think Rafa Benitez looks a bit like René in *Allo, Allo*? Will anyone ever save that great man Arsène Wenger from his dreadful touchline torment?'

Since loving sport is all about keeping up with it, I'm aware I have broken its first commandment by not knowing anything. When you are involved in the world of sport, you are never meant to use the words 'I', 'didn't', 'know' and 'that' in the same sentence, especially not if you put them in that order. But what the hey. It is good to know that at least the spirit of curiosity has survived. And if occasional appalling humiliation is the price, I suppose it must be endured. It is still painful for me to tell the following story, but I think I must, because it lets you see the full horrific extent of how ignorant of sport a person can become if she really sets her mind to concentrate on the cultivation of oregano, parsley and chives. One day in 2002 I happened to meet the lovely John Inverdale in the reception of Broadcasting House, you see, and oh God, I can't go on. It was John Inverdale, you see. And he's such a good bloke. I always craved his good opinion. But it has to be done. The thing is, he mentioned the upcoming Commonwealth Games. And so I said, 'Oh, of course, the Commonwealth Games. Where are they being held this time?' And his eyes actually started out of his head on curly stalks while his jaw dropped right to the floor. You'll have seen the effect in films like *Ace Ventura*. There is usually a cartoony '*Bo-ing*' sound going with it. The answer was Manchester, you see. The Commonwealth Games were about to be held in Manchester, and it was utterly beyond belief for him that I didn't know or care.

Watching Euro 2008 was bliss for several reasons. First, England wasn't represented, having apparently failed to qualify (hooray). Second, the football was good. And third, the turnover of international players meant there were very few left from my era that I could be irritatingly nostalgic about. I was delighted to see that the gigantic striker Jan Koller was still playing for the Czech Republic, but his immense age (35) was often mentioned along with his immense height, and he announced his retirement from the national team when the Czech Republic was knocked out of the competition. Apart from him, it seemed all young blokes, all capable of greatness, and I was in Ignorance Heaven. 'That Fàbregas bloke is terrific,' I would say aloud. 'Perhaps he'll even play in the Premiership when he's old enough.' You see, what I want to argue here is that knowing all about sport may *seem* to enhance one's enjoyment of it, but actually:

a) it's quite time-consuming, and
b) it leads to despair, so
c) in short, it is a trap we should all avoid if we possibly can.

I am in a position to attest all this from experience. But just look at all the dedicated football fans you know and ask yourself: does their deep and wide knowledge of football make them happy? We all know the answer is no.

* * *

Trawling through my old cuttings, I came across the following piece which I had forgotten. It was written at the very end of Euro 2000, and the reason I include it is that I seem to have banged on so much about the discomfort of covering football tournaments that I thought I should offer a straightforward corrective. When I wrote this, I'm pretty sure I was both grumpy and exhausted, having been obliged to drive from Antwerp to Rotterdam and back the day before the final, just to collect my ticket and parking pass, because that's how badly the tournament had been organised. When I had first turned up in Belgium in the week preceding the first match, I had driven to Brussels every day to get the requisite accreditation, and every day they had said, 'Oh, plenty of time yet!' as they looked with equanimity at the empty shelves behind them. 'Will you be able to give me all the parking passes for the matches I'm attending?' I would ask. 'Oh yes, soon, soon, very soon,' they said, vaguely, until the day before the tournament began, at which point they changed the answer to a firm, 'Parking passes will be available at the stadiums.' This didn't sound too good to me, I must say, because it seemed to contain a logical flaw. 'In that case, can you park *without* a parking pass in order to go inside and get your parking pass?' 'No, of course you cannot park without a parking pass!' they said, as if this was a jolly stupid question. Then they turned away to talk to someone else with a more reasonable enquiry. 'Do you have maps to the stadiums, then?' I would plead. 'Maps to the stadiums will also be available *at the stadiums*,' they said.

Anyone who has travelled on the roads in Belgium will know about a) the demonic driving, and b) the strenuous application of the native surreal imagination in the matter of road signage. For one thing, all the major towns have two names (Anvers is also Antwerpen; Liège is also Luik), but the convention is never acknowledged. The name of your destination just depends on which part of the country you are driving from. But it's worse than that. Harry Pearson, in his very funny (and very reassuring) book, *A Tall Man in a Low Land*, perfectly describes the business of following direction signs in Belgium: 'Genk straight on; Genk 24; Genk right; Genk 12; Genk left; Genk 8; Genk You can find your own bloody way from here, surely?' During the tournament, the Belgians added no useful trains or other public transport, but instituted a travel scheme called 'Befoot' which warned in English that 'wild camping' was illegal, and that 'perturbation' would immediately be dealt with. This last made me hopping mad, as you can imagine. How dare the Belgians clamp down on perturbation, when they deliberately caused so much of it? How unfair could you get?

Anyway, here is the piece:

WELL, the party's over, it's time to call it a day. And I have to say it's unsettling. Rarely does a three-week period become so distorted as when a big tournament is on. Only three weeks ago that the gigantic inflated footballer was wheeled, striding elegantly, on to the pitch at the King Baudouin Stadium in Brussels? Only three weeks since, in the opening match against Sweden, Filip De Wilde, the Belgium goalkeeper, took delivery of a back-pass, diddled with it perilously and had it nicked off him for a goal by Johan Mjallby?

Seems like years. Seems like minutes. The European championship has been a colourful dream of astonishingly good football which has, rather too persuasively, created its own world. It's a world in which every time you look up you see Gheorghe Hagi staring into the mental abyss of yet another yellow card; or the dainty Filippo Inzaghi caught offside with his hands in his hair; or a blur where Thierry Henry has just streaked through open country to score a brilliant goal. Over? Euro 2000 is a way of life. How can it possibly be over?

Before the tournament, I noticed with some alarm that Belgium (where I've been stationed throughout) did not appear ready for it. I accepted that I might be an incorrigible fusspot in such matters and that it was always a mistake to arrive at a party too early, while the host was still deciding on his socks and there was only an old half-bottle of Tizer on the kitchen table. But I must whisper, as delicately as possible, now that it's over and we know that the nibbles never did turn up, that hosting a football tournament may be something that Belgium does not do best. Spending all the money on bouncers was a valid choice, but not a particularly endearing one.

But did this matter, in the end? Unless you are a deported England fan, not too much. The Netherlands, the co-hosts, evidently extended a warm welcome to visitors – they even controlled the England fans in Eindhoven without bother. Besides, with the quality of football from the qualifying teams, a good time was absolutely guaranteed. It's the people who make a party, after all. And there is not a single team that didn't turn itself inside out for the sake of this competition, as their fans well know. Even poor old Denmark (played three, lost three) gave their all, with the poignant banner 'TAK FOR ALT BOSSE' displayed in Liège during the Czech Republic match, in genuine gratitude to Bo Johansson, the outgoing coach, for leading Denmark blind and weaponless into the valley of the shadow of the group of death.

So, what I'm saying is, they invited Zinedine Zidane to this party – and memories of this event will rightly focus on Zidane, performing at the height of his talent. From the moment France took the field against Denmark on the first Sunday in Bruges, the pre-eminence of the man was evident.

Unlike Paul Gascoigne, who always suffered from having a brain like a foot, Zidane has a foot like a brain and a brain like a brain. In fact, he is the brainiest footballer I've ever seen. At semi-conductor speed, and with three opponents closing in on him, he simply bends his balding pate over the ball, calculates all coefficients and simultaneous equations, and then not only works out an unfussy way to retain the ball (swivel, counter-swivel, hop, turn, tap), but comes up with a miraculously improvised way to pass it as well.

What everyone has loved about Euro 2000 is the open, forward, dynamic play. More than 80 goals and a million saves; only two goalless draws. High passion, committed athleticism, fabulous hair and great goals. There's nothing to beat it. Hoorah.

England fans will cherish Michael Owen's goal

against Romania and, of course, the glory of beating Germany; less so, perhaps, the false dawn of the two exciting openers against Portugal, before our opponents regrouped and blasted holes through us at close quarters. I was looking at a computer graphic of Luis Figo's goal against England the other day, incidentally – and do you know, it was preposterous. It showed Figo charging directly towards goal, leaving defenders collapsing on both sides, firing through Tony Adams's legs and straight past David Seaman as if he wasn't there. Well, I thought, lucky this was only a graphic. Imagine if such a thing could happen in the real world.

Unsurprisingly, Figo got the man-of-the-match award. It's an award system that has recognised goalscorers in a quite unimaginative way. On the night Martin Keown heroically worked his socks off for England against Germany, for example, it was Alan Shearer who got man of the match.

Goalkeepers, defenders and playmakers don't get a look-in, so the amazing Alessandro Nesta, of Italy, will go officially unrecognised, as will all the goalkeepers, despite the fact that the quality of goalkeeping in Euro 2000 has been one of its great revelations. Toldo's saves in the Holland–Italy match were magnificent; I remember Rustu, of Turkey, taking Emile Mpenza's rocket shot like a bullet to the chest in the match against Belgium; meanwhile, Barthez's vertical salmon-leap to palm a shot from Raul over the bar in the France–Spain quarter-final was frankly unbelievable.

Plus there are players who just physically summed up the tournament. Edgar Davids, in his swimming goggles, proving that even girlie hair and specs can be elevated to footie fashion if the will is strong enough. Patrick Kluivert having the time of his young, strutting life against Yugoslavia (It's three! It's four! No, hang on, it's three again!). Pierluigi Collina giving red cards to players who weren't even on the pitch, with his eyes popping out of his already quite scary head. Christophe Dugarry with his nostril splints. Jan Koller, of the Czech Republic, biggest man in the world, roaming the field as if looking for someone to eat.

What a shame if an event such as this is remembered for the water cannons in Charleroi. So think of Zidane instead, waiting several minutes for the explosive Portuguese protests to die down at the semi-final in Brussels, knowing he must put the penalty away, his whole body whirring and ticking with controlled concentration. This is not only a contested penalty, remember; it is potentially the golden goal.

But though a few more hairs fall out, this is the only sign of the strain he is under. For Zidane is the Pete Sampras of football. The whistle blows. He makes a short run, fires it into the roof of the goal, into Baia's right top corner. And France are in the final, and on this night in June in the year 2000, Zinedine Zidane is the best footballer in the world.

I did love the football, then. But I still don't regret giving it up as a job. On the day in 2000 that Kevin Keegan resigned – and I spent the afternoon watering the sleeve of Brian Glanville with my wet salt tears – one of the chief sports writers said to me, out of the blue, 'You were right

303

about Keegan.' Five words. Five rather kind words. But I get quite tearful recollecting them because of the magnitude of what they signified. They meant that, logically, even if I hadn't just resigned from my job, I was finished. Oh my God. As those words were spoken, all my ambitions as a sports writer sort-of evaporated and rose out of me, like the soul leaving the body. It was like something out of a fairy tale – a fairy tale neatly illustrative of the cruel ironies of life. All this time I had wanted to be accepted by the proper sports writers, you see; but since it was my entire *raison d'être* to barge into their world without ceremony and write only the sort of stuff they would despise, acceptance was out of the question. Being despised had been awful, and I had hated it. However, what turned out to be far harder to take was one of the big boys giving me an unexpected pat on the back on a day when I was emotional enough already. Having someone say 'You were right about Keegan' like this was unbearable. It meant that I had gained a bit of respect from the people I worked with, but at what cost? At the cost of finding out, on my very last day on the job, that I had failed in my main objective, which was never to write anything that a proper sports writer would approve of.

Oh well. Having returned to the non-sports-writing world, I am pleased to say that I can now attend the theatre without feeling weird because the audience doesn't moil about, and sing offensive songs, and keep standing up to get a better view, and chuck stuff at the stage. So there are parts of me that have clearly recovered fully from the experience. But I am mostly very proud of having been a sports writer, and grateful that I was given the chance to do something so extraordinary – and I can be quite sharp with anyone who is snobby about sport, that's for sure. Because people can be very snobby on this subject, did you know? They think that it's an inferior matter suited only to inferior minds. They also seem to think they will be fatally contaminated if exposed to someone else's enthusiasm, so they block their ears and hum a passage from Handel's *Agrippina* until the threat has gone away. I suspect intellectual insecurity lies behind this narrow-mindedness; or at least a rather loathsome fear for reputation. Either way, I find, increasingly, that I want to punch such people in the nose. I have already mentioned the friend who dropped me when I started writing about football – even though she'd known me for several years when I didn't. Before she dropped me, she did a curious thing first, too, which I have pondered ever since. She presented me with a collection of Hugh McIlvanney's football columns with the high-handed words, 'I've taken advice, and apparently everything you'll need to know is in here.'

I often wonder how she would have coped delivering 900 words on the whistle. This is reprehensible in me, I know; it is sheer vanity. But whenever I think of all those deadlines I met from cold, noisy, cramped press boxes, I can't help thinking, 'Not everyone could have done that. Some of these namby-pamby literary novelist types most certainly couldn't have done that.' Now that my everyday working environment is like all those other 'Writers' Rooms' they show in the *Guardian* on Saturdays – a quiet corner of the house with a window I don't look out of; a desk surrounded by heaps of writerly junk; a clock, a phone, a plate with toast crumbs, and a cat on a cushion – I am grateful that I was tested in the fire of football, and I think (rather sternly) that everyone who claims to be a writer should be put through it too. Start your piece at half time. Remember there are no action replay facilities, and no commentary, and that the person sitting next to you happens to hate you on principle. You may need to block out some swearing, and of course someone has nicked all the Yorkies. There is no electricity in the press box, and your laptop has a limited battery capacity. There isn't room for a notepad next to the computer, your feet have turned to ice, and snowflakes keep settling on your eyelashes. You have 15 minutes to get started before play recommences, and then a further 45 to finish, during which period the story of the game (and therefore the thrust of your piece) will change – and even reverse – minute by minute, turning on players being sent off, scoring or assisting goals, diving, fighting, getting substituted, or scoring decisive last-minute penalties against the run of play. Well, deliver on deadline like this a few dozen times, and I think you will be justified in believing there is nothing (as a writer) you cannot do.

When I turn up to cover the golf at the Open every July, I get quite sentimental. I feel I'm coming home. Golf isn't brutal like the footie, and it never was. They have women's lavatories and everything. Now that I've been on the scene for so long, I feel genuinely welcome. Although the venue rotates through different seaside courses, I think I've been to most of them before – and besides, the big white press tent is a familiar space, with its long desks facing the enormous yellow scoreboard, and the same rather improbable job lot of dining chairs upholstered in red velour, which the old hands stack up in twos on arrival to attain a decent height to write from. Before the event each year, I remind myself who won last time, and who won the time before that (there is a small danger I will be expected to know this), and I drive up early in the week so that I can roam the course on practice days, get my picture taken for the paper in unflattering blustery conditions, achieve broadband connection, and try out my waterproofs. The days are long, and involve a great deal more exercise than I'm used to, and I always get an angry red stripe round the back of my neck because I don't have clothes with collars. But the work is stimulating and engrossing, the event is beautifully structured, and my colleagues are not only clever, funny and well-informed, but they are even quite tolerant of all that bloody outdoor survival kit I pile up round my chair.

So this is where I will leave you, I think. At the Open, on a fine day, with half a ton of stuff strapped to my back, binoculars at the ready, crouching behind some gorse so as not to distract the players. From the tee, an almighty crack-whzzz announces that Tiger Woods has taken his shot. 'It's going left,' says one of my colleagues, and I roll my eyes, Gromit-fashion. How can he *possibly* have seen the ball? But then, on the radio, they confirm that, yes, it did go left, and I let out a short scream. As we all scramble forwards over the undulations and tussocks towards the green, I make a squiggly note on damp paper that will be of bugger-all use to me later on, and resist the urge to offer anyone a cup of tea from the thermos or a go with my defibrillator. There isn't much time for reflection here, but I have to admit, it is at times like these, as I travel inside the ropes parallel with one of the greatest sportsmen in the world, that I am overcome with the sense of privilege and awe, and can't help imagining some future scene: of me saying to some hospital carer on my deathbed, 'I used to be a sports writer, you know.' And her patting me on the hand and saying, patiently, 'Of course you did, dear. Of course you did.'

LYNNE TRUSS

Eats, Shoots & Leaves

The Zero Tolerance Approach to Punctuation

Over 3 million copies sold worldwide

Anxious about the apostrophe? Confused by the comma? Or just plain stumped by the semi-colon?

Join Lynne Truss, self-confessed punctuation stickler, in this impassioned and hilarious tour through the rules of punctuation. A runaway bestseller, it is both a brilliantly clear guide for the punctuation challenged and enthralling entertainment for the grammar devotee.

'A punctuation repair kit. Passionate and witty . . . fresh and funny'
Independent

'Truss deserves to be piled high with honours'
JOHN HUMPHRYS, *Sunday Times*

LYNNE TRUSS

Talk to the Hand

The Utter Bloody Rudeness of Everyday Life (or six good reasons to stay at home and bolt the door)

This is not a book about manners, nor a book about etiquette. It is a book about rudeness.

Lynne Truss, bestselling author of *Eats, Shoots & Leaves* and champion of correct punctuation, returns to fight for the cause of politeness. A joyous rant against the everyday rudeness we've all become accustomed to, *Talk to the Hand* brilliantly dissects the incivilities of modern life. Why are other people so crass, selfish and inconsiderate? Whatever happened to 'please' and 'thank you'? Why do we have to put up with so much swearing? And whatever happened to public-spiritedness?

'A lively and witty broadside against the modern "eff off" society'
Sunday Express

'Trademark Truss . . . (very) readable, (very) funny, (very) engaging'
Observer

LYNNE TRUSS

Making the Cat Laugh

One Woman's Journal of Single Life on the Margins

A brilliant collection of Lynne Truss' journalism – recording the life of a metropolitan refugee from coupledom.

For seven years Lynne Truss, in columns for *The Listener*, *The Times* and *Woman's Journal*, tried to make her cat laugh. Along the way, 'Margins', 'Single Life' and 'One Woman's Journal' collected a band of devoted fans, yet the cat remained unimpressed. But, under headings such as 'The Single Woman Considers Going Out but Doesn't Fancy the Hassle' and 'The Single Woman Stays at Home and Goes Quietly Mad', we discover a writer not only obsessed with cats, but prone to overreacting generally – to news stories, shopping, passive smoking, Christmas, coupledom, boy-friends, snails, sheds, Andre Agassi, cooking instructions, requests of 'How's the novel going?' and personal remarks of any kind.

'A small masterpiece of comedy . . . A continual hoot'

The Times

'Trenchant writing, invigorating valour, and a shrewdly observant wit'

Scotland on Sunday